Consumer Vulnerability

Consumer vulnerability is of growing importance as a research topic for those exploring wellbeing. This book provides space to critically engage with the conditions, contexts, and characteristics of consumer vulnerability, which affect how people experience and respond to the marketplace and vice versa.

Focusing on substantive, ethical, social and methodological issues, this book brings together key researchers in the field and practitioners who work with vulnerability on a daily basis. Organised into four parts, it considers consumer vulnerability and key life stages, health and wellbeing, poverty, and exclusion. Methodologically the chapters draw on qualitative research, employing a variety of method from interview, to the use of poetry, film and other cultural artefacts.

This book will be of interest to marketing and consumer research scholars and students, and also to researchers in other disciplines including sociology, public policy, anthropology, and practitioners, policy makers, and charitable organisations working with vulnerable groups.

Kathy Hamilton is Reader in Marketing, University of Strathclyde, UK.

Susan Dunnett is Lecturer in Marketing, University of Edinburgh, UK.

Maria Piacentini is Professor of Consumer Behaviour, Lancaster University, UK.

Routledge Studies in Critical Marketing

Edited by Mark Tadajewski and Pauline Maclaren

Marketing has been widely criticised as being probably the least self-critical of all the business disciplines and has never really been able to escape the charge that it is socially, ethically and morally barren in certain respects. Marketers may talk about satisfying the customer, about building close relationships with their clientele, about their ethical and corporate social responsibility initiatives, but increasingly these claims are subjected to critical scrutiny and been found wanting. In a social, economic and political environment in which big business and frequently some of the most marketing-adept companies' practices are being questioned, there has emerged a very active community of scholars, practitioners and students interested in Critical Marketing Studies.

Using the types of critical social theory characteristic of Critical Marketing Studies, this series will drive the debate on Critical Marketing into the future. It offers scholars the space to articulate their arguments at the level of sophistication required to underscore the contribution of this domain to other scholars, students, practitioners and public-policy groups interested in the influence of marketing in the structuring of the public sphere and society. It is a forum for rigorously theorised, conceptually and empirically rich studies dealing with some element of marketing theory, thought, pedagogy and practice.

1. **Consumer Vulnerability**
   Conditions, contexts and characteristics
   Edited by Kathy Hamilton, Susan Dunnett and Maria Piacentini

Consumer Vulnerability
Conditions, contexts and characteristics

Edited by
Kathy Hamilton, Susan Dunnett
and Maria Piacentini

Routledge
Taylor & Francis Group

LONDON AND NEW YORK

First published 2016 by Routledge

2 Park Square, Milton Park, Abingdon, Oxfordshire OX14 4RN
52 Vanderbilt Avenue, New York, NY 10017

Routledge is an imprint of the Taylor & Francis Group, an informa business

First issued in paperback 2019

British Library Cataloguing in Publication Data
A catalogue record for this book is available from the British Library

Library of Congress Cataloging in Publication Data
Consumer vulnerability : conditions, contexts and characteristics / edited by
Kathy Hamilton, Susan Dunnett and Maria Piacentini.
pages cm
Includes bibliographical references and index.
1. Consumers. 2. Consumer behavior. 3. Consumption (Economics)
I. Hamilton, Kathy. II. Dunnett, Susan. III. Piacentini, Maria.
HC79.C6C656 2015
339.4'7--dc23
2015001814

ISBN: 978-0-415-85858-8 (hbk)
ISBN: 978-0-367-86802-4 (pbk)

Typeset in Bembo
by Taylor & Francis Books

Contents

Illustrations

Figures

Table

Contributors

Stacey Menzel Baker (PhD, University of Nebraska) is Professor of Marketing and Sustainable Business Practices, University of Wyoming. Her research crosses boundaries between transformative consumer research, marketing and public policy, macromarketing and customer experience management. She focuses on attachment to possessions, material wellbeing, marketplace experiences and relationships, consumer vulnerability, and individual and community resilience in contexts such as disaster recovery, disability and social services.

Courtney Nations Baker (PhD candidate, University of Wyoming) has an MS degree in Marketing from Clemson University. Courtney is interested in consumer rituals, agency, and vulnerability for applications in service marketing and policy. She is published in the *Journal of Macromarketing*, has presented at several national conferences, and is currently working on projects in the contexts of death care services and social services.

Wided Batat is Associate Professor of Marketing at the University of Lyon 2 (France) and a United Nations Representative at the UNESCO in Paris. Her works focus on young consumer education, consumption cultures and tourism experience, vulnerability and wellbeing, and food and sustainable consumption. Dr Batat has published several articles in international journals such as the *Journal of Marketing Management,* the *Journal of Business Research, Journal of Research for Consumers, Revue Française de Marketing, International Journal for Consumer Studies* and *Advances in Consumer Research.*

Sara Bryson is Policy & Research Manager at Children North East – a regional children's charity. Founded in 1891 it has over 120 years' experience developing responses to tackling child poverty. Sara leads on the Child Poverty work for the charity, developing initiatives with young people such as Poverty Proofing the School Day. Sara has worked with children and young people for over a decade to ensure their views and experiences inform policy and practice: leading award-winning initiatives at The Children's Society; writing strategies for local authorities; and working for the Office of the Children's Commissioner for England.

http://www.children-ne.org.uk/tackling-child-poverty
www.povertyproofing.co.uk

Follow us on Twitter
@ChildrenNE
@SaraBryson1

Like us on Facebook /ChildrenNorthEast

Elaine Chase is a Senior Research Fellow at the Department of Social Policy and Intervention and a Research Fellow at Green Templeton College, University of Oxford. Her research broadly focuses on the sociological dimensions of wellbeing and the rights of individuals and communities, particularly those most likely to experience disadvantage and marginalization. She has recently completed a study with colleagues in seven countries exploring the link between poverty, shame and social exclusion, and the implications for anti-poverty policies.

Roger Clough is Emeritus Professor of Social Care at Lancaster University, UK. Now an independent researcher, he has written extensively on aging, residential homes, inspection and abuse. His previous publications include *The Practice of Residential Work*, and he has written articles in journals such as the *British Journal of Social Work*, *Education and Ageing* and the *Journal of Elder Abuse & Neglect*. He is a trustee of Age UK Lancashire and was the research director for the project on which his chapter is based. He has written in a personal capacity, not as a representative of the organization.

Catherine Coleman (PhD from the Institute of Communications Research at the University of Illinois, Urbana-Champaign) is an Assistant Professor in the School of Strategic Communication at Texas Christian University, USA. She has professional experience in marketing and advertising and has worked as a prevention educator at a rape crisis center. Her work addresses issues of representation, gender, race, and vulnerability in advertising and consumer culture, and has been published in journals such as the *Journal of Advertising*, *Consumption, Markets & Culture*, the *Journal of Marketing Management* and *Advertising & Society Review*, as well as various book chapters.

Canan Corus is Assistant Professor of Marketing at Lubin School of Business, Pace University, New York. She focuses on consumer health and consumer welfare, as well as corporate social responsibility and stakeholder engagement. Her research relates to and advocates for personal and collective wellbeing of consumers, with a focus on the needs of disadvantaged consumers. She has published in academic journals such as the *Journal of Marketing Research*, *Journal of Business Research*, *Journal of Applied Social Psychology*, *Journal of Consumer Affairs* and *Journal of Public Policy & Marketing*.

Stephen Crossley is a PhD student in the School of Applied Social Sciences at Durham University. Prior to studying he worked on a research and knowledge exchange project based at Durham, working with local authorities and voluntary sector organizations in the North East of England. He has also worked in community development and youth work roles in the public and voluntary sectors.

Susan Dunnett is a Lecturer in Marketing at the University of Edinburgh Business School. Her interest in vulnerability and consumer wellbeing stems from a wider research focus on the sociology of health and illness. Particular areas of investigation are the experience of illness, cultures of self-help, medical consumerism and issues of identity.

Andrea Finney is a Senior Research Fellow at the University of Bristol's Personal Finance Research Centre. With almost 15 years' experience of qualitative and quantitative policy-focused research, Andrea began her social research career at the Home Office, and joined Bristol University in 2007 from the Office for National Statistics. Andrea's current research interests lie in furthering understanding of patterns of saving, borrowing and decision-making, and how these relate to financial and social wellbeing outcomes for individuals and households. Her recent projects have included studies of the financial impacts of cancer and financial wellbeing in later life. Her work can be read in the *Journal of Marketing Management, Journal of Consumer Behaviour* and *Advances in Consumer Research*. Susan was co-organiser of the ESRC seminar series on vulnerable consumers.

Kathy Hamilton is a reader in marketing at the University of Strathclyde, Glasgow. Her research focuses on consumer vulnerability and poverty and the role of community in contemporary culture. Kathy is interested in interdisciplinary research and her work has been published in *Sociology*, the *Journal of Marketing Management, Annals of Tourism Research* and the *European Journal of Marketing*. Kathy was co-organiser of the ESRC seminar series on Vulnerable Consumers.

Sally Hibbert is Associate Professor in Marketing at Nottingham University Business School and former Head of the Marketing Division. Sally's research expertise centres on consumer behaviour and the links between consumer choice/consumption processes and societal and personal welfare. Specifically, her research examines ethical consumption, consumer vulnerability, behaviour change and consumer learning in service contexts. She has published in a wide range of international journals, including the *Journal of Service Research, Journal of Business Research, Psychology & Marketing* and the *European Journal of Marketing*. Sally has led funded research collaborations with charities, the NHS, and local and national government.

Margaret K. Hogg holds the Fulgoni Chair of Consumer Behaviour and Marketing in the Department of Marketing at Lancaster University Management School. Her work has appeared in refereed journals including the *Journal of Advertising, Journal of Business Research, Journal of Marketing Management,*

Journal of Services Marketing, *European Journal of Marketing*, *International Journal of Advertising* and *Consumption, Markets & Culture*. She edited six volumes of papers on consumer behaviour in the Sage Major Works series (2005 and 2006), and, along with Michael Solomon, Gary Bamossy and Soren Askegaard, she is one of the co-authors of the fifth edition of *Consumer Behaviour: A European Perspective* (2013).

Aliakbar Jafari is a Senior Lecturer in Marketing at the University of Strathclyde, UK. His research interests fall within interpretive consumer research and market studies, with a particular focus on cultural consumption, institutional theory, theories of globalization, transformative consumer research and religions/spirituality. His recent work (articles and book reviews) on religion has appeared in *Marketing Theory, Consumption, Markets & Culture*, the *Journal of Islamic Marketing, Journal of Macromarketing, Journal of Marketing Management, International Journal of Market Research* and *European Journal of Marketing*. In 2013 he co-edited (with Professor Özlem Sandıkçı) a special issue of *Marketing Theory* on 'Islamic Encounters in Consumption and Marketing'. Currently he is co-editing two books: *Critical Perspectives on Islamic Marketing* (with Professor Özlem Sandıkçı) (Routledge) and *New Directions in Consumer Research* (with Dr Paul Hewer and Dr Kathy Hamilton) (Sage).

Carol Kaufman-Scarborough has been an active researcher and faculty member in the Rutgers School of Business-Camden for over 30 years. Carol's research is in marketing, particularly in the areas known as consumer behaviour and retailing. Within the disabilities area, her research has focused on the effectiveness of the Americans with Disabilities Act and its impact on shoppers: mobility issues in bricks and mortar stores, usability issues in online shopping for persons with visual impairments, and perceptual and behavioural issues in retail shopping for persons with ADHD. She is currently a member of the Disabilities Committee on campus and has served as a member of the Board of Directors of Goodwill Industries of Southern New Jersey and Philadelphia. Her research appears in the *Journal of Public Policy & Marketing, Journal of Retailing, Journal of Consumer Affairs, Journal of Consumer Policy, Journal of Consumer Research* and *Journal of Business Research*.

Monica LaBarge is an Assistant Professor of Marketing at Queen's University, Kingston (Ontario), Canada. Her research interests centre on public policy issues in marketing and how marketing can positively affect consumer wellbeing. Specifically, she has ongoing research projects in the areas of health promotion, charitable giving and non-profit marketing, as well as how vulnerable populations (such as older adults) cope with and overcome vulnerability in the marketplace.

Marlys J. Mason is Associate Professor of Marketing at the Spears School of Business at Oklahoma State University. Her research interests include consumer health and wellbeing, vulnerability, maladaptive resiliency, risk behavior, anti-tobacco efforts and public policy. Marlys has published in the

Journal of Consumer Research, Journal of Public Policy & Marketing, Journal of Consumer Affairs, Journal of Marketing Management, Journal of Business Research, Journal of Macromarketing, Consumption, Markets & Culture and other journals.

Agnes Nairn is Professor of Marketing at EMLYON Business School, an Associate of the University of Edinburgh Business School, and Visiting Professor at the University of Bath. Her research focuses on the influence of the commercial world on children. She has published award-winning papers in a range of international journals and seeks above all to contribute to social policy and debate. She has advised the Brazilian Justice Ministry, United Nations, UNICEF, Unilever and various UK government departments. She is a frequent keynote speaker and media commentator on the ethics of marketing to children.

Stephanie O'Donohoe is Professor of Advertising and Consumer Culture at the University of Edinburgh. Her research interests include dying and bereaved people's interactions with the marketplace; consumption experiences among new mothers, children and young adults; and advertising creatives' working lives. Her work has been published in journals that include *Human Relations*, the *Journal of Marketing Management* and *Consumption, Markets & Culture*.

Teresa Pavia is Associate Professor of Marketing in the David Eccles School of Business at the University of Utah. Her recent research interests relate to the intersection of health and consumer behaviour. She is particularly interested in the impact that normative expectations for the embodied consumer have on one's lived experience. She has published in the *Journal of Consumer Research, Management Science, Consumption, Markets & Culture, Marketing Management* and other journals.

Maria Piacentini is Professor of Consumer Research at Lancaster University Management School. Her research focuses on consumer vulnerability, and she is concerned with the coping strategies employed by consumers in difficult consumption contexts and situations. She has published her research in top international journals in both marketing/consumer behaviour and the social sciences, including the *Journal of Marketing Management, Journal of Business Research, Sociology of Health and Illness, Journal of Consumer Behaviour* and *Advances in Consumer Research*. With Isabelle Szmigin, Maria is the co-author of the textbook *Consumer Behaviour*, published by OUP in 2014. She is actively involved in various international and national scholarly networks, including the Transformative Consumer Research (TCR) network. Maria was co-organiser of the ESRC seminar series Vulnerable Consumers.

Bige Saatcioglu is Assistant Professor of Marketing at Ozyegin University, Turkey. Her research interests include theoretical and methodological issues in critical and transformative consumer research, the social construction of morality among the poor and vulnerable populations. Her research has appeared in the *Journal of Consumer Research*, *Journal of Macromarketing*, *Journal of Public Policy & Marketing*, *Journal of Business Research*, *Journal of Marketing Management* and *Journal of International Business Studies*.

Jonathan Stearn is a freelance writer and consultant. He was Director of Consumer Vulnerability at Citizens Advice (formerly for Consumer Futures), driving work on empowering consumers, and challenging the poverty premium and market failure. Jonathan was Head of Campaigns at Energy Watch and responsible for developing work on fuel poverty and financial inclusion. Previously, Jonathan was Director of the End Child Poverty Campaign in the UK and seconded as a communication adviser to the Home Office's Active Community Unit. He worked for Age Concern England as Head of Public Affairs. He has worked as a journalist and, in the housing field, as Deputy Editor of *Housing* and *Inside Housing* magazines. He was a campaigner for Shelter. He recently wrote 'The Arsonist' for the anthology *Brighton: The Graphic Novel*, published by QueenSpark Books.

Darach Turley is Emeritus Professor of Marketing at Dublin City University. His research interests have focused primarily on the relationship between consumer behaviour and mortality, with particular emphasis on how goods can be used to negotiate grief and bereavement. In 2007 he was made a Fulbright Scholar.

Robert Walker is Professor of Social Policy at the Department of Social Policy and Intervention and a Fellow of Green Templeton College, University of Oxford. His particular research interests include poverty, shame and social exclusion; family dynamics and budgeting strategies; children's aspirations; and employment instability and progression. He has authored more than 20 books, including his most recent, *The Shame of Poverty* (2014).

Acknowledgement

We are grateful to the *Economic and Social Research Council* for the financial support for our seminar series on vulnerable consumers, which provided the space to gather together researchers working in this area from across the world. We gratefully acknowledge all the speakers from our six seminars who shared their experiences and knowledge of consumer vulnerability, as well as the seminar delegates who contributed to our discussions. Finally, we are grateful to Isobel Speedman from the University of Edinburgh for supporting the administration of the seminar series.

1 Introduction

Kathy Hamilton, Susan Dunnett and Maria Piacentini

The study of consumer vulnerability is a growing and important field within business research: a field which moves beyond managerially focused work to represent those outside the market's profitable mainstream. What began as a few notable studies has coalesced into a nascent research stream that plays a leading role in relating consumption to the rest of human existence. We define consumer vulnerability as an undesirable state catalysed by a number of human conditions and contexts. Vulnerability is not necessarily experienced as a permanent state and can often be felt in times of transition – job loss, bereavement, ill health, natural disaster, ageing, and the identity and lifestyle shifts required in becoming a parent. These conditions and characteristics affect how individuals experience, interpret and respond to the marketplace and often how the marketplace responds to them. The notion of vulnerability has been operationalised as a label for a particular group or demographic within society; we, however, like Baker et al. (2005), view it as a circumstance which all people may experience at some point in their lives.

This text presents a collection of contributions derived from a seminar series funded by the Economic and Social Research Council, UK. Taking consumer vulnerability as an over-arching theme, the seminars explored a number of contemporary concerns relating to issues of individual and societal wellbeing, from poverty to health and wellbeing across a range of life stages. Bringing together key researchers in the field, this volume maps out and explores the conditions, contexts and characteristics of consumer vulnerability from an international and interdisciplinary perspective. Hence, we present work from marketing, consumer research, sociology, geography and anthropology. As the various authors in this volume show, the notion of consumer vulnerability is flexible and can be viewed from a number of vantage points. Methodologically the studies represented here are qualitative in nature, yet they employ a variety of methods, from interview to the use of poetry, film and other cultural artefacts. However, the fundamental aim of this research agenda is to produce work which contributes to consumer and societal wellbeing. The practitioner voice is particularly important in meeting this end; hence we present commentary from practitioners working with vulnerability on a daily basis (see chapters by Stearn, Clough, and Bryson and Crossley).

Above all, we hope this volume provides space to *critically* engage with the conditions, contexts and characteristics of consumer vulnerability. We focus on the role of the market and marketing in both enhancing and ameliorating consumer vulnerability. Demystification is an aim here, as is challenging prevailing stereotypes that persist about such groups, allowing a shift in perception from vulnerable people as potentially frustrated consumers to people experiencing vulnerability as citizens (see chapters by Kaufman-Scarborough and Hibbert et al.). A broader and more nuanced understanding of the lived experience of vulnerability provides the foundation for a critical reassessment of consumerism and the power of market providers (see chapters by Finney and Stearn).

Our aims here, as in the seminar series, are fourfold: to critically explore the terrain of consumer vulnerability; to bring practitioner insight to the academic study of vulnerable people; to share best methodological practice; and to build capacity for new theoretical, methodological and substantive research insight. Through a more complex and nuanced understanding of the conditions and contexts which lead to vulnerability, we hope, lies the route to societal change and improved individual wellbeing.

Language matters

The importance and role of language in shaping reality is explored by several of the authors in this volume (see chapters by Baker et al., Stearn and Clough). Critiquing the notion of vulnerability was important to us throughout the seminar series, and our linguistic and conceptual framing of the concept developed during the process. We began the seminar series under the title 'Vulnerable Consumers' and concluded with the term consumer vulnerability, which more accurately reflected our sensibilities. This simple linguistic shift removed the emphasis on individual responsibility and permanence, creating conceptual space for investigations of the socially constructed and interactive nature of consumer vulnerability. As Hawkins et al. (2001, p. 3) reminds us, 'being aware of the terminology we choose, and the way in which we use it can be critical in determining whose view of 'reality' we are accepting, what power relations we wish to reinforce'. Moving away from conceptualisations of vulnerability based on static notions of individual states, e.g. the elderly as a vulnerable group, allows investigation of more meaningful situational intersections. As such, we seek to highlight the distinction between actual and perceived vulnerability (Smith and Cooper-Martin, 1997), bringing to the fore ways in which so-called vulnerable consumers navigate various marketplace and service interactions with skill.

The notion of falsely labelling conditions, contexts and individuals extends to the use of the term 'consumer'. We are particularly interested in the intersection between consumption and vulnerability, yet the language and practices of business are not always welcome in social service provision and the public sector more widely. Indeed, we suggest that researchers proceed with caution with the notion that individuals in vulnerable situations have access to the marketplace and can act as consumers.

However the consumer discourse can offer agentic power to the vulnerable. Prior (2012) describes how young people using counselling services resist stigma by adopting the position of consumer in order to 'embrace and affirm virtuous problem-solving, agency, individualisation and consumerism. These discourses serve to create opportunities to construct coherent and self-enhancing identities as empowered and entitled consumers of counselling and as competent actors in the social world' (ibid., p. 710). Future research could usefully explore the implications of the consumerist identity among vulnerable groups by investigating how individuals use the consumerist identity, in contexts of both restricted and wide consumer choice.

After considering the power of language, we propose that, conceptually, consumer vulnerability is usefully viewed as a 'sensitizing concept' (Blumer, 1954, p. 7), in much the same way that Chase and Walker interpret poverty (Chapter 16). Rather than simply labelling the contexts, individuals and phenomena under study, it provides a set of conceptual hooks on which to hang ideas, opening up important areas of study to business researchers, giving shape to an otherwise amorphous field of interest and allowing the representation of complex subjectivities.

Relationship matters

The chapters herein illustrate the multi-faceted and complex nature of consumer vulnerability. Understanding its conceptual foundations and reach alongside potential routes to alleviating vulnerability is not an easy task. Following the interdisciplinary nature of the seminar series, we believe that crossing disciplinary boundaries and bringing together fragmented, but related, research has the potential to generate a more comprehensive understanding of the experience of vulnerability. This is well articulated in Chase and Walker's chapter, which refers to research conducted without any real awareness of the literature on consumer vulnerability yet having an unexpected resonance with the concept. Further consideration of the ways in which academics from different disciplinary backgrounds could join forces would be a useful addition to future research in this area.

Our experiences throughout the seminar series demonstrate that engaging with relevant third sector and charitable organisations can support a better understanding of vulnerability and allow academic work to be applied to improving the lives of those in vulnerable positions. Knowledge exchange is now recognised as a central activity for academics, with funding bodies often seeking evidence of research impact to justify public investment in research activities. For example, the Economic and Social Research Council (ESRC), the largest organisation for funding research on economic and social issues in the UK, explain the significance of knowledge exchange as follows:

> Knowledge exchange is a two-way process where social scientists and individuals or organisations share learning, ideas and experiences. We are

committed to knowledge exchange and encouraging collaboration between researchers and the private, public and civil society sectors. By creating a dialogue between these communities, knowledge exchange helps research to influence policy and practice.

(www.esrc.ac.uk/collaboration/knowledge-exchange/)

Our seminar series provided space for processes of sharing, collaboration and dialogue and the feedback received from participants indicated mutual benefit from exploring shared issues and diverse perspectives. From an academic perspective, it led to the identification of new research questions that were informed by the experiences of those working with various vulnerability contexts on a daily basis. Equally, from the third sector perspective it also opened new lines of enquiry – for example, one participant commented that those in third sector organisations are often 'naive to the impact of consumerism on society' (policy and research advisor, global poverty charity). This is in keeping with Bohm's (1996, p. 7) understanding of dialogue as 'a common participation, in which we are not playing a game against each other, but *with* each other. In a dialogue everybody wins.'

However, we do not want to suggest that initiating and maintaining dialogue was free from challenges. Indeed, on occasion we had difficulty in attracting speakers from policy, with many of those we invited expressing concern about the relevance of their contribution to an event organised within a business school and couched within the language of consumers and markets. It also became clear that we work with different timescales – for example, in our seminar on poverty, one participant commented that those working with people living in poverty on a daily basis have 'a different sense of urgency' (policy and business development officer, child poverty charity). In contrast to the lengthy academic research and publication process, those with direct involvement in the daily lives of people experiencing vulnerability are driven by a great immediacy. We therefore suggest that future research consider the following: what practices and processes can academics and representatives from third sector organisations engage in to work more effectively on issues of consumer vulnerability? How can we overcome barriers to collaboration? How can these relationships be sustained?

Context matters

Consumer vulnerability research can be seen as driven by concern for contexts. Contexts may be bounded by geography (see the chapters by Chase and Walker, and Saatcioglu and Corus); by life stage (Nairn's work, for example); by a particular phenomenon such as the experience of illness (as discussed by Mason and Pavia); or broader consumer cultures (seen in the exploration of consumer credit by Finney). The studies contained in this volume reflect this variety while demonstrating that vulnerability is a fluid experience within contexts. Writing about the importance of context in consumer culture theory research,

Arnould et al. (2006, p. 107) discuss how contexts 'engage our emotions and our senses, stimulate discovery, invite description and excite comparison'. Certainly the chapters in this volume reflect this sensibility; O'Donohoe's sensitive chapter exploring childhood grief evokes a strong emotional response in the reader; Jafaris's chapter on religion-related vulnerability stimulates discovery by drawing attention to an under-researched area; and description and comparison can be found in Hibbert et al.'s chapter on care leavers, Kaufman-Scarborough's study of disabled consumers, and Chase and Walker's comparative exploration of poverty and shame in a number of countries.

Contexts are routinely comprehended through theoretical lenses (Arnould et al., 2006, p. 106), yet it is important to remember that contexts themselves bring forth new insights (Aaskegaard and Linnett, 2011). There are several examples in this volume of new thinking and ideas, emanating from specific contexts but providing general guidance, insights and reminders for all working in the area of vulnerability. Turley's focus on the bereavement context highlights the importance of adopting sound ethical practices in our research. The principles he discusses around respect, reciprocity and beneficence are arguably the basis of all good, ethical research, and while there is a heightened need for their consideration in sensitive contexts, Turley's work provides lessons for all social researchers. Similarly, Clough's discussion of older people provides examples from practice that demonstrate new thinking about the way that public–private partnerships can emerge to resolve/reduce felt vulnerability, to ensure wellbeing of vulnerable groups. Nairn's work with children reminds us of the particularities of certain groups who may be particularly vulnerable to aspects of consumer cultures such as advertising. From Batat's chapter we learn about the ways in which consumers passively or actively move in and out of contexts that make them vulnerable. As we suggest above, everyone can experience vulnerability in market interactions; the contexts explored in this volume highlight the market's role and responsibility in this.

Part I, *Mapping the Domain of Consumer Vulnerability*, deals with theoretical, methodological and representation issues relevant to the study of consumer vulnerability. Our opening chapter, by Stacey Menzel Baker, Monica LaBarge and Courtney Nations Baker, provides an overview of the complex and multifaceted field of consumer vulnerability. Reviewing and critiquing the extant literature they ask important and difficult questions which interrogate the nature of our understanding of vulnerability. Through this process they highlight three primary approaches to vulnerability research: isolating particular populations of people; isolating particular environmental conditions; and isolating meanings and processes. People, places, and situations characterized as at-risk, stigmatized, oppressed, powerless, dependent, and/or as transformed via a negative state of being are explored. The authors conclude with directions for future research, critiquing the notion that vulnerability is a purely negative state associated with weakness.

Bige Saatcioglu and Canan Corus examine consumer vulnerability from the perspective of intersectionality, a theoretical position that stems originally from black feminist literature (Crenshaw, 1989), which has been used in the wider social sciences to understand a range of social issues. From this perspective, there is a move away from traditional demographic categorizations to instead recognise, and seek to understand, the more complex intersection of multiple identity axes which together impact on individuals' experience of vulnerability and disadvantage. The authors outline three main types of intersectionality (intracategorical, intercategorical and anti-categorical) and then go on to explain how these might apply in the context of consumer vulnerability, drawing on two key studies, Baker et al.'s (2007) work on tornado recovery processes and Ozanne and Anderson's (2010) study on the social construction of diabetes, from a community action research position. Finally, some key advice and lessons for researchers working in this area are offered.

Catherine Coleman's chapter focuses on representations of vulnerability and empowerment in market-oriented media systems, arguing that media representations are active texts that participate in shaping how we define vulnerability and who is defined as vulnerable. In particular, she considers the role of documentaries and focuses on *The Uncondemned,* a crowd-funded documentary intended to bring greater awareness to the stories of – and give voice to – the women whose testimonies at the International Criminal Tribunal for Rwanda (ICTR) helped secure the first successful prosecutions of rape and sexual violence as crimes of war. Through the lens of dialogic theory, Coleman reflects on the potential for *The Uncondemned* to provide these women with another context to tell their story and build greater understanding of their experiences.

Reflecting on over 25 years of research with bereaved consumers, Darach Turley focuses on what it means to be vulnerable in the bereavement setting, raising a range of issues for researchers and marketers operating in this context. His title, 'Asking for Trouble', signals the challenges and sensitivities that are faced when researching bereaved consumers, and he shares experiences from his own work, and that of others, to bring these challenges to life. He provides guidance for other researchers working in sensitive contexts, discussing the importance of beneficence, respect, rapport, reciprocity and self-disclosure, while recognizing some of the complexities as they apply in the bereavement context. This chapter invites the reader to reflect on the researcher–researched relationship within a specific context, and provides valuable lessons for researchers across a range of settings.

Providing a practitioner perspective, in the final chapter of this section, Jonathan Stearn (from Consumer Focus) writes about the roles and responsibilities of companies and government in the creation of conditions that lead to vulnerability, and also in terms of tackling and addressing the problems of consumer vulnerability. Drawing on a range of contexts (fuel, shopping, banking, water), this chapter pays particular attention to regulators who have a responsibility to oversee markets for essential goods and services and have some legal responsibility for tackling – or at least paying attention to – consumer vulnerability. The chapter finally discusses in detail the British Standard 18477, which was developed to act as a benchmark for organisations, providing clear guidance on how to recognise consumers who could be in vulnerable situations, and how they can provide inclusive services to meet the needs of all consumers.

Part II, *Consumer Vulnerability and Key Life Stages*, focuses on vulnerability as experienced by different age groups or life stages and broadens critical understanding of consumer vulnerability across the life course. Taking as her starting point the fundamental paradox at the centre of the UN Convention on the Rights of Children (1989) in the commercial context (the tension between the right to protection set against the right to be heard), Agnes Nairn draws on research from the UK, Europe and the USA to provide an analysis of vulnerability in childhood and how this is exacerbated by contemporary consumer culture. She demonstrates the links between advertising and materialism, explores how materialism impacts on wellbeing, and argues that, for some children, materialism acts as a form of compensatory consumption. Drivers of compensatory consumption are discussed, including puberty, peer rejection, low socioeconomic status and family disharmony, and Nairn concludes by asking important questions about the role of marketing and advertising in contributing to this sense of vulnerability among children.

In the second chapter of this section, Stephanie O'Donohoe sensitively explores the experience of childhood grief. Her analysis centres on the experiences of toddler Jackson Brookes-Dutton, whose mother was killed in a freak traffic accident while walking with her family in London. Jackson's father Ben Brooks-Dutton records their early experiences of loss and grief in his memoir, *It's Not Raining Daddy, It's Happy*. O'Donohoe draws from this text to interrogate the interplay between grief and consumption, illuminating the role of consumer goods – such as toys or his mother's belongings – in Jackson's experience of grief. Through objects and things meaning is made, and grief can be expressed, shared and escaped. At a time of great vulnerability, such objects and things also allow the continuation of bonds with the lost loved one.

Wided Batat's chapter provides an overview of adolescents' experiences of vulnerability. Many recent studies have pointed to this group being particularly vulnerable (Pechmann et al. 2011; Mason et al. 2013), mainly due to the changes in their cognitive, physiological and psychological make-up, which leads to greater impulsivity, heightened self-consciousness and self-doubt, and an elevated risk from consumption of products such as alcohol and tobacco. Batat presents an adolescent-centric framework of consumer vulnerability, in which she distinguishes between the different types of vulnerability as experienced by adolescents. *Imposed vulnerability* refers to those consumption behaviours that young feel obliged to adopt to fit in with their peers, whereas *deliberate vulnerability* relates to the vulnerability associated with the sought after consumption experiences adolescents are engaging in as an act of transgression against the adults in their worlds. These types of vulnerability are unpacked in the chapter, and discussed in relation to a range of risky consumption practices. Finally, implications for public policy are presented.

In the following chapter Sally Hibbert, Maria Piacentini and Margaret Hogg explore the transition to adulthood of young people who have been fostered or were care users in their childhood. Viewing transition as a process, they observe that moving to adult roles and statuses are times of great disruption and uncertainty. Vulnerability is heightened as these young people typically face the transition to adult roles much earlier than their peers, without the same level of support and are exposed to multiple risk factors associated with life chances, which interact to affect their experiences of assuming new consumer roles. Focus group data reveals their anxiety over new roles coupled with satisfaction in market prowess. What emerges is that managing marketplace/service interactions is central to the destabilisation of identity and the cementing of new, adult, selves.

In the final chapter of this section, Roger Clough provides a practitioner perspective on consumer vulnerability, describing a programme of research undertaken for Age UK, which adopts a participatory action research approach. The research aimed to explore the range and types of services and facilities available to older people and how these might support them to lead fuller lives, and was concerned with the role of older people in society, and also the mechanics of participation in the research. The chapter challenges perceptions of vulnerability in old age and discusses the issues around terminology and service use, including how appropriate the use of the word 'consumer' is in this context. Clough discusses some of the outcomes of this work, including an initiative involving a local independent cinema which put on dedicated film screenings for people with dementia.

The two chapters in Part III, *Consumer Vulnerability, Health and Wellbeing,* explore experiences of illness and disability within consumer culture. First, Marlys Mason and Teresa Pavia explore how health challenges deeply affect the agency and identity of the consumer. Drawing four empirical studies together, this chapter presents data from interviews with those living with late-stage AIDS, breast cancer patients, individuals with a chronic illness and parents of children with a significant disability. Informants express feeling shock, a sense of loss and confusion as to how to proceed as a consumer with the onset of health difficulties. The authors highlight that illness causes barriers to accessing the marketplace, due to physical or financial constraints. Yet from the high involvement to the mundane, consumption is found to be central to the recovery of self and group identity. The chapter ends with a call to develop a deeper understanding of the how illness affects vulnerability in the marketplace.

Second, Carol Kaufman-Scarborough discusses the social exclusion that consumers with disabilities may encounter. Using her prior studies related to mobility disabilities, vision impairments and cognitive disabilities, she suggests the Ability/Inclusion Matrix as a new analytical framework. The Ability/Inclusion Matrix is based on the intersection between the ability/disability continuum and the inclusion/exclusion continuum. The following four quadrants are proposed: (1) *Selective inclusion* is when access is based upon criteria established by decision-makers in the social environment, (2) *Unintended Exclusion* occurs when the exclusion is due to a lack of understanding of the needs of persons with disabilities, (3) *Universal Inclusion* is characterized as a situation in which everyone regardless of ability or disability is included, (4) *Rejected Exclusion* occurs when the market-place establishes clear criteria for access which results in the denial of membership for particular groups. Overall the matrix captures the potential for vulnerability based on various externalities in the marketplace.

The final section of the book, *Consumer Vulnerability, Poverty and Exclusion*, explores consumer experiences of exclusion from both religious and financial perspectives. In 'Towards an Understanding of Religion-related Vulnerability in Consumer Society', Aliakbar Jafari considers how and why religion matters to discussions of consumer vulnerability. There has been limited research attention given to experiences of consumer vulnerability on the basis of religion. Drawing on a range of anecdotal examples including potentially offensive advertisements and the conversion of churches into secular places of entertainment, Jafari highlights the need for further conceptualization and empirical investigations in this area. Overall he argues that, in the changing landscape of religion, vulnerability should be understood primarily against the backdrop of macro-environmental factors that impact public perceptions of and engagement with religion and religiosity.

In the following chapter, Andrea Finney, moving away from a focus on the individual, considers the households' vulnerability to financial difficulties in the post-financial crisis environment of the late 2000s and early 2010s. She explores the clear, if nuanced, role of consumer credit in compounding vulnerability to financial difficulties, reflecting on the intersection of: the difficult economic context; the legacy of a booming credit market and consumer culture; a mis-match between credit supply and consumer needs; and consumers' responses to changing situations. The chapter concludes by identifying roles for industry and government in helping consumers to recognise and respond to early signs of financial difficulty and help them avoid the escalation of debt.

Elaine Chase and Robert Walker explore the psychosocial dimensions of poverty, with a focus on the concept of shame. They present findings from an ESRC research project undertaken in seven countries that was largely informed by the disciplines of social policy, sociology and anthropology. The study is based on an analysis of the representation of poverty through a range of cultural media (including film and literature) alongside interview data on the lived experience of poverty across the seven countries. Their findings reveal that people in poverty struggle to consume in ways which enable them to meet both their own and societal expectations, resulting in vulnerability to ridicule and feelings of inadequacy. They also discuss findings from focus groups with more affluent consumers on the negative assumptions held about people living in poverty, drawing conclusions on the challenges they encounter in being valued as 'viable' consumers.

Chase and Walker's chapter indicates that the school is one arena where competitive consumption is particularly prominent. This theme is continued in the final chapter, by Sara Bryson and Stephen Crossley, on 'Poverty-Proofing the School Day', an initiative developed by a regional children's charity in the UK to tackle child poverty. Input from children and young people revealed that policies and practices across the school day often unintentionally stigmatise children from poorer backgrounds and create barriers to their learning. Examples include the expectation that parent will provide resources for class activities, uniform requirements (such as branded sportswear) or debt letters sent to parents who are behind in their payments for school meals. In response to these findings, the charity developed a toolkit to poverty-proof the school day, to reduce the stigma and remove the barriers to learning.

References

Arnould, E., L. Price, and R. Moisio (2006), 'Making contexts matter: Selecting research contexts for theoretical insights'. In R. W. Belk (ed). *Handbook of Qualitative Research Methods in Marketing*, Cheltenham, UK: Edward Elgar, 106–125.

Askegaard, Søren, and Jeppe TrolleLinnet (2011), 'Towards an epistemology of consumer culture theory: Phenomenology and the context of context', *Marketing Theory* 11(4), 381–404.

Baker, S.M., J.W. Gentry, and T.L. Rittenburg (2005), 'Building understanding of the domain of consumer vulnerability', *Journal of Macromarketing*, 25(2), 128–139.

Baker, S.M., D.M. Hunt, and T.L. Rittenburg (2007), 'Consumer vulnerability as a shared experience: Tornado recovery process in Wright, Wyoming', *Journal of Public Policy & Marketing*, 26(1), 6–19.

Blumer, H. (1954), 'What is wrong with social theory?', *American Sociological Review*, 19(1), 3–10.

Bohm, D. (1996), *On Dialogue*, Routledge: London.

Crenshaw, K. (1989), 'Demarginalizing the intersection of race and sex: A black feminist critique of antidiscrimination doctrine, feminist theory, and anti-racist politics', *University of Chicago Legal Forum*, 139–167.

Hawkins, L., J. Fook, and M. Ryan (2001), 'Social workers' use of the language of social justice', *British Journal of Social Work*, 31(1), 1–13.

Mason, M.J., J.F. Tanner, M. Piacentini, D. Freeman, T. Anastasia, W. Batat, W. Boland, M. Canbulut, J. Drenten, A. Hamby, P. Rangan, and Z. Yang (2013), 'Advancing a participatory approach for youth risk behavior: foundations, distinctions, and research', *Journal of Business Research*, 66(8), 1235–1241.

Ozanne, J. L. and L. Anderson (2010), 'Community Action Research', *Journal of Public Policy and Marketing*, 29 (Spring), 123–137.

Pechmann, C., E.S. Moore, A.R. Andreasen, P.M. Connell, D. Freeman, M.P. Gardner, D. Heisley, R.C. Lefebvre, D.M. Pirouz, and R.L. Soster (2011), 'Navigating the central tensions in research on consumers who are at risk: challenges and opportunities', *Journal of Public Policy and Marketing*, 30(1), 23–30.

Prior, S. (2010), 'Overcoming stigma: how young people position themselves as counselling service users', *Sociology of Health & Illness*, 34(5), 679–713.

Smith, N.C. and E. Cooper-Martin (1997), 'Ethics and target marketing: The role of product harm and consumer vulnerability', *Journal of Marketing*, 61 (July), 1–20.

Part I

Mapping the domain of consumer vulnerability

2 Consumer vulnerability

Foundations, phenomena, and future investigations

Stacey Menzel Baker, Monica LaBarge and Courtney Nations Baker

Approaches to vulnerability analysis

Vulnerability analysis has a rich history throughout the social and professional sciences, with scholars studying people, conditions, and experiences characterized as vulnerable (a status) or by vulnerability (a state). In essence, vulnerability analysis encompasses a set of theories and methods whereby the human experience of the *potential* for harm or the *materialization* of harm is explored. People, places, and situations characterized as at-risk, stigmatized, powerless, dependent, and/or as transformed via a physical, psychological, or social harm are explored. The diversity of theories and methods encompassed by the vulnerability analysis label provides a window into the multifaceted and complex nature of the experience of consumer vulnerability, as well as what it means to be a vulnerable consumer.

We discuss three different methodological approaches to vulnerability analysis. First, researchers may isolate particular populations based on their biophysical or psychosocial characteristics, such as age or race. Second, scholars may isolate particular environmental conditions, such as poverty or disaster recovery in communities. Third, academics may focus on the meaning and experience of vulnerability, allowing biophysical, psychosocial, and environmental conditions to vary. As each approach is unpacked, we identify extant research, discuss conceptual and methodological issues, and consider benefits and pitfalls.

Isolating particular populations of people

A particular population of "vulnerable consumers" may be isolated on the basis of biophysical or psychosocial characteristics. From Andreasen's (1975) *The Disadvantaged Consumer* forward, researchers working in the vulnerability space have commonly foregrounded individual difference variables including gender (Bristor and Fischer 1995), age (LaBarge and Pyle 2011; Moschis 1992), race (Ainscough and Motley 2000), mobility impairment (Kaufman-Scarborough 1999), sensory impairment (Kaufman-Scarborough and Childers 2009), sexual orientation (Kates and Belk 2001); social variables including ethnicity (Crockett and Wallendorf

2004) and socioeconomic status (Hill 2001); institutionalization (Hill and Rapp 2014); states of body such as addiction (Hirschman 1995); or states of mind such as grief (Gentry et al. 1995). By isolating groups of people with particular character-istics or in a particular state of being, researchers tend to make one of two points with respect to vulnerability: (1) people with these characteristics are "at risk" for harm and their risk is associated with their status in society or their state of being, or (2) people with one (or more) of these characteristics are not homogeneous, are under-represented, provide unique insights, *deserve* a voice and can cope in the marketplace.

At-risk populations

Some biophysical or psychosocial characteristics are identified as "at risk" because historical trends reveal that people with particular characteristics are more likely to experience harm than those without the characteristics (Pechmann et al. 2011). Individual characteristics are assumed to be limitations and the appropriate market and policy response is assumed to be protection. For example, empirical work shows adolescents are more vulnerable than adults to advertisements for cigarettes and alcohol due to 1) greater impulsivity, 2) greater self-consciousness and self-doubt, and 3) an elevated long-term risk from product use (Pechmann et al. 2005). This type of stimulus-response analysis helps to easily identify who is vulnerable, as well as who should be the target of any protective measures. Data are used to bring awareness to the susceptibility of harm for particular groups, and then, through social negotiation, it is determined which particular population characteristics and situations should be protected, as well as what type of interventions should be used. Public policies, such as the Civil Rights Act of 1964 and the American Disabilities Act of 1990, established precedent through legal opinions over the last century, and business practices may be created or adjusted to recognize and address different types of at-risk groups (Baker and Kaufman-Scarborough 2001; Pechmann et al. 2011).

One difficulty with this approach is that generalizations may be made beyond the historical patterns to project into the future that a particular individual with a particular characteristic is vulnerable, or susceptible to harm, all of the time (Baker and Gentry 2006). The "elderly," who are often conceptualized as anyone over 65 years old, are frequently given as a proto-typical example of a vulner-able group. However, empirical evidence suggests that the factors that might make older adults more vulnerable, including reduced sophistication, lower literacy, or poverty, in the marketplace are also present in younger populations. Thus, there is little empirical evidence to suggest that being "old" is a sufficient criterion for being weak or dependent (Moschis 1992).

When results are generalized beyond the intent of the data, the method may be criticized as being paternalistic and incapable of distinguishing between perceived and actual vulnerability in the marketplace (Baker et al. 2014; Smith and Cooper-Martin 1997). In other words, when vulnerability is treated as a status characteristic it is difficult to distinguish between those with elevated risk and those who would or could engage in risky behaviours. It is also difficult to determine under what conditions a person with those status characteristics may experience harm in the marketplace. These types of limitations have catalyzed a series of studies that isolate particular population characteristics, but which flow from a subjective (versus stimulus-response) perspective.

The subjective perspective of under-represented populations

Research flowing from the subjective perspective shares four key characteristics. First, it embraces the notion that people within a population group are heterogeneous and experience situations differently (Bristor and Fisher 1995). For instance, Adkins and Ozanne (2005) identify tremendous differences between people with low literacy skills. Social isolates accept the label of illiterate and feel shame. Social deceivers accept their stigma, but actively work to manage social interaction. Identity exchangers and enhancers challenge the stigma of low literacy and empower themselves by learning to read. Finally, proficient consumers reject the label of illiterate and make use of the resources they have.

Second, the subjective perspective assumes a great deal of variance exists within and between people, and the meaning of an experience depends on the receiver and how she or he experiences a situation. Baker, Stephens, and Hill (2001) reveal how consumers with visual impairments may be simultaneously dependent and independent in a particular domain of interaction. In other words, psychological meanings derive from dependence and independence, and these meanings vary by environmental conditions, personal characteristics, and the domain of behavior. Importantly, a person with a visual impairment is not dependent in every situation or domain of behaviour. Further, consumer research shows that for people with mobility impairments, the sociological meanings of marketplace access go well beyond structural accommodation (Kaufman-Scarborough 1999) and that while minority groups may perceive the functional and identity meanings of brands similar to how the majority perceives them, meanings also include broader social meanings (Bennett, Hill, and Oleksiuk 2013). For some consumers, these deeper social meanings relate to inclusion (versus exclusion) and participation (versus stigma or scrutiny) in society (see also Baker 2006).

Third, a particular population is isolated because the population can provide unique insights that are not typically generated for theoretical and empirical development. Baker's (2006) research conducted among people with visual impairments shows that *any* person may value shopping, because shopping allows them to participate or just *be* in the marketplace, achieve distinction, demonstrate competence and control, and be perceived as an equal.

Finally, research conducted within under-represented groups may empower members by articulating their under-represented voices to the marketplace and to public policymakers (Adkins and Ozanne 2005; Baker 2006; Baker, Stephens, and Hill 2001; Bristor and Fisher 1995; Lee, Ozanne, and Hill 1999). Hill and Martin (2014) call attention to the fact that most of the pages of consumer research scholarship have been devoted to 15 percent of the world's population: those who are able-bodied, affluent, educated, and primarily Anglo-Saxon – those who have an abundance of choice. In other words, the theory and methods of consumer behaviour have largely failed to account for 85 percent of the world's population. The research, which flows from the subjective perspective and which isolates people in particular, under-represented populations, is an attempt to rectify this oversight. And, it may give voice to people typically excluded from participation. For example, Baker's (2006) research was employed by lawmakers in the province of Manitoba, Canada who were wrestling with how barriers to participation could be removed so that a more "inclusive" Manitoba could be achieved (Howard and Rondeau 2010).

Isolating particular environmental conditions

A second approach to vulnerability analysis is to isolate environmental conditions, and then explore how people respond and how situations unfold within these conditions. Research in this vein approaches the context in one of two ways. First, the research approach may examine a particular environmental context and show how the context disables the human beings operating within it. Second, the research approach may take a subjective perspective, showing boundary conditions when people are and are not vulnerable within a particular environmental condition.

Disabling environments

In this approach, a particular environmental condition may be assumed as disabling all the time, or at least all the time for some groups of people. Researchers foreground a particular type of social problem, structural issue, environmental disruption, or business practice that disempowers the people who must operate within it. Assumptions about placing blame on the population are critically evaluated and conclusions are tested against other plausible explanations. For instance, Hill (1994, 2001) raises awareness on the social problem of homelessness. Unemployment, deinstitutionalization, scarcity of low-cost housing, drug addiction, and abusive living conditions create systemic circumstances that disempower human beings and contribute to the issue of homelessness. In other words, homelessness is not necessarily a result of characteristics of the person; rather, homelessness may be due to environmental conditions.

In terms of structural issues, Crockett and Wallendorf (2004) raise awareness on how the distribution of large food stores (100–249 employees) in a major city (Milwaukee) creates inequalities and disparities of consumption choice for people in particular ethnoracial groups. Housing patterns and store locations mean that blacks and Hispanics living in the area of Black Milwaukee, where there is only one large food store, typically face a smaller assortment of goods and higher prices than those shopping outside of Black Milwaukee. Similarly, multiple studies within the healthcare space illuminate how structural factors limit treatment options and create disparities, particularly for some consumer groups (Lee, Ozanne, and Hill 1999; Scammon, Li, and Williams 1994). For instance, Franzak, Smith, and Desch (1995) show how structural issues, including public policies that limit treatments available in particular geographic regions, contribute to a lack of appropriate care for the treatment of cancer for people living in rural areas.

Disrupted environments also may be foregrounded to highlight vulnerability and the potential or realization of physical, psychological, or social harm. Following natural hazard events, some people lose homes and meaningful possessions, and these losses fundamentally alter their self-identity (Sayre 1994). Because of the nature of disasters, an entire community of people simultaneously experiences the loss of lives, infrastructure, homes, and possessions. Such losses diminish the ability of the people surrounding an individual to provide the type of social support witnessed in times of personal crisis. People share a sense of vulnerability where personal losses are compounded by losses felt by neighbours and damages to the fabric of social life and environmental conditions (Baker, Hunt, and Rittenburg 2007). Social groups have to make sense of these losses, and members often use marketing and consumption activities to do so (Baker 2009). The processes of working with damaged and donated material objects help community members reconstitute a shared sense of "we," as well as an individual sense of "me" (Baker and Hill 2013). Working through the meanings of damaged and donated goods can exacerbate or create new vulnerabilities, in part because of tensions inherent in collective versus individual identities as understood by the group.

Unscrupulous business practices also may be highlighted in this approach. For instance, advertising that depicts sexualized violence in ads may increase acceptance of cross-gender aggression and rape and increase the vulnerability of potential or actual victims, even though it has little impact on marketing success (Capella et al. 2010). Further, the practice of target-marketing tobacco, alcohol, entertainment violence, and unhealthful foods to children, adolescents, ethnic minority populations is related to adverse public health consequences felt disproportionately by the segments targeted (Grier and Kumanyika 2010). And the practice of locating fast-food restaurants, which serve high-caloric foods, close to urban schools is related to higher body weight, particularly for black and Hispanic students (Grier and Davis 2013).

Ultimately, the studies that foreground particular environmental issues make three principal contributions. First, they show how particular structural conditions, social and material environments, or business practices contribute to the vulnerabilities people face. In doing so, the studies make salient conditions and practices of which people (policymakers, managers, consumers) may not be aware. Second, they illuminate how some social groups, because of their geographic location and social composition, may experience greater impacts. Finally, they show how structural characteristics of the environment limit access and constrain consumer choice. These contributions are important because in many situations it is unlikely that individuals can effect change on their own, such as in racial and ethnic minority consumers seeking loans, yet being constantly faced with systemic, chronic, and controlled restrictions on loan options, especially when compared to similar white consumers (Bone, Christensen, and Williams 2014). Thus, identifying and trying to address environmental conditions that create vulnerabilities may be the biggest source of relief for those human beings made vulnerable by particular environmental forces.

The subjective experience of disabling environments

One potential pitfall to treating the environment as disabling is that the approach may not recognize when or how people actively and constructively resist oppressive environments. People who experience homelessness seek work in nontraditional ways, by scavenging or by becoming a member of the homeless community where possessions are shared (Hill and Stamey 1990). People imprisoned in the Buchenwald concentration camp actively resisted their commoditization by staging performances and creating artistic works such as songs and poems (Hirschman and Hill 2000). And some people may willingly take on the elevated prices and be subject to what some may see as unscrupulous business practices in the rent-to-own industry simply because it is easy to obtain credit, credit is unavailable elsewhere, quick transactions are desired, and ownership is important (Hill, Ramp, and Silver 1998).

This body of work contributes by showing that even in dire environmental circumstances people still may find ways to be active agents in their own consumption choices. In addition, the work reveals the spirit of what it means to be human. It honours the identities of people against whom structural inequities work and those whom oppressors attempt to dehumanize and commoditize.

Isolating meanings and processes

In the third approach, researchers isolate the meanings and processes of vulnerability, allowing both the population and the environmental condition to vary. Research in this space explores the experiential and symbolic aspects of vulnerability. The work in this space varies by perspective and unit of analysis. The first perspective focuses on the subjective experience of individual vulnerability, and the second perspective explores the socially constructed vulnerability of a social group.

Individual vulnerability

Vulnerability may be conceptualized as a dynamic state of powerlessness and dependence. Baker, Gentry, and Rittenburg (2005) comprehensively reviewed the literature in marketing and consumer research, which they classified as 'on vulnerability' as defined by a particular population or a particular environmental condition. By drawing upon this extensive body of empirical work and thereby allowing population and environmental condition to vary, the authors offer a conceptual definition of the construct.

> Consumer vulnerability is a state of powerlessness that arises from an imbalance in marketplace interactions or from the consumption of marketing messages and products. It occurs when control is not in an individual's hands, creating a dependence on external factors (e.g. marketers) to create fairness in the marketplace. The actual vulnerability arises from the interaction of individual states, individual characteristics, and external conditions within a context where consumption goals may be hindered and the experience affects personal and social perceptions of self.
>
> (Baker et al. 2005, p. 134).

This conceptualization indicates that vulnerability resides in a relationship between person and a stimulus object, e.g. an interaction in a retail store, consumption of a consumer good, receiving an advertising message. A damaged relationship greatly reduces or nullifies consumer agency (see also Baker et al. 2014). The lack of power or control experienced by an individual in this damaged relationship makes a person dependent on external factors (environmental conditions) to ensure the reduction or amelioration of that vulnerability. The model embraces and flows from the first two approaches to vulnerability analysis, but here the focus is clearly on how a particular individual subjectively experiences a particular situation as disempowering and as a threat to their physical, psychological, or social safety. This work also conceptualizes consumer vulnerability as a multi-dimensional latent construct that sits within a nomological network whose antecedents include individual states, individual characteristics, and external conditions, and whose outcomes include identity reconstitution and coping.

Baker and Mason (2012) extend the original (2005) model to illuminate that a trigger event (e.g. job loss, severing of a relationship), as well as subsequent aftershocks (e.g. discontinued bus route), may expose our vulnerabilities (e.g. powerlessness, dependence). In addition, the extended model accounts for the resiliency of people, acknowledges that different stakeholder groups have interests that may reduce or exacerbate vulnerability, and recognizes the transformative potential of exposing vulnerabilities.

Conceptual and empirical research consistent with this perspective has contributed by providing a deeper understanding of the experiential aspects of vulnerability and the practical application of that understanding. In terms of theoretical development, Botti and her colleagues (2008) focus on particular choices made in restricted environments. This work highlights important dimensions of restriction, including the source (internally imposed vs. externally imposed), duration (temporary, intermittent, permanent), and immediacy of the decision. Further, the relationship between the experience of vulnerability and particular outcomes has been addressed. For example, Pavia and Mason (2004) show how breast cancer survivors shed clothes and possessions which they associate with their disease, as a precondition for their eventual, long-term wellbeing and status as a "survivor."

Numerous practical applications flow from this type of approach. Service providers may understand better how to recover after a service delivery failure due to dysfunctional consumer participation (Hibbert, Piacentini, and Hogg 2012), and service providers and policymakers may understand better how to create website accessibility for people with disabilities and why accessibility is important (Kaufman-Scarborough and Childers 2009). In addition, research insights may help to discern which unscrupulous business practices should be addressed. Empirical work with over 24,000 complaints filed with a local Better Business Bureau office over a 13-year period provides evidence that the BBB is better able to understand and address consumer complaining behavior when they focus on the experience of vulnerability (What happened? What did the experience feel like?), rather than on the demographics (age, income, education, race) of who complains (Garrett and Toumanoff 2010).

Collective vulnerability

In this research approach, vulnerability is recognized as socially constructed, dynamic, and systemic (Baker, Hunt, and Rittenburg 2007; Baker and Mason 2012; Shultz and Holbrook 2009; Layton 2007; Sachs 2005). Shared vulnerability can unite people and give them strength in the face of adversity (Baker, Hunt, and Rittenburg 2007), such as when community members share possessions and experience a sense of communitas at various point throughout disaster recovery (Baker and Hill 2013). Similarly, members of a Weight Watcher's community may share their feelings of personal inadequacy, and this helps members realize they are not alone in their quest to shed weight and anxieties and desire to enhance their overall wellbeing (Moisio and Beruchashvili 2010).

To capture the dynamic nature of collective vulnerability, Shultz and Holbrook (2009) adopt a macro perspective to classify four different types of vulnerability experiences based upon cultural and economic capital: (1) the doubly vulnerable (low knowledge, low resources), (2) economically vulnerable (knowledge, but low resources), (3) culturally vulnerable (resources, but low knowledge or care), and (4) invulnerable (high knowledge, high resources, and can avoid vulnerability). This model embraces the assumption that people enter and exit various states of security based upon their cultural and economic capital. In contrast, the variables of analysis used when we isolate a population as at risk assume a static conception of people.

Also from a macro perspective, Saatcioglu and Ozanne (2013) explore how the consumption practices of low-income, working-class residents of a mobile home community are shaped by different moral identities. Each identity derives from how people enact their economic, cultural, social, and symbolic resources in the practices of their daily lives. This model embraces the assumption that identity is fluid; thus, the practices in which individuals engage can change throughout the course of their lives. Further, the model articulates that the people living in the trailer park are not a homogeneous segment of society.

In terms of a nomological network for collective vulnerability, structural and systemic factors may contribute to collective perceptions of vulnerability. For example, medical contexts, legal factors, economic resources, media, and public policy all contribute to the social construction of motherhood ideologies (Davies et al. 2010). These dominant ideologies contribute to and exacerbate the vulnerability experienced by women as they transition into a mothering role. Outcomes of collective vulnerability include a changed sense of collective identity and a transformed collective understanding of the nature of what it means to live well and do well (Baker and Hill 2013).

Analysis of collective vulnerability can be practically applied, such as by offering an ethical framework for businesses seeking to address human beings living at the bottom of the economic pyramid (Santos and Laczniak 2009). According to the Integrative Justice Model for Engaging Impoverished Marketing Segments (Santos and Laczniak 2009), to diffuse the charge of exploitative marketing, businesses must consider it a moral imperative to authentically engage with impoverished customers (see also Hill 2005; Shultz and Holbrook 2009). Further, businesses must co-create value with impoverished consumers, represent the interest of all customers, and focus on long-term, rather than short-term, profits (Santos and Laczniak 2009).

Summary of approaches

Table 2.1 summarises the three different approaches to vulnerability analysis (population, environment, meanings) that are generally foregrounded to high-light research contributions. While each approach is treated as distinct, it is important to note that some studies simultaneously address and make contributions to our understanding of all three aspects (population characteristics, environmental conditions, and meanings). For example, Chaplin, Hill, and John (2014) address children living in poverty and their self-esteem as tied to material possessions. They find that impoverished youth are more materialistic and have lower self-esteem than their wealthier counterparts, indicating the importance of public policy solutions aimed at reducing vulnerability for a particular population, in a particular environmental condition (neighborhood), and with particular meanings (reducing materialistic values that impact identity).

At times different approaches are contrasted to see which approach provides a better explanation of a phenomenon. Garrett and Toumanoff (2010) contrasted the explanatory power of isolating populations to the power of isolating meanings and found that the latter approach allowed the Better Business Bureau to better address consumer complaining behavior. At other times, approaches are combined to isolate meanings and processes for particular populations (Baker, Gentry, and Rittenburg 2005; Kaufman-Scarborough and Baker 2005). Kaufman-Scarborough and Baker (2005) analyzed perceptions of people with disabilities following the implementation of the Americans with Disabilities Act

Table 2.1 Vulnerability approaches

	Isolating particular populations of people	Isolating particular environmental conditions	Isolating meanings and processes
	At-risk populations	Disabling environments	Individual vulnerability
Core assumptions	• People with these characteristics are at risk for harm, based on status in society or state of being • Perceived homogeneity of group and its experience • Characteristics as limitations • Protection as appropriate response (intervention and public policy) • The subjective perspective of under-represented populations • Heterogeneity of group • Variance within and between people • Unique experiences and insights • Empowering group members through articulating their voices	• Environmental condition as constantly disabling • Disempowering social problems, structural issues, environmental disruptions, or business practices • Vulnerabilities specific to geographic region or social composition • Limited access or constrained consumer choice • The subjective experience of disabling environments • Finds boundary conditions for when to expect vulnerability • People find ways to exert agency in disabling environments • Reveals the human spirit	• Dynamic state of powerlessness and dependence • Interaction of individual states, individual characteristics, and external conditions • Goals may be hindered and self-perception may be affected • Reduced consumer agency • Identity reconstitution as an outcome • Collective vulnerability • Vulnerability as socially constructed, dynamic, and systemic • Shared vulnerability may unite and strengthen a group • Structural and systemic factors contribute to collective perceptions of vulnerability
Contextual domains in extant research	• Sex, age, race, mobility impairment, sensory impairment, sexual orientation, ethnicity, socioeconomic status, institutionalization, addiction, grief	• Homelessness, low-income housing, natural disaster, sexualized violence in advertising, loan restrictions, rent-to-own	• Job loss, severed relationship, weight loss, service delivery failure, business/service complaints, disaster recovery, nutrition, working-class residential areas, motherhood

(continued overleaf)

Table 2.1 (continued)

	Isolating particular populations of people	Isolating particular environmental conditions	Isolating meanings and processes
Methodological issues	• Groups often excluded from research studies • Difficult to access members • Difficult to mimic in lab setting • Must use caution to not exacerbate vulnerability or risk through research	• May not be able to recognize active resistance to oppressive environments • Difficult to create realistic disabling environment in lab • Impossible to capture all aspects of environment and its influence	• Vulnerability as multi-dimensional latent construct within a nomological network
Benefits of approach	• Gives attention to under-represented groups • Offers concrete solution to policymakers • Represents the unique voices of group members • Facilitates target marketing	• Better understanding of external (and possibly preventable) sources of vulnerability • Allows for planning to control or prepare for environmental circumstances • Shows boundary conditions • Tests and critically evaluates assumptions about blame	• Both the population and environmental condition can vary • More genuine depiction of conditions for vulnerability • Accounts for resiliency of people • Acknowledges various stakeholder groups • Recognizes transformative potential of exposing vulnerabilities • Recommends practices for avoiding conditions of vulnerability
Detriments of approach	• Overgeneralizations • Neglect other relevant factors • Wrongly perceive group as constantly susceptible to harm • Respond to all members of groups in the same way • Assumes vulnerability is constant	• Focus solely on externalities, rather than on human contribution to situation • Environments are complex and difficult to fully understand	• Extremely complex • Requires extended research endeavors employing multiple techniques • Requires case-by-case analysis

of 1990 in the U.S. In their analysis, they combined the medical model (isolating particular populations) with the social model (isolating particular environmental conditions) to develop the Consumer Response Model (isolating meanings and processes) as an explanation for the vulnerability that people with disabilities may perceive in the marketplace. These results suggest that if policymakers want to examine the true impact of an intervention such as the ADA, they should assess its outcomes by looking at population impacts, environmental impacts, and the social and psychological meanings derived from its outcomes (i.e. use all three approaches to vulnerability analysis).

In a practical sense, there is no one "best" approach to vulnerability analysis. Rather, we advocate pluralism with the ultimate aim of enhancing the human condition. However, we do note the political and social ramifications for how vulnerability is conceptualized. The conceptualization and approach affects how interventions are designed, who or what is seen as the target of the intervention, and how and where resources are distributed.

Future research on vulnerability

The previous section demonstrated the richness and variety of perspectives and contexts for examining vulnerability. In this section, we consider some possible questions for future research.

Should vulnerability be eliminated?

Shultz and Holbrook (2009) argue that we have "a moral imperative to protect vulnerable consumers – ideally in a way that eliminates their vulnerability completely or, at least, that turns [it] into temporary invulnerability." This assertion is predicated on the assumption that vulnerability is always a negative consequence. In much of the literature on vulnerability there is an implicit assumption that vulnerability necessarily detracts from consumer wellbeing (Baker, Gentry, and Rittenburg 2005). Certainly, in the case of individuals who do not have access to basic income or some adequate level of resources that will allow them to live healthfully or even hope for a better future, vulnerability can be a source for frustration and despair and an impediment to survival. For consumers considered more fortunate, for whom thoughts of survival rarely surface and who instead strive for more lofty goals such as personal growth and fulfillment, might some degree of vulnerability provide an opportunity?

In the relationship literature in psychology, it is well-established that vulnerability is necessary to achieve intimacy. Clearly, allowing oneself to be vulnerable (open to love or rejection) is a prerequisite for an authentic, lasting relationship. Further, when individuals seek personal transformation, vulnerability may be necessary to create lasting change. Consider weight loss regimes where individuals share their experiences of vulnerability and success (Moisio and Beruchashvili 2010). The process of sharing requires the individual to admit their vulnerability, such as the control food has over their life, and their own biological and psychological factors, and to discuss the role of outside forces (locations of fast-food chains, commercials, family rituals) in nurturing their eating habits. The sharing of our vulnerabilities may allow individuals to turn away from emotions like guilt and shame and toward emotions like self-compassion and courage. Thus, surely there are times when vulnerability might result in positive consequences. Under what conditions can the experience of vulnerability create uplifting changes for individuals? Are there cases in which negative circumstances of vulnerability could create uplifting changes for groups? For example, particularly in cases where a whole community experiences the same traumatizing event – such as being nearly decimated by a tornado – collective action and community-driven reconstruction can breathe new life into and produce new opportunities (Baker and Baker 2014).

There are implicit assumptions in our notion that vulnerability *should* be eliminated and that we *can* eradicate it. But we cannot. Management activities are often predicated on the implicit assumption that outcomes can be controlled. For example, disaster management, to a certain extent, assumes nature can be controlled. Such an illusion may inhibit the planning necessary for withstanding (and occasionally for surviving) a powerful natural hazard event, and it may also inhibit responses in the face of an event. What is the appropriate level of sensitivity to vulnerability? How does sensitivity to vulnerability relate to coping, resilience, identity, and overall wellbeing?

How do temporal factors relate to vulnerability?

When we embrace the assumption that vulnerability is situational, we embrace the possibility that individuals and social groups can move beyond circumstances that may render them powerless and dependent. Clearly, this is a normative position, an ideal for which to strive. Just as clearly there are circumstances when it seems nearly impossible to surmount adversity. At the extreme abject poverty, incarceration, mass imprisonment, and genocide seem nearly impossible to tackle. Yet, individuals, communities, countries, and global networks do respond, though sometimes these responses take time, and sometimes such responses never come to fruition. We know little about how and why individuals and social groups move in and out of states of vulnerability. How do our perceptions about the potential for harm influence the materialization of harm? What are the impacts of the materialization of harm when the potential for harm was never perceived? Under what conditions is vulnerability more or less enduring? Are individuals and social groups who have already experienced vulnerability in a particular domain (e.g. discrimination, disaster recovery) more or less prepared for future vulnerability experiences? If so, how?

In the face of vulnerability, what should the baseline of material support be?

Hill (2005, p. 217) asserts that we [marketers, researchers, citizens] have a "moral obligation as a society embedded in a consumer world," to ensure that "all persons should have reasonable access to those items that sustain healthful living as well as goods and services that support a better future." His assertion is predicated on the idea that *consumer* wellbeing spills over onto other life domains (*environmental, spiritual*) affecting overall, subjective wellbeing. Consider that the ramifications of not fulfilling obligations to fellow citizens may include political uprisings, terrorism and war, community conflict, and human suffering. Clearly, a baseline of support is a moral imperative, and it likely makes economic sense as well. Is there a standard package of sorts for a baseline of consumption? What types of goods are included? Are services part of the package, and, if so, which ones? How does the environmental context (material abundance or lack of abundance in a particular neighbourhood, region, country) affect the contents of a baseline of consumption? Further, when people are dependent on market mechanisms or policy interventions, they rely on a consistent availability of the goods and services necessary for survival, self-determination and dignity. Under what circumstances might the market or sources of aid not ensure a baseline of support? What responses could be initiated in those circumstances?

What are the trade-offs between individual and collective vulnerability?

Because how vulnerability is conceptualized affects how, where, and to whom resources are allocated, the concept of vulnerability can become a tool in the struggle for resources (Baker 2009). The approaches of isolating a particular population or environmental condition seem to suggest a uniform response where anyone in the population or who is impacted by the environment could be the recipient of resources or protection. In contrast, when meanings and processes of vulnerability are isolated, this allows for response on a case-by-case basis. Are there conditions where one approach is better than the other? Could models be developed to determine alternative scenarios?

How are trade-offs between individuals and groups made and with what effects? Baker and Hill (2013) show how disaster recovery in community can result in some individuals being forced to sacrifice for the good of the group, or in the group sacrificing for the good of some individuals. On a practical level, how could we move decision-making in disaster management beyond the transactional approach, where there are clear winners and losers in particular decisions, to a broader relational approach, where decision-making accounts for outcomes in previous situations? We can envision that the pluralistic methods and guiding precepts of participatory action research (e.g. Ozanne and Saaticioglu 2008), as well as choice models on different decision-making scenarios (e.g. Botti et al. 2008), would be helpful in further exploring these trade-offs.

Concluding remarks

In much of the vulnerability literature, including much of the work by the first author of this chapter, vulnerability is assumed to be a negative state of being, all of the time. But this assumption is flawed. Human beings have imperfections, and they experience hardship. Real life includes difficult circumstances, such as the dissolution of marriage, the death of a loved one, the loss of a job, a tornado that tears at the social life of community, or a fire that destroys a family's home. All of these are possibilities. None of us is immune.

Brené Brown (2012), an academician who studies vulnerability, shame, and the power of positive thinking, believes: "Vulnerability is not weakness. And that myth is profoundly dangerous." Following that logic, there are at least three potential negative consequences of human beings not allowing themselves to experience vulnerability. First, people may not expect to experience hardship and, therefore, have a difficult time coping when they experience it. Second, some people may not allow themselves the "luxury" of being vulnerable, such as in the deepening of a relationship or in really feeling the losses that come from the death of a loved one or from the loss of homes and meaningful possessions. If people never allow themselves to feel love and loss, then they miss out on essential emotions that are a fundamental part of what it means to be human. Finally, vulnerability may be a catalyst, an opportunity, for individual and social transformation. Over 2,000 years ago, a Greek poet, Horace, said, "Adversity is wont to reveal genius, prosperity to hide it." In our moments of vulnerability (adversity), perhaps we might want to lean in and learn its lessons.

References

Adkins, Natalie Ross and Julie L. Ozanne (2005), "The Low Literate Consumer," *Journal of Consumer Research*, 32(1), 93–105.

Ainscough, Thomas L. and Carol M. Motley (2000), "Will You Help Me Please? The Effects of Race, Gender and Manner of Dress on Retail Service," *Marketing Letters*, 11(2), 129–136.

Andreasen, Alan R. (1975), *The Disadvantaged Consumer*, New York: The Free Press.

Baker, Stacey Menzel (2006), "Consumer Normalcy: Understanding the Value of Shopping Through Narratives of Consumers with Visual Impairments," *Journal of Retailing*, 82(1), 37–50.

Baker, Stacey Menzel (2009), "Vulnerability and Resilience in Natural Disasters: A Marketing and Public Policy Perspective," *Journal of Public Policy & Marketing*, 28(Spring), 114–123.

Baker, Stacey Menzel and Carol Kaufman-Scarborough (2001), "Marketing and Public Accommodation: A Retrospective on the Americans with Disabilities Act," *Journal of Public Policy & Marketing*, 20 (Fall), 297–304.

Baker, Stacey Menzel and James W. Gentry (2006), "Framing the Research and Avoiding Harm: Representing the Vulnerability of Consumers," in *Handbook of Qualitative Research Methods in Marketing*, Russell W. Belk, ed. Brookfield: Edward Elgar Publishing, 322–332.

Baker, Stacey Menzel and Marlys Mason (2012), "Toward a Process Theory of Consumer Vulnerability and Resilience: Illuminating its Transformative Potential," in *Transformative Consumer Research: For Personal and Collective Well-Being*, David Glen Mick, Simone Pettigrew, Cornelia Pechmann, and Julie L. Ozanne, eds. Abingdon: Taylor & Francis/Routledge, 543–563.

Baker, Stacey Menzel, and Ronald Paul Hill (2013), "A Community Psychology of Object Meanings: Identity Negotiation during Disaster Recovery," *Journal of Consumer Psychology*, 23(3), 275–287.

Baker, Stacey Menzel and Courtney Nations Baker (2014), "Keeping the Bounce in our Steps: Community Narratives of Vulnerability and Resistance and their Relationship to Shared Material Resources," Working Paper, University of Wyoming.

Baker, Stacey Menzel, Debra Lynn Stephens, and Ronald Paul Hill (2001), "Marketplace Experiences of Consumers with Visual Impairments: Beyond the Americans with Disabilities Act," *Journal of Public Policy and Marketing*, 20 (Fall), 215–224.

Baker, Stacey Menzel, James W. Gentry, and Terri L. Rittenburg (2005), "Building Understanding of the Domain of Consumer Vulnerability," *Journal of Macromarketing*, 25(2), 128–139.

Baker, Stacey Menzel, David M. Hunt, and Terri L. Rittenburg (2007), "Consumer Vulnerability as a Shared Experience: Tornado Recovery Process in Wright Wyoming," *Journal of Public Policy & Marketing*, 26 (Spring), 6–19.

Baker, Stacey Menzel, James W. Gentry, Stephanie Geiger-Oneto, and Courtney Nations Baker (2014), "Identity Degradation in Consumption: The Phenomenology of Consumer Vulnerability across Time and Space," Working Paper, University of Wyoming.

Bennett, Aronté Marie, Ronald Paul Hill, and Daniel Oleksiuk (2013), "The Impact of Disparate Levels of Marketplace Inclusion on Consumer–Brand Relationships," *Journal of Public Policy & Marketing*, 32, Special Issue, 16–31.

Bone, Sterling A., Glenn L. Christensen, and Jerome D. Williams (2014), "Rejected, Shackled, and Alone: The Impact of Systemic Restricted Choice on Minority Consumers' Construction of Self," *Journal of Consumer Research*, 41(2), 451–474.

Botti, Simona, Susan Broniarczyk, Gerald Häubl, Ron Hill, Yanliu Huang, Barbara Kahn, Praveen Kopalle, Donald Lehmann, Joe Urbany, and Brian Wansink (2008), "Choice Under Restriction," *Marketing Letters*, 19 (July), 183–199.

Bristor, Julia, and Eileen Fischer (1995), "Exploring Simultaneous Oppressions Toward the Development of Consumer Research in the Interest of Diverse Women," *American Behavioral Scientist*, 38(4), 526–536.

Brown, Brené (2012), "Listening to Shame," Ted Talk, online, http://www.ted.com/talks/brene_brown_listening_to_shame, accessed July 25, 2014.

Capella, Michael L., Ronald Paul Hill, Justine M. Rapp, and Jeremy Kees (2010), "The Impact of Violence Against Women in Advertisements," *Journal of Advertising*, 39(4), 37–51.

Chaplin, Lan Nguyen, Ronald Paul Hill, and Deborah Roedder John (2014), "Poverty and Materialism: A Look at Impoverished Versus Affluent Children," *Journal of Public Policy & Marketing*, 33(1), 78–92.

Crockett, David and Melanie Wallendorf (2004), "The Role of Normative Political Ideology in Consumer Behavior," *Journal of Consumer Research*, 31(3), 511–528.

Davies, Andrea, Susan Dobscha, Susi Geiger, Stephanie O'Donohue, Lisa O'Malley, Andrea Prothero, Elin Brandi Sørensen, Thyra Uth Thomsen (2010), "Motherhood, Marketization, and Consumer Vulnerability: Voicing International Consumer Experiences," *Journal of Macromarketing*, 30(4), 384–397.

Franzak, Frank J., Thomas J. Smith, and Christopher E. Desch (1995), "Marketing Cancer Care to Rural Residents," *Journal of Public Policy & Marketing*, 14(1), 76–82.

Garrett, Dennis E. and Peter G. Toumanoff (2010), "Are Consumers Disadvantaged or Vulnerable? An Examination of Consumer Complaints to the Better Business Bureau," *Journal of Consumer Affairs*, 44 (Spring), 3–23.

Gentry, James W., Patricia F. Kennedy, Katherine Paul, and Ronald Paul Hill (1995), "The Vulnerability of Those Grieving the Death of a Loved One: Implications for Public Policy," *Journal of Public Policy & Marketing*, 14 (Spring), 128–142.

Grier, Sonya and Brennan Davis (2013), "Are All Proximity Effects Created Equal? Fast Food Near Schools and Body Weight Among Diverse Adolescents," *Journal of Public Policy & Marketing*, 32 (Spring), 116–128.

Grier, Sonya A. and Shiriki Kumanyika (2010), "Targeted Marketing and Public Health," *Annual Review of Public Health*, 31, 349–369.

Hibbert, Sally A., Maria G. Piacentini, and Margaret K. Hogg (2012), "Service Recovery Following Dysfunctional Consumer Participation," *Journal of Consumer Behaviour*, 11 (July/August), 329–338.

Hill, Ronald Paul (1994), "The Public Policy Issue of Homelessness: A Review and Synthesis of Existing Research," *Journal of Business Research*, 30(1), 5–12.

Hill, Ronald Paul (2001), *Surviving in a Material World: The Lived Experience of People in Poverty*. Notre Dame, IN: University of Notre Dame Press.

Hill, Ronald Paul (2005), "Do the Poor Deserve Less Than Surfers? An Essay for the Special Issue on Vulnerable Consumers," *Journal of Macromarketing*, 25(2), 215–218.

Hill, Ronald Paul and Kelly D. Martin (2014), "Broadening the Paradigm of Marketing as Exchange: A Public Policy and Marketing Perspective," *Journal of Public Policy & Marketing*, 33 (Spring), 17–33.

Hill, Ronald Paul, David L. Ramp, and Linda Silver (1998), "The Rent-to-Own Industry and Pricing Disclosure Tactics," *Journal of Public Policy & Marketing*, 17(1), 3–10.

Hill, Ronald Paul and Justine Rapp (2014), "Codes of Ethical Conduct: A Bottom-up Approach," *Journal of Business Ethics*, forthcoming.

Hill, Ronald Paul, and Mark Stamey (1990), "The Homeless in America: An Examination of Possessions and Consumption Behaviors," *Journal of Consumer Research*, 17 (December), 303–321.

Hirschman, Elizabeth C. (1995), "Professional, Personal, and Popular Culture Perspectives on Addiction," *American Behavioral Scientist*, 38(4), 537–552.

Hirschman, Elizabeth C. and Ronald Paul Hill (2000), "On Human Commoditization and Resistance: A Model Based upon Buchenwald Concentration Camp," *Psychology & Marketing*, 17 (June), 469–491.

Howard, Jennifer and Jim Rondeau (2010), "Discussion Paper for Made in Manitoba Accessibility Legislation," November, online, http://www.gov.mb.ca/dio/discussionpaper/pdf/discussionpaper.pdf, last accessed June 26, 2014.

Kates, Steven M. and Russell W. Belk (2001), "The Meanings of Lesbian and Gay Pride Day: Resistance through Consumption and Resistance to Consumption," *Journal of Contemporary Ethnography*, 30 (August), 392–429.

Kaufman-Scarborough, Carol (1999), "Reasonable Access for Mobility-Disabled Persons is More Than Widening the Door," *Journal of Retailing*, 75(4), 479–508.

Kaufman-Scarborough, Carol and Stacey Menzel Baker (2005), "Do People with Disabilities Believe the ADA Has Served Their Consumer Interests?," *Journal of Consumer Affairs*, 39 (Summer), 1–26.

Kaufman-Scarborough, Carol and Terry L. Childers (2009), "Understanding Markets as Online Public Places: Insights from Consumers with Visual Impairments," *Journal of Public Policy & Marketing*, 28 (Spring), 16–28.

LaBarge, Monica C. and Martin Pyle (2011), "Old Age Isn't So Bad When You Consider the Alternative: How Older Adults Make Good Decisions," *Society of Consumer Psychology Proceedings*, Atlanta, GA.

Layton, Roger (2007), "Marketing Systems: A Core Macromarketing Concept," *Journal of Macromarketing*, 27 (September), 227–242.

Lee, Dong-Jin, M. Joseph Sirgy, Val Larsen, and Newell D. Wright (2002), "Developing a Subjective Measure of Consumer Well-Being," *Journal of Macromarketing*, 22(2), 158–169.

Lee, Renee Gravois, Julie L. Ozanne, and Ronald Paul Hill (1999), "Improving Service Encounters Through Resource Sensitivity: The Case of Health Care Delivery in an Appalachian Community," *Journal of Public Policy & Marketing*, 18 (Fall), 230–248.

Moisio, Risto and Mariam Beruchashvili (2010), "Questing for Well-Being at Weight Watchers: The Role of the Spiritual-Therapeutic Model in Support Group," *Journal of Consumer Research*, 36 (February), 857–875.

Moschis, George C. (1992), *Marketing to Older Consumers: A Handbook of Information for Strategy Development*. Westport, CT: Quorum Books.

Ozanne, Julie L. and Bige Saatcioglu (2008), "Participatory Action Research," *Journal of Consumer Research*, 35(3), 423–439.

Pavia, Teresa M. and Marlys J. Mason (2004), "The Reflexive Relationship between Consumer Behavior and Adaptive Coping," *Journal of Consumer Research*, 31 (December), 441–454.

Pechmann, Cornelia, Linda Levine, Sandra Loughlin, and Frances Leslie (2005), "Impulsive and Self-Conscious: Adolescents' Vulnerability to Advertising and Promotion," *Journal of Public Policy & Marketing*, 24(2), 202–221.

Pechmann, Cornelia (Connie), Elizabeth S. Moore, Alan R. Andreasen, Paul M. Connell, Dan Freeman, Meryl P. Gardner, Deborah Heisley, R. Craig Lefebvre, Dante M. Pirouz, and Robin L. Soster (2011), "Navigating the Central Tensions in Research on At-Risk Consumers: Challenges and Opportunities," *Journal of Public Policy & Marketing*, 30(1), 23–30.

Saatcioglu, Bige and Julie L. Ozanne (2013), "Moral Habitus and Status Negotiation in a Marginalized Working-Class Neighborhood," *Journal of Consumer Research*, 40(4), 692–710.

Sachs, Jeffrey (2005), *The End of Poverty: How We Can Make it Happen in our Lifetime*. United Kingdom: Penguin.

Santos, Nicholas J.C. and Gene R. Laczniak (2009), "Marketing to the Poor: An Integrative Justice Model for Engaging Impoverished Market Segments," *Journal of Public Policy & Marketing*, 28(1), 3–15.

Sayre, Shay (1994), "Possessions and Identity in Crisis: Meaning and Change for Victims of the Oakland Firestorm," in *Advances in Consumer Research, 11*, Chris T. Allen and Deborah Roedder John, eds. Provo, Utah: Association for Consumer Research, 109–114.

Scammon, Debra L., Lawrence B. Li, and Scott D. Williams (1994), "Increasing the Supply of Providers for the Medically Underserved: Marketing and Public Policy Issues," *Journal of Public Policy & Marketing*, 13(2), 35–47.

Shultz, Clifford J., II and Morris B. Holbrook (2009), "The Paradoxical Relationships Between Marketing and Vulnerability," *Journal of Public Policy & Marketing*, 28(1), 124–127.

Smith, N. Craig and Elizabeth Cooper-Martin (1997), "Ethics and Target Marketing: The Role of Product Harm and Consumer Vulnerability," *Journal of Marketing*, 61 (July), 1–20.

3 An inclusive approach to consumer vulnerability

Exploring the contributions of intersectionality

Bige Saatcioglu and Canan Corus

Introduction

This chapter introduces the basic premises of the intersectionality paradigm and explores its potential theoretical and methodological contribution to the study of consumer vulnerability. Originating from the critical feminist thought, intersectionality has been described as "as a way of mediating the tension between assertions of multiple identity and the ongoing necessity of group politics" (Crenshaw 1991, p. 1296), multi-level analysis (Winker and Degele 2011), "a normative theoretical argument…to conducting empirical research that emphasizes the interaction of categories of difference" (Hancock 2007, p. 63–4), and even as "buzzword" (Davis 2008). Despite this wide array of meanings, the core insight offered by intersectionality is that every individual within a social group is positioned at the intersection of multiple identity axes (e.g. race, gender, social class, health status). As a result, everyone is subject to multiple overlapping advantages or disadvantages that are peculiar to their intersectional position.

The concept of intersectionality also denotes a set of theoretical and methodological tools to explore social inequalities and how individuals and groups manage their oppressed position (McCall 2005, Choo and Ferree 2010). Consequently, intersectionality offers insights into the ways in which the disadvantaged manage interdependent forms of vulnerability such as economic, structural, and social vulnerabilities.

Although intersectionality has been an integral part of feminist and critical thinking, particularly within the last two decades, it is a relatively new concept in consumer research [see, for an overview, Crockett et al. (2011), Gopaldas and Fischer (2012), and Gopaldas (2013)]. However, intersectionality is particularly valuable for the study of multiple interlocking forms of consumer vulnerability for a variety of reasons. First, an intersectional approach is committed to analyzing the interaction of co-existing disadvantages that are not merely additive but mutually constitutive in nature (Hancock 2007). Oftentimes, a person's vulnerability in one domain (e.g. low income) is exacerbated by other types of vulnerability (e.g. poor health, age) and can even lead to other forms of vulnerability (e.g. exclusion from the consumption domain, social stigmatization). Second, by recognizing the heterogeneous nature of social positions, intersectionality researchers delve deeper into the multiple different realities that might exist even within the same social group or setting (McCall 2005, Choo and Ferree 2010). Understanding differences in lived experiences across individuals is important because this might reveal distinct types of vulnerability, depending on the individuals' social position within a group. Finally, intersectionally driven research seeks to make visible the workings of underlying macro-level processes (e.g. racism, gender discrimination, social stigmatization) by exploring the dynamics between individual and institutional actors (Hankivsky, Cormier, and de Merich 2009). This is vital in understanding the collective, systemic, and status-based form of vulnerability that has been understudied in consumer research.[1]

A brief overview of the intersectionality paradigm

Historical roots and theoretical foundations

Emerging from Black feminist thought, the term intersectionality has been coined by Kimberlé Crenshaw (1989, 1991) in her work on violence against women of color. Initially, intersectionality researchers have relied on typically favored categorizations such as race, gender, and class to understand how oppression operates in different contexts. As the idea of intersectionality has evolved, analyses have expanded beyond traditional demographic categorizations to include the impact of simultaneously interacting identity structures such as socio-economic status, sexuality, health, religion, age, and marital status (Hankivsky, Cormier, and de Merich 2009).

Perhaps the most central theoretical principle of an intersectional approach is that social groups are rarely homogeneous and cannot be reduced to categorizations organized solely around race, gender, income, or any other single, stand-alone dimension (McCall 2005, Ozanne and Fischer 2012). Instead, an individual is positioned at the intersection of multiple "interlocking matrices of privilege and oppression" (Collins 2000). For example, a person might experience co-existing and intersecting vulnerabilities if he/she is unemployed as well as disabled, lives in a marginalized community, does not have access to necessary social networks, and feels stigmatized. On the other hand, a more privileged individual can benefit simultaneously from dimensions of being White, male, straight, and middle class. Consequently, the conceptual scope of the intersectionality has expanded to take into account "the interaction [among] categories of difference in individual lives, social practices, institutional arrangements, and cultural ideologies and the outcomes of these interactions in terms of power" (Davis 2008, p. 68).

Second, intersectionality recognizes that social positions and experiences can greatly differ even within the same social group or setting. In her book on how power relations and ideologies influence African American women's social construction of reality, Collins (2000) defines intersectionality as "matrix of domination" and demonstrates multiple ways in which Black women experience subordination. While domestic and sexual abuse is a common form of oppression among many Black women, social stigmatization related to racial, socio-economic, and cultural dynamics also constitutes a significant type of oppression that contributes to vulnerability. There are multiple, degrading stereotypes (e.g. "welfare mother," "Jezebel") attributed to African American women depending on their social position within a group. Hence, the notion of vulnerability can differ greatly across the same race, gender, or social class.

Third, while intersectionality researchers study underrepresented social groups (e.g., low-income people, African American workers), special emphasis is given to multiplicatively oppressed social groups (e.g. Black gay elderly). This allows for moving beyond overlooked or understudied groups to unravel the multiple realities surrounding extremely marginalized and deeply vulnerable populations. *The Stigma Project* by Benoit and colleagues (2007) provides an exemplar approach to such vulnerable groups; in this study, the experiences of Canadian sex workers are compared to the experiences of other workers who provide "emotional labour," such as hairstylists and food servers.

Different types of intersectionality

As the concept of intersectionality has begun to evolve as an interdisciplinary field of studies, researchers have developed typologies that help facilitate different theoretical and methodological orientations within this domain of research (McCall 2005, Verloo 2006). We review McCall's (2005) well-known typology to illustrate the potential of this approach for the study of consumer vulnerability.

Intracategorical intersectionality

Researchers interested in understanding the heterogeneous experiences within the same social group rely on intracategorical intersectionality. Also referred to as "locational or micro-level intersectionality" (Collins 2000), this form of intersectionality is useful for exploring how members of a social group or people who share the same social setting can have multiple realities and hence, can constitute distinct subgroups (Ozanne and Fischer 2012). As such, an intracategorical perspective challenges the notion of essentialism, which defines social groups as homogenously categorized under race, gender, or any other unifying dimension (McCall 2005) and sheds light on the heterogeneous and complex nature of social positions and identities. Although not informed by the intersectionality literature per se, studies on the homeless (Hill 1991) and low-income African Americans (Crockett and Wallendorf 2004) within the larger category of "the poor" are examples of such an approach.

The methods best appropriate to this approach include qualitative interviews, observation, ethnography, and case study. Gopaldas and Fischer (2012) define the methodological aim of this approach as "within-intersections" analysis that helps answer such questions as "what are the unique experiences of this group?"

and "what are the similarities and differences across group members in terms of their experiences and social positions?"

Intercategorical intersectionality

This form of intersectionality is well suited to investigate the similarities and differences between two different social groups or across a number of social groups within the same research study. Deriving from the literature on social class and habitus, Henry (2005) investigates how working-class and upper-middle-class males differ in terms of financial planning and budgeting. Researchers working in this tradition first determine which social identity axes deem appropriate for the study and then compare groups along these axes. What differentiates this type of research from traditional approaches is a focus on the interaction effects, for example the interaction of gender, social class, and employment status, rather than merely considering one type of social identity dimension such as gender or social class alone. If Henry (2005) were to adopt an intercategorical perspective, he would have considered other relevant categories in addition to social class and analyzed the interaction effects of these dimensions. For instance, age and ethnicity could be considered along with gender and social class as the budgeting habits might differ across different age groups and people from different ethnic backgrounds.

Both quantitative and qualitative methods have been used to arrive at an "among-intersections analysis" (Gopaldas and Fischer 2012). Several interesting examples of such analyses exist. In an ethnographic study, Lareau (2003) offers a rich account of American childrearing dynamics in working-class and middle-class families through a comparison across gender, race, and class. Similarly, Lamont (1992, 2000) explores working-class males' worldviews in France and the United States, and particularly investigates how moral boundaries are socially constructed between Black and White men. Veenstra (2011), on the other hand, relies on survey data and compares the self-rated health outcomes across Asian, South Asian, and Aboriginal Canadians.

Anticategorical intersectionality

Unlike the first two approaches, anticategorical perspective does not deal with categories because categories are perceived to be too simplistic to account for the complexity of lived experience. Rather than focusing on the interaction effects across different categories of identity, anticategorical view attempts at understanding the underlying processes behind any type of categorization. Consequently, researchers explore *racism* instead of race, *sexual discrimination* instead of gender, or *structural vulnerability* instead of social class. Historical and genealogical analyses are the most suitable methods that "deconstruct analytical categories" (McCall 2005, p. 1773). Questions such as "by what processes are the focal categories constructed, reproduced, opposed, or possibly transformed over time" and "what mechanisms might alter current distribution of power among stakeholders" (Gopaldas and Fischer 2012, p. 398) help illuminate how persistent and systemic forms of vulnerability as well as social positions of advantage and privilege are shaped. As a case in point, Karababa and Ger's (2011) historical analysis on the formation of an "active consumer" within the context of sixteenth and seventeenth-century Ottoman coffeehouse demonstrates how positions of advantage and disadvantage can be shaped through both individual (e.g. coffeehouse dwellers, preachers) and institutional (e.g. Ottoman state, marketers) actors.

Analyzing consumer vulnerability through an intersectional lens

In this section, we briefly review consumer vulnerability literature, distinguish between two distinct approaches to vulnerability, and highlight the relevance of the intersectionality paradigm for an inclusive look at the lived experience of vulnerable populations.

A brief overview of consumer vulnerability

Like intersectionality, the notion of vulnerability has been of interest to scholars and practitioners interested in exploring power relations and issues of social justice. Across different disciplines, diverse conceptualizations have led to different ways of measuring it. For example, while the asset-based perspective treats vulnerability as inadequate access to both tangible and intangible resources, the sociological approach focuses on the institutional and structural conditions leading to vulnerability (Alwang, Siegel, and Jorgensen 2001). One shared premise across these diverse approaches is the notion of risk or harm and welfare-related outcomes of being susceptible to harm.

In consumer research, reviewing much of the literature on the topic, Baker, Gentry, and Rittenburg (2005, p. 134) conceptualize vulnerability as a multi-dimensional "state of powerlessness … [that] arises from the interaction of individual states, individual characteristics, and external conditions." Echoing this view, much of the consumer research on the topic highlights the multi-dimensional nature of vulnerability, including individual (i.e. socio-economic status, literacy level, health), collective (i.e. community characteristics and resources), and external (i.e. weather, marketplace dynamics) conditions causing vulnerability (Peñaloza 1995, Hill 2001, Ringold 2005, Baker, Hunt, and Rittenburg 2007, Commuri and Ekici 2008). This view of vulnerability reflects a similar perspective on intersectionality whereby a multitude of factors and dynamics plays a role in shaping human experiences. However, research that deals with consumer vulnerability mostly focuses on one category as the basis of analysis while alternative, overlapping categories recede to the background and are out of focus. For example, in Lee, Ozanne, and Hill's (1999) work on rural poverty, gender and health status are the main identity categories, while geographical setting and socio-economic level are secondary categories that overlap with gender.

Intersectionality, however, treats categories as equally important and builds on the assumption that they are interdependent. If Lee, Ozanne, and Hill were to take an intersectional angle, they would have considered the interaction effects of all these categories simultaneously. A deep intersectional analysis might help reveal complex interplay of factors that shape health inequities. Disadvantaged positions of women in health settings are hardly only a matter of gender-based power situation. Social positions, roles, and identities are co-constructed and shaped in relation with geographic stratification, racism, ageism, heterosexism, and other systems of oppression, some of which may be more dominant in shaping these women's experiences.

While consumer researchers agree on the multidimensional nature of vulnerability, there are differing views on the nature, level, and outcomes of experiencing vulnerability. One perspective treats vulnerability as a temporary and dynamic state of powerlessness that people actively work to cope with to get their lives back to normal (Hill 2001, Baker, Gentry, and Rittenburg 2005, Baker, Hunt, and Rittenburg 2007). According to this research stream, vulnerability is a dynamic, context-dependent, and manageable state that cannot be equated to single, class-based categories such as race, gender, income, or any other demographic characteristic. Both individual and structural conditions might have a role in causing vulnerability, yet people most often choose to fight back to improve their conditions. Even though this approach highlights the temporary and state-based nature of vulnerability, it also recognizes the pre-existing individual and communal characteristics that trigger exposure to risk (Baker, Hunt, and Rittenburg 2007). Accordingly, this view of vulnerability both bears some resemblance to anticategorical intersectionality and differs from it in some ways. The rejection of categories in exploring vulnerable states and positions and a focus on pre-existing conditions are the two core principles of an anticategorical perspective. On the other hand, equating vulnerability to a dynamic, fluid, and transient state challenges one of the core assumptions of intersectionality: certain groups are multiplicatively oppressed and their oppression can be permanent and systemic due to underlying macro dynamics such as persistent poverty, chronic unemployment, or racial segregation (Mechanic and Tanner 2007). Moreover, some social groups might experience persistent vulnerability because they are positioned at the intersection of multiple identity categories (e.g. being Black, unemployed, disabled, and gay). While managing interlocking disadvantages is possible to some degree, vulnerable conditions will persist unless there is a significant shift in underlying power relations and mechanisms (Hankivsky et al. 2009, Choo and Ferree 2010).

In contrast with the state-based view, another stream of research focuses on the systemic, institutionalized, and collective nature of vulnerability (Commuri and Ekici 2008, Shultz and Holbrook 2009). Here, vulnerability is treated as more of a status than a state; some groups are more vulnerable than the others because they belong to a certain race, gender, ethnicity, or they merely share some collective characteristics that lead to systemic oppression. Examples of such groups include, but are not limited to, ethnic minorities, the elderly, low income consumers, gays and lesbians, and stigmatized communities such as people living in substandard housing forms like low-income housing projects and mobile home parks. With its emphasis on multiplicatively oppressed groups and power relations between individual and institutional actors, an intersectional perspective would be more sympathetic to this second approach to vulnerability.

Another key benefit of intersectionality for vulnerability research is to help illuminate who is vulnerable, what causes actual vulnerability, and who is perceived to be vulnerable but may not be so. Within the context of product harm and ethics in marketing, Smith and Cooper-Martin (1997) distinguish between actual and perceived vulnerability. Actual vulnerability occurs when people experience vulnerable states and/or statuses, and gives an account of what causes their vulnerability. All three types of intersectionality can help reveal actual forms of vulnerability by giving voice to different social groups. Perceived vulnerability, on the other hand, refers to people's misconception about who is or can be vulnerable, but in reality, those perceived to be vulnerable may not be so. Likewise, since many vulnerable states can be context-dependent; what one group of people defines as actual vulnerability might be viewed as perceived vulnerability by another group. An intersectionality-driven approach that looks at the matrices of being exposed to risk across different social groups, and contexts can help reveal the "real" forms of vulnerability people experience.

Intersectional vulnerability: exemplar studies

We re-examine two vulnerability-based, empirical consumer research studies via an intersectional lens. Although these studies are not directly informed by the intersectionality paradigm per se, they share some of its tenets. We review these studies with particular attention to intersectionality-driven insights and discuss how intersectionality can offer useful guidance for better understanding the dynamics of vulnerability.

"Consumer Vulnerability as a Shared Experience: Tornado Recovery Process in Wright, Wyoming"

In this paper, Baker et al. (2007) examine vulnerability as "a shared experience" and a temporary state that can be overcome through individual and communal resources. Extending Baker, Gentry, and Rittenburg's (2005) model that treats vulnerability as an individual state, this work takes a more collective approach and suggests that multiple stakeholders (e.g. individuals, communities, and policymakers) can shape the shared lived experience of vulnerability. Echoing an intersectional approach, several intersecting dynamics such as individual characteristics, external conditions, and pre-existing communal characteristics are taken into account. Methodologically, the researchers focus on experiences of vulnerability across three distinct groups within the community: community members, city officials and support staff, and businesspeople. Hence, this study is an example of both an intracategorical and intercategorical approach to intersectionality. It is intracategorical because the authors investigate vulnerability experience within a particular community in the aftermath of a tornado. It can also be considered as intercategorical because the researchers compare and contrast three subgroups within the larger category of "survivors of a natural disaster." Attention to nuances within and across groups challenges the notion that all survivors of natural disasters have similar experiences, which would have been closer to the essentialist approach to poverty that assumes all poor people share the same characteristics.

A pure intersectional lens could further inform the shared experience of vulnerability. The authors highlight insurance status and roles within the community as the primary categories in analysing how community members perceive and manage threats to safety, health, and material possessions. Yet, other categories such as age, income, and gender could also be relevant within this context. For instance, the survivors of the tornado could differ in their perception of safety or health across different life stages and income levels. In addition, a historical discussion on how natural disasters are socially constructed and perceived across different regions and communities – hence, adopting an anticategorical view – could be helpful in understanding why and how responses to tornado vary within this Wyoming community. Since the aftermath of natural disasters is very context-dependent – a community might either benefit or suffer from governmental and local actions – it would be helpful to investigate how other communities with similar characteristics experience physical and psychological losses and how policymakers handle such disasters.

On the other hand, intersectionality researchers could also benefit from this study. The authors discuss various individual and collective coping strategies in the aftermath of tornado and demonstrate how personal recovery processes operate and intersect with the collective negotiation of "a new understanding of self and community" (p. 17).

"Community Action Research" (CAR)

Inspired by community action research, Ozanne and Anderson (2010) investigate the social construction of diabetes across Native Americans and Mexican Americans in a southwestern community of the United States. This is an example of intercategorical intersectionality that compares and contrasts the lived experience of two social groups. Consistent with the goals of CAR, the authors also seek to reveal and improve local capacities by including various stakeholders (i.e. community members, community partners such as doctors, healthcare workers, and community leaders) within the research process and by giving the informants the ownership of the research. Intersectionality researchers would share a similar interest in a practical problem like diabetes that has social and policy implications and they would be sympathetic to an action research-driven design. In fact, this is an area where intersectional researchers can benefit from: including many stakeholders in the research process, giving the ownership of the research to the community, and forging collaborative relationships to understand and solve a practical problem.[2]

While Ozanne and Anderson provide an account of multiple overlapping disadvantages such as poor health, lack of access to necessary resources, and economic vulnerability, an intersectional approach would include the intersectional effects of all other possibly relevant identity axes (e.g. health literacy, gender, age, pre-existing personal risk factors to diabetes). Diabetes is a condition whereby the interactive effects of several broader dynamics and individual conditions take a role (Vissandjée and Hyman 2011). In addition, a closer look at the similarities and differences in individual conditions and in the ways of handling diabetes between the two groups (i.e. Native Americans and Mexican Americans) would be at the forefront of an intersectional angle.

Recommendations and conclusion

In this final section, a few key recommendations are offered to researchers who are interested in utilizing intersectionality to explore consumer vulnerability. First, researchers are advised to consider all relevant categories of social identity (e.g. race, gender, age, income, health status, ethnicity, living conditions) that seem to be interdependent in the chosen vulnerability context. Here, the challenge facing researchers is to avoid sounding too simplistic by considering one or two categories only or to create unnecessary complexity as a result of taking too many categories into account (Cole 2009). The following questions might be useful to think about when determining the scope of the study: Which identity axes have been overlooked and/or under-theorized in the chosen vulnerability context? Which identity axes seem most relevant and which ones not so directly relevant in the chosen context? Can the chosen identity axes be useful to investigate diverse lived experiences within and across groups? What types of vulnerability (e.g. actual vs. perceived vulnerability; structural vs. cultural vs. economic vulnerabilities) are the researcher(s) most likely to find in the chosen context and which identity dimensions might help reveal these vulnerabilities?[3]

Second, identifying vulnerable sample(s) to be explored and consequently deciding on the research design necessitates a close look at the multiplicatively oppressed groups. Researchers might find the following questions helpful to determine the right population of interest: Who is most likely to experience vulnerability at the intersection of chosen identity axes? Is there a need to compare a vulnerable group to another and why? Does this comparison advance our understanding of vulnerability and, if so, in what ways? What could be the consequences of including certain vulnerable groups and excluding other groups? Which methodologies seem most suitable to untangle vulnerable states or statuses?[4]

Third, the research should be designed in such a way to reveal the dynamics of all applicable social exchanges. In the context of a research study on vulnerability, this would necessitate a close look at the power relations among all the stakeholders involved. If vulnerability has two components (i.e. a transient, status-based component and a systemic, group-based component) as theorized by Commuri and Ekici (2008), then power relations should be analysed not only across individuals but also between individuals and institutional actors.

In sum, we suggest that researchers who adopt an intersectional lens attend to relevant within- or across-group categories of diversity. An intersectional analysis would take into account that these categories are dynamically produced and shaped by both individual and institutional actors. It is only through a closer analysis of the relations across various social actors, identity categories, and underlying macro-level processes that systemic, persistent, and collective forms of vulnerability can be understood in depth.

Notes

1   Consumer researchers distinguish between two approaches to vulnerability: a temporary, state-based view (Baker, Gentry, and Rittenburg 2005, Baker, Hunt, and Rittenburg 2007) and a systemic, class-based or collective view (Commuri and Ekici 2008, Shultz and Holbrook 2009). More on these two perspectives can be found in our discussion on consumer vulnerability.
2   One of the outcomes of this research was the development of an advisory board and a tribal youth program that serve as action partners to improve the well-being of the community.
3   These questions were inspired by Hancock (2007), Cole (2009), and Hankivsky, Cormier, and de Merich (2009).
4   These questions were inspired by Cole (2009) and Winker and Degele (2011).

References

Alwang, Jeffrey, Paul B. Siegel, and Steen L. Jorgensen (2001), "Vulnerability: A View From Different Disciplines," Social Protection Discussion Paper Series No. 0115, Human Development Network, The World Bank.

Baker, Stacey Menzel (2009), "Vulnerability and Resilience in Natural Disasters: A Marketing and Public Policy Perspective," *Journal of Public Policy & Marketing*, 28(1), 114–123.

Baker, Stacey Menzel, James W. Gentry, and Terri L. Rittenburg (2005), "Building Understanding of the Domain of Consumer Vulnerability," *Journal of Macromarketing*, 25(2), 128–139.

Baker, Stacey Menzel, David M. Hunt, and Terri L. Rittenburg (2007), "Consumer Vulnerability as a Shared Experience: Tornado Recovery Process in Wright, Wyoming," *Journal of Public Policy & Marketing*, 26(1), 6–19.

Benoit, Cecilia, Leah Shumka, Bill McCarthy, Mikael Jansson, Rachel Phillips, Helga Hallgrimsdottir (2007), *Laborers, Managers and Counselors: A Comparative Analysis of Intimate Work in the Sex Industry*, Intimate Laborers Conference, University of Santa Barbara, California.

Choo, Hae Yoon and Myra Marx Ferree (2010), "Practicing Intersectionality in Sociological Research: A Critical Analysis of Inclusions, Interactions, and Institutions in the Study of Inequalities," *Sociological Theory*, 28(2), 129–149.

Cole, Elizabeth R. (2009), "Intersectionality and Research in Psychology," *American Psychologist*, 64(3), 170–180.

Collins, Patricia Hill (2000), *Black Feminist Thought: Knowledge, Consciousness, and the Politics of Empowerment*, New York, NY: Routledge.

Commuri, Suraj and Ahmet Ekici (2008), "An Enlargement of the Notion of Consumer Vulnerability," *Journal of Macromarketing*, 28 (June), 183–186.

Crenshaw, Kimberle (1989), "Demarginalizing the Intersection of Race and Sex: A Black Feminist Critique of Antidiscrimination Doctrine, Feminist Theory, and Anti-Racist Politics," *University of Chicago Legal Forum*, 139–167.

Crenshaw, Kimberle (1991), "Mapping the Margins: Intersectionality, Identity Politics, and Violence Against Women of Color," *Stanford Law Review*, 43(6), 1241–1299.

Crockett, David and Melanie Wallendorf (2004), "The Role of Normative Political Ideology in Consumer Behavior," *Journal of Consumer Research*, 31 (December), 511–528.

Crockett, David, Laurel Anderson, Sterling A. Bone, Abhijit Roy, Jeff Jianfeng Wang, and Garrett Coble (2011), "Immigration, Culture, and Ethnicity in Transformative Consumer Research," *Journal of Public Policy & Marketing*, 30 (May), 47–54.

Davis, Kathy (2008), "Intersectionality as Buzzword: A Sociology of Science Perspective on What Makes a Feminist Theory Successful," *Feminist Theory*, 9(1), 67–85.

Gopaldas, Ahir (2013), "Intersectionality 101," *Journal of Public Policy & Marketing*, 32 (Spring), 90–94.

Gopaldas, Ahir and Eileen Fischer (2012), "Beyond Gender: Intersectionality, Culture, and Consumer Behavior," *in Gender, Culture, and Consumer Behavior*, ed. Cele C. Otnes and Linda Tuncay Zayer, New York, NY: Routledge, 393–410.

Hancock, Ange-Marie (2007), "When Multiplication Doesn't Equal Quick Addition: Examining Intersectionality as a Research Paradigm," *Perspectives on Politics*, 5(1), 63–79.

Hankivsky, Olena, Renée Cormier, and Diego de Merich (2009), *Intersectionality: Moving Women's Health Research and Policy Forward*, Vancouver: Women's Health Research Network.

Henry, Paul (2005), "Social Class, Market Situation, and Consumers' Metaphors of (Dis)Empowerment," *Journal of Consumer Research*, 31 (March), 766–778.

Hill, Ronald Paul (1991), "Homeless Women, Special Possessions, and the Meaning of Home: An Ethnographic Case Study," *Journal of Consumer Research*, 18 (December), 298–310.

Hill, Ronald Paul (2001), *Surviving in a Material World: The Lived Experience of People in Poverty*, Notre Dame, IN: University of Notre Dame Press.

Karababa, Eminegul and Guliz Ger (2011), "Early Modern Ottoman Coffeehouse Culture and the Formation of the Consumer Subject," *Journal of Consumer Research*, 37(5), 737–760.

Lamont, Michele (1992), *Money, Morals and Manners: The Culture of the American and French Upper-Middle Class*, Chicago, IL: University of Chicago Press.

Lamont, Michele (2000), *The Dignity of Working Men*, New York, NY: Russell Sage.

Lareau, Annette (2003), *Unequal Childhoods: Class, Race, and Family Life*, Berkeley, CA: University of California Press.

Lee, Renee G., Ozanne, Julie L., and Ronald Paul Hill (1999), "Improving Service Encounters Through Resource Sensitivity: The Case of Health Care Delivery in an Appalachian Community," *Journal of Public Policy and Marketing*, 18 (Fall), 230–248.

Mechanic, David and Jennifer Tanner (2007), "Vulnerable People, Groups, and Populations: Societal View," *Health Affairs*, 26(5), 1220–1230.

McCall, Leslie (2005), "The Complexity of Intersectionality," *Signs*, 30(3), 1771–1800.

Ozanne, Julie L. and Laurel Anderson (2010), "Community Action Research," *Journal of Public Policy and Marketing*, 29 (Spring), 123–137.

Ozanne, Julie L. and Eileen Fischer (2012), "Sensitizing Principles and Practices Central to Social Change Methodologies," in *Transformative Consumer Research for Personal and Collective Well-being*, ed. David Glen Mick, Simone Pettigrew, Cornelia Pechmann, and Julie L. Ozanne, NY: Taylor and Francis, 89–106.

Peñaloza, Lisa (1995), "Immigrant Consumers: Marketing and Public Policy Considerations in the Global Economy," *Journal of Public Policy & Marketing*, 14 (Spring), 83–94.

Ringold, Debra Jones (2005), "Vulnerability in the Marketplace: Concepts, Caveats, and Possible Solutions," *Journal of Macromarketing*, 25(2), 202–214.

Shultz, Clifford J., II and Morris B. Holbrook (2009), "The Paradoxical Relationships Between Marketing and Vulnerability," *Journal of Public Policy & Marketing*, 28(11), 124–127.

Smith, Craig N. and Eliabeth Cooper-Martin (1997), "Ethics and Target Marketing: The Role of Product Harm and Consumer Vulnerability," *Journal of Marketing*, 61 (July), 1–20.

Veenstra, Gerry (2011), "Race, Gender, Class, and Sexual Orientation: Intersecting Axes of Inequality and Self-rated Health in Canada," *International Journal for Equity in Health*, 10 (January), 1–11.

Verloo, Mieke (2006), "Multiple Inequalities, Intersectionality and the European Union," *European Journal of Women's Studies*,13(3), 211–228.

Vissandjée, Bilkis and Ilene Hyman (2011), "Preventing and Managing Diabetes: At the Intersection of Gender, Ethnicity, and Migration," in *Health Inequities in Canada: Intersectional Frameworks and Practices*, ed. Olena Hankivsky,Vancouver: UBC Press, 257–273.

Winker, Gabriele and Nina Degele (2011), "Intersectionality as Multi-Level Analysis: Dealing with Social Inequality," *European Journal of Women's Studies*, 18(1), 51–66.

4 A story of *The Uncondemned*

Seeking justice and empowerment in marketed representations of vulnerability

Catherine A. Coleman

> It is impossible to talk about the single story without talking about power... .
> How they are told, who tells them, when they're told, how many stories are
> told, are really dependent on power.
>
> (Adichie, 2009: 9:37)

The Uncondemned is a documentary currently in production (at the time of
writing) by Film at 11, intended to bring greater awareness to the stories of –
and give voice to – the women whose testimonies at the International Criminal
Tribunal for Rwanda (ICTR) helped secure the first successful prosecutions of
rape and sexual violence as crimes of war. In *The Uncondemned*, the women
who testified about the violence they endured and observed, known only
through the trial by identification letters, reveal their identities publicly for the
first time. Financed through crowdfunding, charity events, and benefit sales of
jewellery and clothing, and currently in preparation for a global audience, this
documentary is both media and market commodity. The concealment of the
women's identities during the trials, intended for their protection, and the
subsequent disclosure of their identities in the documentary invite questions
about representations of vulnerability, as well as the market-oriented development
and consumption of these representations.

Specifically, how are we to understand representations of vulnerability and
empowerment in light of critiques of contemporary cinematic and consumer
cultures that employ tools, such as interviews, "as a social technique for construction and reconstruction of fragile selves" (Kvale, 2006: 492) and turn
"transgressive experience into consumable commodity" (Denzin, 2001: 28)? In
line with previous scholarship on the formative nature of discourse and representation (e.g. Foucault, 1972; Shankar et al., 2006), this chapter proceeds on
the notion that conceptualizations of vulnerability, enacted through various
forms of representation (e.g. speech, written text, visual imagery, tone, pre-
sence/absence, targeting) are active texts – that is, they are discourses that
construct meaning. As Hall (2000: 81) has argued, media representations shape
ideologies and "provide the frameworks through which we represent, interpret,
understand, and 'make sense' of some aspect of social existence," such as
vulnerability.

This context further invites questions of who has the power to represent whom (Belk, 2011; FitzSimons, 2009) and what it might mean for documentary film subjects to be "given a voice" (Winston, 2013: 11) through representations that are marketed and consumed. These issues are informed by epistemological, creative, constructive, and social characteristics of documentaries. As Nigerian novelist Chimamanda Ngozi Adichie (2009) reminds us in her popular TED talk on *The Danger of the Single Story*, "power is the ability not just to tell the story of another person, but to make it the definitive story of that person." The charge of this edited collection is to focus on issues relevant to consumer vulnerability. If representations of vulnerability presented *to* consumers participate in shaping ideologies and experiences *of* consumer vulnerability, then media representations of vulnerability and the individual and structural practices that shape these representations are important sites of critical examination in furthering scholarship on consumer vulnerability. To this end, I reflect on the potential for the documentary *The Uncondemned*, as one opportunity among others (e.g. Mukamana and Collins, 2006), to participate in telling *a* story that builds understanding of the lives and experiences of the women presented.

The discussion unfolds as follows: first, the history of victim testimonies at the International Criminal Tribunal for Rwanda (ICTR) provides context for circumstances recounted in *The Uncondemned*. Next, I point to literature on vulnerability and representation in consumer culture. As Film at 11 is promoting *The Uncondemned* as a documentary, I introduce prior scholarship on documentaries: in light of market logic through which documentaries increasingly are understood, in terms of epistemology and representation, or the "problematics of documentary definition" (Winston, 2013: 6), and at intersections of representation and othering. Through the lenses of dialogic theory and a theory of "justice as reconciliatory practice" (Isasi-Díaz, 2010), I examine *The Uncondemned* as a complicated artifact embedded in, representing, and disrupting multiple apparatuses of power and vulnerability. I argue that the project of *The Uncondemned* has the potential to be empowering insofar as it offers alternative texts through which the women can tell their stories and encourages continued writing of the texts through ongoing engagement. At the same time, these circumstances are calls to actively enter into what Hall (1997: 277) refers to as "the politics of representation" and seek ways of representing vulnerability that are reflexive, dialogical, and empowering, rather than culturally hegemonic, fetishizing, and exoticizing (Denzin, 2001, 2012; Hietanen et al., 2014). This calls for sustained critical reflection on representations of vulnerability and empowerment in market-oriented media systems, and the ways in which those representations shape the world.

Letters and words: testimonies and interviews of victims

In 1994, the International Criminal Tribunal for Rwanda (ICTR) obtained the first successful prosecution of rape as a crime of war. Their success was achieved, significantly, through the testimonies of a handful of women who spoke of the brutalities they experienced as victims of rape and sexual violence. With crimes of rape and sexual violence en masse historically silenced, the testimonies heard at the International Criminal Tribunal for Rwanda (ICTR) and the "sister court" of the International Criminal Tribunal for the Former Yugoslavia (ICTY) were unprecedented challenges to "the gendered foundations of international criminal law" (Koomen, 2013: 254). As Koomen (2013: 254) argues, "the Rwandan women who came to tell their stories at the ICTR exposed and tested the taken-for-granted practices and presumptions of international tribunals." This process gave individual and collective voice to women made vulnerable in various ways by the brutalities inflicted on them – including physically, emotionally, and through community ostracization – and sought justice and the promotion of norms respecting human rights (Lu, 2013).

While the tribunal testimonies may have offered victims a means to seek justice and a previously unheard voice in the process, success and empowerment are contested readings of the outcomes of these trials. For example, Nowrojee (2005) has questioned the lack of sustained political will amongst investigators and prosecutors in pursuing gendered crimes of rape and sexual violence within the mandate of ICTR. Further, various works have pointed to the problematic influences on the tribunal system of international bureaucracy and politics and of the realities of interview collection, translation and presentation of witness testimony (e.g. Koomen, 2013; Nowrojee, 2005).

Kvale (2006: 497) has argued that while interviews are important tools for producing knowledge and giving voice to people otherwise marginalized, the complex relationships of power between interviewer and interviewee, interpreter and interpreted, and the more macro-oriented political and ethical issues of interview cultures should give pause to consider the "ethical-political" concerns. The critical perspective he takes resonates both in the context of interview collection for the trials and for the interviews collected for the documentary. Data collection and testimony for international tribunals surely are subject to complex power dynamics that affect the kind of knowledge produced through the process. The tribunal process, empowering as its potential may be by giving victims a forum to seek justice, put quotes around their experiences and assigned them letters rather than identities (Jeltson, 2014; The Prosecutor v. Sylvestre Gacumbitsi, 2003). In interviews conducted with Rwandan women in the midst of the ICTR trials, including rape victims who had or were scheduled to testify before the ICTR, Nowrojee (2005) learned that many of them were concerned that their stories and experiences were not being heard, acknowledged, and chronicled appropriately. These accounts assuage the implications for empowerment and justice for victims through court systems. As Noworojee (2005: 6) concludes, "The documenting of historical truth is another important function of justice, because history is not simply what happened in the past, but rather the scribe's interpretation of events. In this case, the ICTR serves not only as an arbiter of justice, but also a documenter of the narrative of Rwandan genocide."

The needs of the justice system drove the development of the victims' stories (Koomen, 2013), posing "the danger of the single story" against which Adichie (2009) warned. The presentations of the victims' narratives in tribunal records are but one telling of broader and more complex truths experienced by the women who testified, and are but one telling of sexual violences experienced by thousands of victims during the Rwandan genocide.

A reading of the post-genocide Human Rights Watch Report, *Shattered Lives: Sexual Violence During the Rwandan Genocide and its Aftermath* (Nowrojee 1996), reveals numerous ways in which Rwandan women – including the women in *The Uncondemned* – may have experienced and may continue to experience multiple "states of powerlessness" or vulnerabilities that arise when there is an "interaction of individual states, individual characteristics, and external conditions" (Baker et al., 2005: 134). A few such states, characteristics, and conditions engendering vulnerability and highlighting the problematics at the intersections of representation include: a legacy of European racism imposing spurious categories of racial identity (Hutu and Tutsi) used to incite violence; gender and class discrimination within and between these identities; traditions of patriarchy; underrepresentation of women in education and politics; poor or inaccessible health care for women; disparities in female labour production and women's abilities to have control over and enjoy what they produce; laws prohibiting women's land ownership; discriminatory lending practices; displacement; significant psychological and emotional abuse; and stigmatization of victims of sexual violence (Nowrojee, 1996).

Further, the women who reveal their stories in *The Uncondemned* were made vulnerable by time and place, or quite literally where they happened to be when the genocide began and militia entered their villages. They were made vulnerable through their participation in the tribunal system, evidenced in the variety of ways the court tried to protect their identities, at the same time that they represented a message of empowerment through the impact of their testimonies.

Representation and vulnerability

Baker et al.'s (2005) focus on experiences of vulnerability (rather than who is vulnerable) serves as a reminder of the complexity and potential transience of, as well as our shared potential for, vulnerability. Yet media have been criticized for representing vulnerabilities in ways that set up boundaries, distancing and othering vulnerability (Hodgetts et al., 2006; Shugart, 2008). When packaged through media, these messages are consumed by privileged audiences. The vulnerable "other" becomes commodity. Hodgetts et al. (2006) argue media images can reproduce social inequalities that affect the lives of people experiencing vulnerability, often without giving them the opportunity to name their own conditions. However, they suggest that while scholars have argued empowerment can be achieved when people have the opportunity to describe their own conditions, this is insufficient because they "cannot simply locate themselves within their own discourses" outside of the bounds of dominant social discourse. Instead, they focus on "cultures of resistance" (Hodgetts et al., 2006: 514) in which people appropriate dominant representations, which hold symbolic power, to construct alternative meanings. Nisbet and Aufderheide (2009: 454) have proposed research agendas that look further at how "films designed to inform and provoke publics alert a wider public to a problem, potentially by reframing a problem so that it connects to a wider set of values or so that it can be addressed differently."

Creation and consumption: documentaries

Defining documentary and market logic

The term "documentary" has been used to describe a wide variety of "filmic and photographic products" (Ball, 2005: 518) with multiple subgenres (Aufderheide, 2007; Belk, 2011). The documentary's major – though contested – claim is in its ability to truthfully represent its subjects. Despite prior "negative connotations" arising from the historical record on documentaries (Renov, 1993: 5), they have experienced renewed public interest in recent decades (Maccarone, 2010), as celebrities and well-known patron organizations lend their names and support to documentary films of all sorts, giving them a reputation as "the new rock 'n' roll" (Fraser, 2013: x). The historical use of documentary films to educate the public on social issues (Hodes, 2007) may appeal to those who wish to promote and associate their names with social causes. The economic realities of production and distribution surely serve to drive market discourse, with marketing pressures affecting what is defined as documentary (Aufderheide, 2007). Documentaries are increasingly understood through market logic – whether through calls for market-based distribution solutions, higher incomes for professionals often working under poor pay standards despite increasing audiences (Fraser, 2013), or discourses of commodification. Fraser (2013: x) writes of the increasing popularity of documentaries, "They're among the least valued, and most interesting cultural forms of our time… . And they are now being sold as a means to save the world," even if their potential to do this may be unrealistic (Winston, 2013).

Further, with contemporary media culture's heavy reliance on visual technologies and the rising interest in documentary films, scholars have noted their potential as resources of information about marketing, consumers, and the social world and as opportunities to communicate about topics of import in marketing (Belk, 2011; Belk and Kozinets, 2005; Shultz et al., 2013). The documentary tradition, as a practical mode of recording the world, supports the assumption that visual reality can be truthfully or factually captured and communicated (Hodes, 2007), giving the format "representational legitimacy" (Hamilton, 1997: 87).

Truth, knowledge, and representation

The documentary tradition has held a position of privilege over truth in representation (Renov, 1993; Trinh, 1993). In fact, epistemology and representation are at the centre of documentary discourses, their defining characteristics and ethical concerns, both lending them legitimacy and repudiating it (Hodes, 2007; Nichols, 1991). Any discussion of documentary is susceptible to what Winston (2013: 6) has called the "problematics of documentary definition": "the specific conflict between the assumptions governing the ethics of documenting 'life as lived' (which can be thought of as journalistic requirements of objectivity) and those behind processing this as 'life as narrativised' (which implies creative intervention, that is to say: art" (Winston, 2013: 10). Rather than delineating the field, a look at the subgenres betrays the permeable borders of fiction and nonfiction, objective and subjective, truth and representation (Aufderheide, 2007).

A variety of traditions including postmodernist, poststructuralist, cultural, and critical theories have focused on the inescapably representational nature of documentary (Ball, 2005). These critiques of realism are reminders that documentaries are products of creativity, technical skill, and storytelling ability; they are constructed texts (Belk and Kozinets, 2005; Kellner, 2013; Renov, 1993). They further pose ethical concerns about such issues as authenticity, power and voice (Belk, 2011; Hamilton, 1997; Hodes, 2007; Maccarone, 2010; Nash, 2011; Winston, 2013), and point to ideologies created, presented, maintained or changed through representational politics of gender, race, sexuality, other, and even emotion (Hall, 1997; Rabinowitz, 1994; Smaill, 2010).

Given this, we must ask what potential there is for a project such as *The Uncondemned* to be realized through the documentary format and as a media commodity working within market-based logic. Can *The Uncondemned* tell the story of women whose testimonies secured the first successful prosecution of rape as a war crime, provide a forum for these women to voice their experience in the tribunal system without subsuming them as objects of knowledge, and bring awareness to issues of (dis)empowerment? Can the project build relationships to disrupt power structures that create and maintain vulnerabilities? Or is mediation of the women's stories in this format, packaged and consumed, itself creating and maintaining vulnerabilities?

Development of *The Uncondemned*

On the heels of their award-winning documentary, *Haiti: Where Did the Money Go*, Film at 11 began development of *The Uncondemned*. Despite a willing financial backer, the Film at 11 team, led by executive editor and co-founder Michele Mitchell, turned to crowdfunding to support the development and dissemination of the film in an effort to build community around the project. Halfway through their Kickstarter campaign, launched in November 2013, they had reached their $7,000 goal to support a scouting trip to Rwanda and the

Democratic Republic of Congo (www.filmat11.tv/kickstarter-2013-backers). The Kickstarter raised nearly $14,000, allowing the team to begin production (the total cost of the film is $465,000). According to Mitchell, the over-whelming response they received from both men and women is testament to the fact that this is a border-crossing human rights issue: "people care very much about the suffering inflicted by the use of rape as a weapon of war, and they are willing to put their money towards bringing this issue to the broadest possible audience" (www.filmat11.tv/kickstarter-2013-backers). The quotes provided by Kickstarter backers on the organization's website suggest they wanted to participate in affecting change. One writes, "I wanted to be a part of this story which aims to bring awareness in to [sic] suffering of many women victims of rape, to help to end these atrocities so that they cannot ever happen again in their lives" (www.filmat11.tv/kickstarter-2013-backers). Another indicates, "Not only are those without a voice now heard, but an audience who might otherwise remain complacent is moved to take action" (www.filmat11.tv. kickstarter-2013-backers). Mitchell (2014) has argued that crowdfunding created an engaged community impassioned by the story, waiting to see it, and most likely prepared to promote it among their own communities. Mitchell suggests this kind of engagement facilitates a shift in the narrative of rape. She perceives the film as an active text in this sense. The FilmAt11 website indicates, "We realized with our first film that audience engagement doesn't stop there – actually, it begins after the final frame fades. We actively build communities around our films… ."

The Uncondemned features interviews with three women who testified at the ICTR. The code names of these three women as they went through the tribunal process were JJ, NN, and OO, code names they will discard in the film. Of the story the women have told her, Mitchell noted that after the genocide the women had not been sitting around hoping justice would prevail. They were healing themselves. But when the opportunity to testify arose, they wanted to be heard. Through the trial, they spoke of the experience of rape and violence that they endured and observed. The trial ended and they returned to their communities to continue rebuilding their lives, yet with little recognition among the global community of the lived experiences of these women – that is, the individual human stories that predate and proceed their testimonies. Thus, the focus of the documentary is not intended to have them recount the violence they endured, but rather to discuss their experiences in coming before the tribunal to seek justice. The name *The Uncondemned* is to represent the journey of the women:

> The perpetrators raped the women, which condemned them in the eyes of the communities, etc., while the men remained uncondemned. This made the women 'victims.' They then became 'survivors' with their process of healing. Then they testified and became 'witnesses'; this made them 'heroes.' And, finally, their perpetrators become the 'condemned' by being found guilty, and they became the 'uncondemned'.
>
> (Mitchell, 2014)

Thus, the documentary is named to present the story of transition from vulnerability toward empowerment through voice. The potential of the documentary is for the women to reclaim their testimonies in the tribunal, reconnecting their testimonies to their lived experiences as individuals, and to name their own story.

Further, *The Uncondemned* as a project is compelling in its potential because it has been consciously designed as a platform for broader conversations about sexual violence in ways that are encouraged by but are not under the control of the producers. The documentary is "'braided, a form of stranded singularity in which 'coming to voice' typically includes the input of many individuals and institutions" (FitzSimons 2009: 131). For example, the related initiative *Action After Fade* is to "create a cultural shift towards justice, emphasizing the critical role that the world community plays in protecting the human rights of vulnerable populations" and to engage with audiences "to take action after the final frame of the film fades" (http://www.actionafterfade.org/mission/). *Action After Fade* promotes a campaign to "End the Myth" about sexual violence, to position it as a human rights issue, and to promote global dialogue about various forms of sexual violence historically and as enacted today. The campaign provides educational resources and ways for people to join the conversation and take action against the injustices of sexual violence against individuals and communities. Even before the documentary is released, people are taking up the charge. Various salons are being organized to build dialogue of resistance to global rape culture, and at my own university students are actively seeking ways to participate in the conversation, to build understanding of their relatedness to issues of sexual violence on campus, and to encourage others to join. The potential exists for these initiatives to accomplish a goal of connectedness without subsuming the alterity – the alternative history and phenomenological otherness – of the women who come forward to name their world in the documentary. To better understand this potential, I propose the lenses of reconciliatory justice (Isasi-Díaz, 2010) and dialogic theory, which serve simultaneously as reminders to maintain a critical stance toward consumption of representations.

Justice and dialogue

In her work on the ethics of documentary, Nash (2011: 230) warns that Western philosophy "has most often been violent towards the Other, neutralizing difference and subsuming the other under its own categories. It is a philosophy of power, a philosophy that transforms the Other into an object of knowledge" and consumption (Denzin, 2001). In response, a reconciliatory justice may guide us toward non-violence in our interactions with the Other (Isasi-Díaz, 2010). A dialogic approach that is premised on difference (Arnett et al., 2010) and engages people in the transformative potential of naming their world (Freire, 2000) may guard against neutralizing difference and totalizing the Other as an object of knowledge and consumption. Isasi-Díaz's (2010: 42) theory of reconciliatory justice takes "injustice as the starting point"; dialogic theory is built on mutual acceptance of vulnerability as a foundation for empowerment

(Nash, 2011; Freire, 2000). Therefore we may, at the same time, locate the potential for justice and empowerment in injustice and vulnerability, even as we are called upon to maintain a critical stance to representation.

Rape and sexual violence are wielded to dehumanize individuals and to dismantle communities. A community-based reconciliatory practice of dialogue seems appropriate. The injustice of sexual violence tacitly bonds individuals and communities made vulnerable by these crimes with the "majority of humanity, [whose] reality is one of injustice" (Isasi-Díaz, 2010: 42). Isasi-Díaz's (2010: 42) theory of justice as reconciliatory praxis decolonizes epistemologies, shifting orientations. She considers "knowledge as emerging necessarily from the historical and material mediations in which one is immersed, for which one takes responsibility and, in taking responsibility, one changes." In twenty-first-century, globalized contexts, we must understand the interdependence of privilege and oppression, particularly as cast through mediated and consumed representations of vulnerability, through the historical record, and with an eye to the future. Isasi-Díaz (2010: 44) promotes reconciliation through care and tenderness, which focuses not on punishment but on relationships – building a "common future" – achieved through dialogue.

According to Arnett et al. (2010: 111), "dialogue privileges the understanding of difference"; dialogic ethics requires that we come to an encounter with difference to learn. One can imagine that there is much to learn from the women who lend their stories to *The Uncondemned*. *Action After Fade* further promotes and facilitates learning through texts and actions. A dialogic approach embraces multiplicity and, drawing from Levinas, "requires us to turn toward the Other, never subsuming the Other," never colonizing the Other (Arnett et al., 2010: 115; Nash, 2011). At the same time, the dialogic encounter emphasizes the importance of being vulnerable, of conceding the limitations of our power and knowledge (Nash, 2011: 238). Documentary projects "that engage sensitively and reflexively to tell the stories of others" (Nash, 2011: 238) may offer a form of resistance (Hodes, 2007) that challenges monolithic interpretations and fosters ownership of the message by those being represented, by giving them a voice, an opportunity to participate in their own naming – "a perspective that seeks to be epistemologically emancipatory rather than reductionist" (Hietanan et al. 2014: 2). While the documentary will always be framed by those who produce it and this must be continually examined, *The Uncondemned* provides the women whose testimonies influenced a global change in legal justice another context to tell their story, providing a "fuller and more complex picture" (FitzSimons, 2009). As Freire (2000: 88) writes, "If it is in speaking their word that people, by naming the world, transform it, dialogue imposes itself as the way by which they achieve significance as human beings. Dialogue is thus an existential necessity."

Conclusion

In considering ethics as "a questioning stance" (Nash 2011: 230), it is not my intention to overstate the emancipatory potential of projects such as *The*

Uncondemned, but rather to explore it. We must continue to question important issues such as voice, the power complexities of representation that can lead to othering, and unreflective consumption of representations. *The Uncondemned* is a project that, in its mission to promote a cultural and discursive change, attempts to produce "new realities" and promote "new ways of thinking" (Hietanen et al. 2014) in representing a story "braided" (FitzSimons, 2009) with the polyvocal realities of the women in the documentary and of global communities embattled by sexual violence. Its further development as a project should be examined critically and reflexively as a reminder of continued attention to representations of vulnerability. We might see *The Uncondemned* and continued praxis through *Action After Fade* as a form of dialogic storytelling "that functions as an interpretive map – displaying conversation between interpreter and text that invites the reader into the conversation" and brings us to a historical consciousness (Arnett et al., 2008) from which new ways of knowing – cultural shifts – may emerge.

References

Action After Fade (2014). [Online] Available at: http://www.actionafterfade.org/ [accessed 1 Nov 2014].

Adichie, C. (2009). *The Danger of the Single Story*. TED talk, available at: http://www.ted.com/talks/chimamanda_adichie_the_danger_of_a_single_story?language=en#t-6 01005 [accessed 15 Jan 2015].

Arnett, R., Arneson, P. and Holba, A. (2008). Bridges not walls: The communicative enactment of dialogic storytelling. *Review of Communication*, 8(3), 217–234.

Arnett, R., Bell, L. and Fritz, J. (2010). Dialogic learning as first principle in communication ethics. *Atlantic Journal of Communication*, 18(3), 111–126.

Aufderheide, P. (2007). *Documentary Film*. Oxford: Oxford University Press.

Baker, S., Gentry, J. and Rittenburg, T. (2005). Building understanding of the domain of consumer vulnerability. *Journal of Macromarketing*, 25(2), 128–139.

Ball, M. (2005). Working with images in daily life and police practice: An assessment of the documentary tradition. *Qualitative Research*, 5(4), 499–521.

Belk, R. (2011). Examining markets, marketing, consumers, and society through documentary films. *Journal of Macromarketing*, 31(4), 403–409.

Belk, R. and Kozinets, R. (2005). Videography in marketing and consumer research. *Qualitative Market Research: An International Journal*, 8(2), 128–141.

Denzin, N. (2001). The reflexive interview and a performative social science. *Qualitative Research*, 1(1), 23–46.

Denzin, N. (2012). The cinematic society and the reflexive interview. *Society*, 49(4), 339–348.

Film at 11 (2014). [Online] Available at: http://www.filmat11.tv/ [accessed 1 Nov 2014].

FitzSimons, T. (2009). Braided Channels: A Genealogy of the Voice of Documentary. *Studies in Documentary Film*, 3(2), 131–146.

Foucault, M. (1972). *The Archaeology of Knowledge and the Discourse on Language*. New York: Pantheon Books.

Fraser, N. (2013). Foreword: Why Documentaries Matter. In: B. Winston, ed., *The Documentary Film Book*, 1st ed. London: Palgrave MacMillan, x–xv.

Freire, P. (2000). *Pedagogy of the Oppressed*. New York: Continuum.

Hall, S. (1997). The Spectacle of the "Other". In: S. Hall, ed., *Representation: Cultural Representation and Signifying Practices*, 1st ed. London: Sage Publications, 223–290.

Hall, S. (2000). Racist Ideologies and the Media. In: P. Marris and S. Thornham, ed., *Media Studies: A Reader*, 1st ed. New York: New York University Press, 271–282.

Hamilton, P. (1997). Representing the Social: France and Frenchness in Post-war Humanist Photography. In: S. Hall, ed., *Representation: Cultural Representations and Signifying Practices*, 1st ed. London: Sage Publications, 75–150.

Hietanen, J., Rokka, J. and Schouten, J. (2014). Commentary on Schembri and Boyle (2013): From representation towards expression in videographic consumer research. *Journal of Business Research*, 67(9), 2019–2022.

Hodes, R. (2007). HIV/AIDS in South African documentary film, *c.* 1990–2000. *Journal of Southern African Studies*, 33(1), 153–171.

Hodgetts, D., Hodgetts, A. and Radley, A. (2006). Life in the shadow of the media: Imaging street homelessness in London. *European Journal of Cultural Studies*, 9(4), 497–516.

Isasi-Díaz, A. (2010). Justice as reconciliatory praxis: A decolonial mujerista move. *International Journal of Public Theology*, 4(1), 37–50.

Jeltson, A. (2014). A look back at the trial that made rape a war crime. *Huffington Post*. [Online] Available at: http://www.huffingtonpost.com/2014/07/29/rwanda-genocide-rape_n_5602108.html?cps=gravity [accessed 1 Nov 2014].

Kellner, D. (2013). On Truth, Objectivity and Partisanship: The Case of Michael Moore. In: B. Winston, ed., *The Documentary Film Book*, 1st ed. London: Palgrave Macmillan, 59–67.

Koomen, J. (2013). "Without these women, the Tribunal cannot do anything": The politics of witness testimony on sexual violence at the International Criminal Tribunal for Rwanda. *Signs*, 38(2), 253–277.

Kvale, S. (2006). Dominance through interviews and dialogues. *Qualitative Inquiry*, 12(3), 480–500.

Lu, I. (2013). Curtain call at closing: The multi-dimensional legacy of the International Criminal Tribunal for Rwanda. *University of Pennsylvania Journal of International Law*, 34, 859–899.

Maccarone, E. (2010). Ethical responsibilities to subjects and documentary filmmaking. *Journal of Mass Media Ethics*, 25(3), 192–206.

Mitchell, M. (2014). *A few follow-up questions*. [Email].

Mukamana, D. and Collins, A. (2006). Rape survivors of the Rwandan genocide. *International Journal of Critical Psychology*, 17, 140–166.

Nash, K. (2011). Documentary-for-the-Other: Relationships, ethics and (observational) documentary. *Journal of Mass Media Ethics*, 26(3), 224–239.

Nichols, B. (1991). *Representing Reality*. Bloomington: Indiana University Press.

Nisbet, M. and Aufderheide, P. (2009). Documentary film: Towards a research agenda on forms, functions, and impacts. *Mass Communication and Society*, 12(4), 450–456.

Nowrojee, B. (1996). *Shattered Lives: Sexual Violence during the Rwandan Genocide and its Aftermath*. HRW Index: 2084. [Online] New York: Human Rights Watch. Available at: http://www.hrw.org/reports/1996/Rwanda.htm [accessed 1 Nov. 2014].

Nowrojee, B. (2005). *"Your Justice is Too Slow": Will the ICTR Fail Rwanda's Rape Victims?* Occasional Paper 10. Geneva: United Nations Research Institute for Social Development.

Rabinowitz, P. (1994). *They Must Be Represented*. London: Verso.

Renov, M. (1993). *Theorizing Documentary*. New York: Routledge.

Shankar, A., Cherrier, H. and Canniford, R. (2006). Consumer empowerment: A Foucauldian interpretation. *European Journal of Marketing*, 40(9/10), 1013–1030.

Shugart, H. (2008). Sumptuous texts: Consuming "otherness" in the food film genre. *Critical Studies in Media Communication*, 25(1), 68–90.

Shultz, C., Peterson, M., Zwick, D. and Atik, D. (2013). My Iranian road trip: Comments and reflections on videographic interpretations of Iran's political economy and marketing system. *Journal of Macromarketing*, 34(1), 87–94.

Smaill, B. (2010). *The Documentary*. Basingstoke, UK: Palgrave Macmillan.

The Prosecutor v. Sylvestre Gacumbitsi (Trial Judgement) [2004] ICTR-2001–2064-T (International Criminal Tribunal for Rwanda; Trial Chamber III).

Trinh, T. (1993). The Totalizing Quest of Meaning. In: M. Renov, ed., *Theorizing Documentary*, 1st ed. New York: Routledge, 90–107.

Winston, B. (2013). Introduction: The Documentary Film. In: B. Winston, ed., *The Documentary Film Book*, 1st ed. London: Palgrave Macmillan, 1–29.

5 Asking for trouble

Reflections on researching bereaved consumers

Darach Turley

When someone close to us dies, we lose them, we lose part of ourselves, and we can also lose many of our customary cognitive and emotional ways of functioning. Many survivors find themselves traumatised, confused, and bewildered in surreal, uncharted territory where everyday personal and social functioning is highly problematic. Fundamental assumptions can be shattered, and they find themselves having to adapt to a new reality – life without their loved one – at a time when physical and mental resources are sorely depleted. The emotional maelstrom in which they find themselves can significantly impair their judgement, concentration, confidence, and ability to assess risks (Parkes 1995). Against this daunting and debilitating backdrop, bereaved people are often called upon to make arduous, emotionally charged, and costly consumer acquisition and disposition decisions. On the other hand, the routine and mundane consumer decisions that still have to be made underscore what Wright and Flemons (2002) term the 'doubleness of death', that sense of survivors having to wrestle with profound existential issues of life and death while simultaneously attending to the nuts and bolts of daily living. Grief occasioned by the loss of a close family member or acquaintance is obviously not the sole form of grief: those mourning the passing of a celebrity (Walter 1999), pet (Hirschman 1994, Wrobel and Dye 2003), brand (Muniz and Schau 2005), or cherished television series (Russell and Schau 2014) have also featured in both consumer and thanatological literatures, however the focus of this chapter are those who have been bereaved by the loss of a close personal loved one.

Vulnerability and sensitivity

'Bereaved people, particularly those who are newly bereaved, are vulnerable' (Parkes 1995: 173). The effects of proximate bereavement can manifest themselves in diametrically opposite ways, giving vulnerability two distinct complexions. In the first case, people are driven to accept support from whatever quarter it can be accessed, while in the second they feel hurt and devastated, viewing other people with distrust and suspicion. The credulity and gullibility of the former group leave them open to potentially harmful interventions from commercial, medical, or research agencies, the wariness of the latter can mean a reluctance to entertain any overtures whatsoever from them and the risky resolve to try and 'go it alone'.

One aspect of vulnerable populations is that they are often overlooked. Thankfully, within consumer research, this situation no longer holds, courtesy of a cadre of scholars who have established vulnerability as an accepted focus of study in its own right (Baker et al. 2005, Hill 1995, Ringold 2005, Wolberg 2005). Gentry et al.'s (1994) foundational study on the consumer behaviour of bereaved families was arguably the first in the discipline to explicitly conjoin the notions of grieving and vulnerability. Grieving consumers experience many aspects of vulnerability: liminality (Gentry et al. 1995), lack of personal control (Baker et al. 2005), being at risk of diminished autonomy (Liamputtong 2007), and 'motivational limitation' (Wolberg 2005). If bereaved consumers represent a vulnerable segment of the population, research that broaches the source of their vulnerability will, in all probability, raise issues that are experienced as sensitive.

The search for an agreed definition of what constitutes 'sensitive research' has been a lengthy and inconclusive one; however, the views of Lee and Renzetti (1990) and Lee (1993) appear to have gained wide acceptance in the social sciences. Rather than designate specific topics as intrinsically sensitive, they contend that sensitive research is research that poses one or more of three potential threats: intrusion, stigmatisation and the political. As its name suggests, the first of these threats may be experienced in any studies that intrude into spheres of people's lives that are viewed as private, stressful, or sacred; studies on grief and bereavement would seem to fall within the ambit of this form of threat. Characterising sensitivity in terms of anything survivors perceive as intrusive is quite apposite in the present context. First, it underscores how sensitivity does not inhere *a priori* in any given topic or group; it is contextually conditioned and socially negotiated during the research encounter. Second, the potential threat can be experienced by both participants and researcher (Bahn and Weatherill 2012). Third, in conducting research on sensitive private spheres, academics should be aware of the possibility of complicity in a contemporary media and academic zeitgeist, 'a novelty-hungry world' (Bettany and Woodruffe-Burton 2009), with an insatiable appetite for 'lifting the lid' and uncovering what lies hidden beneath the patina of people's seemingly pedestrian lives (Lee 1993).

Although, the sensitivity of any research encounter is, in the final analysis, determined contextually by the interaction of the participants, it can still be maintained in a general sense that research is more likely to prove sensitive in some areas of consumers' lives than in others (Johnson and Clarke 2003). This chapter looks at one such group of consumers, and asks how their vulnerability, coupled with the likelihood that research with them will prove sensitive, informs appropriate research practice. It does so by reflecting on over 25 years of conducting research, mainly through in-depth interviews, with bereaved consumers. The chapter also responds to Bettany and Woodruffe-Browne's (2009) provocative call to consumer researchers to pin their reflexive colours to the mast and ask themselves: 'what is our relation with the individual who participates in our research … what is our relation with the *vulnerable* individual?' (662). It should be remembered that reflexivity encompasses more than self-conscious awareness of one's role as researcher/interpreter; it can also entail awareness of the ramifications of the topic under discussion for oneself. Indeed, as Dickson-Swift et al. (2009) note, qualitative researchers often undertake research in areas that resonate with unresolved aspects of their own lives, albeit with the intention of contributing to both the advancement of academic knowledge and the welfare of those with whom they research.

A growing number of authors in sociology and thanatology have commented on issues that arise in researching sensitive matters with bereaved people, much of it driven by the need to assuage the concerns of Research Ethics Boards over potential damage to vulnerable participants (Cook 1995, Dyregrov 2004, Goodrum and Keys 2007, Rosenblatt 1995, Rowling 1999, Valentine 2007, Williams et al. 2008). Baker et al. (2005) emphasise that, in assessing levels of vulnerability, it must be borne in mind that, properly speaking, it is a state or condition that people experience, usually intermittently, rather than a designated status such as age or ethnicity. Put another way, it is the actual vulnerability the participant is experiencing, rather than the perceived vulnerability which others assume the participant is experiencing, that should matter most. My experience with survivors suggests that the most common manifestation of this pivotal distinction is that actual vulnerability often goes hand in hand with perceived invulnerability. In other words, many bereaved people are actually vulnerable, while those about them, often for the best of reasons, either do not see or do not wish to see them as vulnerable, and interact with them accordingly. This aptly named variant of vulnerability captures precisely how others can sometimes perceive what they want to perceive and choose to interpret external signs of normality in their bereaved relative or friend as a form of reassurance that, when their time of loss inevitably comes round, their grief will be short-lived and finite. It is precisely in this ambivalent context that many research interviews with bereaved persons take place. Indeed, I have found that such research interviews can represent one among an increasingly infrequent number of social encounters where free articulation of actual vulnerability is sanctioned and supported. Ironically, in the peri-mortem period, the corollary can occur. Both concern for the survivors and perceived vulnerability are high, while the recently bereaved are valiantly doing battle with actual vulnerability, to prove to others, and to themselves, that they *can* manage. This resolve can sometimes translate into precipitate, and what others perceive as irrational, consumer decisions such as immediate domestic refurbishments, speedy disposal of the deceased person's personal inventory, or a hasty home sale. High perceived vulnerability can also give rise to over-protective relatives dissuading or preventing access by researchers to their bereaved family member.

This distinction between actual and perceived grief, initially coined by Smith and Cooper-Martin (1997), sits well with current understandings among thanatologists that grief is a sporadic and intermittent experience for most bereaved individuals and does not follow any linear phasic trajectory (Bradbury 1999,

Neimeyer 2001, Valentine 2006). A variety of cues, many of them unpredictable and serendipitous, can serve to trigger its reoccurrence; indeed, the researchers should be alert to the possibility that the interview itself may have this effect. The most vivid and poignant example I came across featured the bereaved parent of a teenage daughter finding himself in tears after picking up a tin of peas in a supermarket bearing the same sell-by date as his daughter's upcoming anniversary.

Beneficence and respect

The intermittent and fluid nature of actual grief understandably heightens the need for bereavement researchers to be especially alert to the principles of beneficence and respect, irrespective of the recency of the bereavement (Cook 1995). Beneficence, the requirement to maximise positive outcomes and minimise risk, asks researchers to assess potential damage or harm to their bereaved participants during or following their engagement with them. Research on death and loss probably cannot be carried out without rendering participants, at least potentially, more vulnerable to harm; both the sensitivity of the topics during the interview and the confidentiality of the information that is disclosed make this almost unavoidable. However, despite this possibility, and the attendant risk of 're-victimising' participants during the interview, the bereavement literature is virtually unanimous that beneficence has been well-served by academic researchers over the years (Buckle et al. 2010, Corbin and Morse 2003, Dyregrov 2004, Johnson and Clarke 2003). Benefits reported by participants have included the welcome and rare opportunity to speak of their loss (Carverhill 2002, Valentine 2007), healing, catharsis, and a sense of purpose and self-awareness (Kavanaugh and Ayres 1998), helping and giving hope to others (Buckle et al. 2010).

The distinction between harm and distress seems pertinent in this context. Most of my research participants have cried or shown distress at some stage during the interview – however, on reflection I have wondered if they would not have been doing the same if they were speaking to friends or family members on the same topic. As Corbin and Morse (2003) suggest, the operative question when considering beneficence may be whether 'this manifestation of distress is normal and of a nature that one might find in everyday life?' (337). Added to this has been the impression that my encounters were affording participants an opportunity to express what they were *already* feeling as a result of their bereavement and not what they were feeling as a direct result of being interviewed.

Blurring of the boundary between therapist and researcher can impact on beneficence by giving rise to unrealistic expectations on the part of some survivors, an expectation that is more likely to arise in the context of qualitative interviews than surveys. Both therapy session and interview involve protracted, intimate, face-to-face contact on topics that are sensitive, emotionally charged, and often secret, and in settings that are supportive, empathetic and non-judgemental.

Both also require the same practitioner skill set. That said, each has distinct goals; for therapy it is personal change in the participant, in research it is change in the researcher's understanding (Romanoff 2001); in the former participants need help, in the latter they possess power (Rowling 1999). Possible harm can be minimised at the outset by clarifying that the researcher is not a therapist and that any subsequent therapeutic dividend, though welcome, is not the main purpose of the encounter. A note of healthy realism is probably in order here. Researchers cannot pre-empt the possibility that participants often volunteer in the hope that the exercise will 'do them good', neither can they or should they prevent them from feeling this way (Dickson-Swift 2008), and, in my experience, virtually all will tell you as much when it is over.

Beneficence also involves the question of timing, in other words, how close to the bereavement should participants be approached. This is obviously a matter of striking a balance between optimising recall and minimising harm and should ultimately be determined by bearing in mind that 'the willingness of the respondent to revisit the experience both factually and emotionally is more important than the chronological time since the death' (Williams et al. 2008). This willingness could be assessed either by asking a close third party or by checking with participants who are long-term bereaved how long after the death they would have felt comfortable being interviewed. Whatever the interval, care should be taken not to schedule interviews around anniversaries or birthdays of the deceased.

Despite the fact that bereaved people report little or no long-term adverse effects of being interviewed, Corbin and Morse (2003) admit to a lingering doubt, to residual misgivings that they might, after all, have caused such effects even though they never evidenced them in their own research careers. Whatever its basis in fact, this doubt could still serve as a healthy antidote to complacency by ensuring that sensitivity to any threats to beneficence remains foremost in researchers' minds. Reliance on in-depth interviews as opposed to quantitative surveys serves as an additional guarantor; here the bereaved person can assume greater control of the content and conduct of the research encounter and thereby promote more beneficent outcomes (Brannen 1988).

The principle of respect involves protecting the participant's autonomy and freedom and, in the context of bereaved people, has to do mainly with ensuring their participation is based on informed consent and is freely given. The issue of informed consent presents a particular challenge in qualitative studies where the objectives may be vague and emergent, the method(s) flexible, and the exchange between researcher and participant idiosyncratic and on-going. In these circumstances it is difficult to make an *a priori* determination of potential risks – and benefits – to both participant and researcher. Neither can be fully informed in advance. As Corbin and Morse (2003) and Cutcliffe and Ramcharan (2002) note, the upshot of adopting an epistemological position that sees both the ebb and flow, and outcome of each interview as a discrete co-construction, is that informed consent represents a gamble, a 'shot in the dark'. In qualitative studies with bereaved people this dilemma appears to be even more acutely felt, with some critics questioning whether, in the absence of full information at the outset, such studies can ever be ethically justified (Rosenblatt 1995). One increasingly popular stratagem for addressing this quandary is to adopt what has been termed 'processual consent' (Rosenblatt 1995) or 'ethics as process' (Cutcliffe and Ramcharan 2002). Such an approach sees consent being continuously negotiated throughout the interview by both parties, with participants being asked to re-consent (Williams et al. 2008), particularly at moments when fresh sensitive topics are being introduced or when they appear distressed. Essentially this is reading the ethical topography as it reveals itself during the interview, the researcher remaining vigilant for any adverse reactions, and making use of a prepared battery of suitable prompts ('Are you happy to continue on?'), reminders of the right to withdraw, and, where appropriate, temporary exit suggestions ('Maybe we should take some time out here and …').

Free participation is the second element of the principle of respect and arises primarily when participants are being recruited. The key concern here is that they are not made to feel obligated to participate. This can be particularly relevant where the researcher is in some way attached to an institution – medical, ecclesiastical or social – with which the deceased person had some connection and the survivor may feel obligated to participate for the sake of their deceased loved one. As a general rule, the roles of researcher and recruiter should remain separate and direct requests to bereaved people from the researcher should be avoided. My experience has been that 'open call' requests through local media coupled with requests through third parties – relatives, acquaintances, organisation members – make it easier to decline. Indeed, researchers need to be alert to the possibility that unwillingness may be communicated indirectly through repeated postponements, cancellations, late arrivals, or unanswered messages. By way of reassurance it is worth recalling Parkes' (1995) observation that those most at risk of harm in an interview situation will probably not volunteer in the first place or will be discouraged from doing so by family or care-givers.

Rapport, reciprocity, and self-disclosure

The process of putting participants at ease, of creating an environment that will facilitate disclosure, requires a modicum of rapport between both parties, with the initiative typically lying with the researcher. In other words, a friendship of sorts has to be established at the outset either during recruitment or in the preamble to the interview. One of the more remarkable findings in the reflexive accounts of researchers working with vulnerable participants is the pervasiveness of scruples over the nature of this friendship or rapport (Bahn and Weatherill 2012, Jafari et al. 2013, Watts 2008). These scruples seem to centre on concerns that these contrived 'friendships' are phoney, feigned, and ephemeral. Rapport has been manipulatively conflated with ruse. Terms such as 'hit and run', 'smash and grab', and 'exploitation' are not uncommon (Liamputtong 2007), all giving rise to feelings of deceit and dissemblance, especially when exiting the interview (Woodthorpe 2007). Lofland and Lofland (1984) liken this experience to:

> an ethical hangover … a persistent sense of guilt or unease over what is viewed as a betrayal of the people under study … that in transforming personal knowledge into public knowledge, you have committed a kind of treason.
>
> (156)

These remorseful feelings can be exacerbated when researchers realise that the most enticing verbatims usually come from the most distressed participants (Dickson-Swift et al. 2008) and admit to wondering how well they will read on the pages of some highly rated academic publication (Dickson-Swift et al. 2007).

One wonders whether these misgivings are somewhat overstated and whether they underestimate the nous of most bereaved people who, in my experience, harbour quite a realistic grasp of the nature and outcomes of research interviews. Attention to reciprocity can also go some way in alleviating and mitigating these concerns. 'Give and take' are essential components of any relationship; researchers should try to counterbalance the inevitable and sizeable 'take' from their interactions with bereaved persons with what they try to give back in return. Such efforts can go some way towards 'levelling the playing field' and redressing the power differential inherent in all encounters with vulnerable people (Harrison et al. 2001). In the process, they may also go some way towards assuaging any residual exploitation-induced guilt. Goodrum and Keys (2007) propose three types of reciprocity: financial, follow-up and personal. On occasions I have made financial donations to charities connected with the deceased person or given token lottery tickets; both proved acceptable. However, follow-up and personal reciprocity are seen as far more effective. Follow-up initiatives could include soliciting their assistance with member checks, sending letters of appreciation, forwarding them summary findings, accompanying the participant to a cinema or restaurant, or furnishing details of relevant support and coun-selling services (Dickson-Swift et al. 2008, Sque 2000). Personal reciprocity, while critical, appears to be a matter of considerable debate, much of it centering on the degree to which the researcher should be 'in' the research (Rowling 1999) or the appropriate 'distance' that should be maintained between researcher and participant (Watts 2008). Interviews with bereaved survivors tend to be highly emotionally charged for both parties, with this charge oscil-lating considerably over the course of each interview. Against this backdrop determining the optimal distance tends to be a matter of contextual judgement, with most bereavement researchers choosing to err on the side of caution, 'staying close but not too close' (Watts 2008), exercising a non-judgemental 'empathetic distance', and keeping in mind that distance need not mean detach-ment (Rowling 1999, Valentine 2007). In the case of those who are grieving, other non-tangible personal reciprocal gestures could include acknowledging the depth of their loss, assurance that they are not losing their minds, and thanking them for making their stories available to others.

Arguably the most potent form of personal reciprocity during the interview is self-disclosure, in which researchers, prompted or unprompted, share their experience of loss and bereavement; acknowledgement of this commonality can engender trust and minimise power asymmetry (Williams et al. 2008). Participants will certainly assume this is the case, i.e. that the researcher has lost someone; the only question is whether it surfaces during the interview and how the researcher reacts. Stonewalling is clearly not an option, so researchers might consider preparing a succinct account of their own experience in advance, making sure that, in sharing it, they are not seen as 'trumping' the participant's narrative. Self-disclosure should always serve to foster the flow of the encounter, not to disrupt it (Valentine 2007). If self-disclosure is not solicited during the interview, researchers might turn the tables at the end and ask participants whether they wish to ask them anything about their personal lives (Goodrum and Keys 2007).

Any discussion of potential harm or risk to bereaved participants in interviews has to take cognisance of how the research encounter fits into the broader tableau of the survivor's grief. There has been a seismic change in the understanding of functional grieving over the past 20 years. A growing number of thanatologists and therapists now argue that grief should be about reconfiguring our bonds and relationships with the deceased rather than relinquishing them (Klass et al. 1996). A critical part of reconfiguring these bonds is trying to make sense of the meaningless biographical disruption occasioned by the death, 'an on-going venture in constructing new meanings that may last as long as the griever lives' (Harvey et al. 2001: 236). Gilbert's (2002) aphorism that 'we live in stories, not statistics' might well be rephrased as 'we grieve in stories, not statistics'. Each time survivors tell their story, including in the research interview, they are simultaneously reconfiguring both their own and the dead person's identities, and affirming the continuing centrality of that person in their lives. These stories are more than poignant replays of life without the lost loved one. Two related considerations arise from this continuing-bonds perspective, both relating to researchers' duty of care to survivors. First, researchers may have to show that they are comfortable in interviews where the presence of the deceased person seems potent and palpable, where they are asked to hold the interview in a particular room where a mother feels she is 'with' her dead son each day, or when they are kindly requested not to sit in the deceased father's chair. Second, unlike research with other vulnerable groups, estimations of benefits and potential risks in this case should properly embrace the interests of three parties: participant, researcher, and the deceased person. Put another way, the interview can be just as much for the deceased as it is about them. Seen through the survivor's eyes, the distress and tears of the research interview may represent a small price to pay for the opportunity to 'do something' for the deceased; solicitude on the part of academic researchers for their well-being, though understandable and necessary, should not be at the expense of depriving them of the increasingly rare opportunity to tell the story of their loss and their loved one.

References

Bahn, Susanne and Pamela Weatherill (2012). 'Qualitative social research: a risky business when it comes to collecting "sensitive" data', *Qualitative Research*, 13, 1: 19–35.

Baker, Stacey Menzel, James W. Gentry and Terri L. Rittenburg (2005). 'Building understanding of the domain of consumer vulnerability', *Journal of Macromarketing*, 25, 2: 128–139.

Bettany, Shona and Helen Woodruffe-Burton (2009). 'Working the limits of method: the possibilities of critical reflexive practice in marketing and consumer research', *Journal of Marketing Management*, 25, 7/8: 661–679.

Bradbury, Mary (1999). *Representations of Death: A Social Psychological Perspective*, London: Routledge.

Brannen, Julia (1988). 'The study of sensitive subjects', *The Sociological Review*, 36, 3: 552–563.

Buckle, Jennifer L., Sonya Corbin Dwyer and Marlene Jackson (2010). 'Qualitative bereavement research: incongruity between the perspectives of participants and research ethics boards', *International Journal of Social Research Methodology*, 13, 2: 111–125.

Carverhill, Philip A. (2002). 'Qualitative research in thanatology', *Death Studies*, 26, 3: 195–202.

Cook, Alicia Skinner (1995). 'Ethical issues in bereavement research: an overview', *Death Studies*, 19, 2: 103–122.

Corbin, Juliet and Janice M. Morse (2003). 'The unstructured interactive interview: issues of reciprocity and risks when dealing with sensitive topics', *Qualitative Inquiry*, 9, 3: 335–354.

Cutliffe, John R. and Paul Ramcharan (2002).'Leveling the playing field: exploring the merits of the ethics-as-process approach for judging qualitative research proposals', *Qualitative Health Research*, 12, 7: 1000–1010.

Dickson-Swift, Virginia, Erica Lyn James, Sandra Kippen, and Pranee Liamputtong (2007). 'Doing sensitive research: what challenges do qualitative researchers face?', *Qualitative Research*, 7, 3: 327–353.

Dickson-Swift, Virginia, Erica Lyn James and Pranee Liamputtong (2008). *Undertaking Sensitive Research in the Health and Social Sciences: Managing Boundaries, Emotions and Risks*, Cambridge: Cambridge University Press.

Dickson-Swift, Virginia, Erica Lyn James, Sandra Kippen and Pranee Liamputtong (2009). 'Researching sensitive topics: qualitative research as emotion work', *Qualitative Research*, 9, 1: 61–79.

Dyregrov, Kari (2004). 'Bereaved parents' experience of research participation', *Social Science and Medicine*, 58, 2: 391–400.

Gentry, James W., Patricia F. Kennedy, Catherine Paul and Ronald Paul Hill (1994). 'The vulnerability of those grieving the death of a loved one: implications for public policy', *Journal of Public Policy and Marketing*, 13, 2: 128–142.

Gentry, James W., Patricia F. Kennedy, Catherine Paul and Ronald Paul Hill (1995). 'Family transitions during grief: discontinuities in household consumption patterns', *Journal of Business Research*, 34, 1: 67–79.

Gilbert, Kathleen R. (2002). 'Taking a narrative approach to grief research: finding meaning in stories', *Death Studies*, 26, 3: 223–239.

Goodrum, Sarah and Jennifer L. Keys (2007). 'Reflections on two studies of emotionally sensitive topics: bereavement from murder and abortion', *International Journal of Social Research Methodology*, 10, 4: 249–258.

Harrison, Jane, Lesley MacGibbon and Missy Morton (2001). 'Regimes of trustworthiness in qualitative research: the rigors of reciprocity', *Qualitative Inquiry*, 7, 3: 323–345.

Harvey, John H., Heather R. Carlson, Tamara M. Huff and Melinda A. Green (2001). 'Embracing their memory: the construction of accounts of loss and hope' in Robert A. Neimeyer (ed.), *Meaning Reconstruction and the Experience of Loss*, Washington, DC: American Psychological Association, 231–244.

Hill, Ronald Paul (1995). 'Researching sensitive topics in marketing; the special case of vulnerable populations', *Journal of Public Policy and Marketing*, 14, 1: 143–148.

Hirschman, Elizabeth (1994). 'Consumers and their animal companions', *Journal of Consumer Research*, 20, 4: 616–632.

Jafari, Aliakbar, Susan Dunnett, Kathy Hamilton and Hilary Downey (2013). 'Exploring researcher vulnerability: contexts, complications, and conceptualisation', *Journal of Marketing Management*, 29, 9/10: 1182–1200.

Johnson, Barbara and Jill Macleod Clarke (2003). 'Colleting sensitive data: the impact on researchers', *Qualitative Health Research*, 13, 3: 421–434.

Kavanaugh, Karen and Lioness Ayres (1998). '"Not as bad as it could have been": assessing and mitigating harm during research interviews on sensitive topics', *Research in Nursing and Health*, 21, 1: 91–97.

Klass, Dennis, Phyllis R. Silverman and Steven L. Nickman (eds) (1996). *Continuing Bonds: New Understandings of Grief*, Washington: Taylor & Francis.

Lee, Raymond M. (1993). *Doing Research on Sensitive Topics*, Thousand Oaks: Sage Publications.

Lee, Raymond M. and Claire M. Renzetti (1990). 'The problems of researching sensitive topics: An overview and introduction', *American Behavioral Scientist*, 33, 5: 510–528.

Liamputtong, Pranee (2007). *Researching the Vulnerable: A Guide to Sensitive Research Methods*, London: Sage Publications.

Lofland, John and Lyn H. Lofland (1984). *Analyzing Social Settings*, 2nd ed., Belmont, CA: Wadsworth.

Muniz, Albert M. Jr. and Hope Jensen Schau (2005).'Religiosity in the abandoned Apple Newton community', *Journal of Consumer Research*, 31, 4: 737–747.

Neimeyer, Robert A. (2001). 'Introduction' in Robert A. Neimeyer (ed.), *Meaning Reconstruction and the Experience of Loss*, Washington, DC: American Psychological Association, 1–9.

Parkes, Colin Murray (1995). 'Guidelines for conducting ethical bereavement research', *Death Studies*, 19, 2: 171–181.

Ringold, Debra Jones (2005). 'Vulnerability in the marketplace: concepts, caveats, and possible solutions', *Journal of Macromarketing*, 25, 2: 202–214.

Romanoff, Bronna D. (2001). 'Research as therapy: the power of narrative to effect change' in Robert A. Neimeyer (ed.), *Meaning Reconstruction and the Experience of Loss*, Washington, DC: American Psychological Association, 245–260.

Rosenblatt, P. (1995). 'Ethics of qualitative interviewing with grieving families', *Death Studies*, 19: 139–155.

Rowling, Louise (1999). 'Being in, being out, being with: affect and the role of the qualitative researcher in loss and grief research', *Mortality*, 4, 2: 167–182.

Russell, Cristel A. and Hope Jensen Schau (2014). 'When narrative brands end: the impact of narrative closure and consumption sociality on loss accommodation', *Journal of Consumer Research*, 40, 6: 1039–1062.

Smith, N. Craig and Elizabeth Cooper-Martin (1997). 'Ethics and target marketing: the role of product harm and consumer vulnerability', *Journal of Marketing*, 61, 3: 1–20.

Sque, Magi (2000). 'Researching the bereaved: an investigator's experience', *Nursing Ethics*, 7, 1: 23–34.

Valentine, Christine (2006). 'Academic constructions of bereavement'. *Mortality*, 11, 1, February, 57–78.

Valentine, Christine (2007). 'Attending and tending to the role of the researcher in the construction of bereavement narratives'. *Qualitative Social Work*, 6, 2: 159–176.

Walter, Tony (ed.) (1999). *The Mourning for Diana*, Oxford: Berg.

Watts, Jacqueline H. (2008). 'Emotion, empathy and exit: reflections on doing ethnographic qualitative research on sensitive topics', *Medical Sociology*, 3, 2: 3–14.

Williams, Beverly R., Lesa L. Woodby, F. Amos Bailey and Kathryn L. Burgio (2008). 'Identifying and responding to ethical and methodological issues in after-death interviews with next-of-kin', *Death Studies*, 32, 3: 197–236.

Wolberg, Joyce M. (2005). 'Drawing the line between targeting and patronizing: how "vulnerable" are the vulnerable?' *Journal of Consumer Marketing*, 22, 5: 287–288.

Woodthorpe, Kate (2007). 'My life after death: connecting the field, the findings and the feelings', *Anthropology Matters*, 9, 1: 1–11.

Wright, Kristin and Douglas Flemons (2002). 'Dying to know: qualitative research with terminally ill persons and their families', *Death Studies*, 26: 255–271.

Wrobel, Thomas A. and Amanda L. Dye (2003). 'Grieving pet death: normative, gender and attachment issues', *Omega: Journal of Death and Dying*, 47, 4: 385–393.

6 Consumer vulnerability is market failure

Jonathan Stearn

Introduction

Nearly all our essential goods and services are provided through 'liberalised' markets. The UK government Department for Business, Innovation & Skills (BIS) argued in its 2012 report *Better Choices: Better Deals* that 'Markets rely heavily on active and informed consumers to drive competition' (BIS 2011: 4). BIS therefore outlines a consumer empowerment strategy to 'put information and influence into the hands of consumers and help secure a significant power shift to citizens and communities' (BIS 2011: 4) A key element in achieving this goal is the realisation that 'not everybody is a confident consumer – which is why *Better Choices: Better Deals* is also about helping to support the vulnerable in becoming more confident as consumers' (BIS 2011: 2). However, following the publication of *Better Choices, Better Deals*, a number of organisations (Consumer Futures, Citizens Advice and Citizens Advice Scotland) submitted a report to BIS, written by Jonathan Stearn (Stearn 2012), arguing that consumer vulnerability is not just resolved by people gaining more confidence as consumers. Consumer vulnerability cannot simply be seen as consumers' failure to engage with the market when markets are failing to engage with consumers.

Consumer Futures also challenges the notion of 'the vulnerable'. Personal circumstances clearly have an impact on whether people find themselves in vulnerable situations, but we cannot simply or easily divide society into static 'vulnerable groups' and 'the rest'. People's circumstances change and anybody can become vulnerable at any time. To tackle consumer vulnerability the focus of action needs to go beyond individuals and individual solutions. We must recognise that the policies and practices of product and service suppliers in different markets can heavily influence the choices available, the decisions people make and the extent to which people are in vulnerable positions. People, for example, may 'choose' more expensive energy tariffs, credit or purchase deals because it is the only real option available to them. While it is important that everyone has the tools to use and develop their power as consumers, this chapter argues that changes in the behaviour of the companies providing essential goods and services and their regulators are as important as developing the 'empowered' behaviour of consumers in vulnerable situations.

This chapter investigates consumer vulnerability and the role and responsibilities of companies and government in making markets work. In addition it pays particular attention to regulators who have a responsibility to oversee markets for essential goods and services and have some legal responsibility for tackling – or at least paying attention to – consumer vulnerability.

Vulnerable groups and 'the rest'

There is a tradition of producing lists of categories of people considered to be vulnerable. There is such a list in the Consumers, Estate Agents and Redress Act 2007 that set up Consumer Focus (later Consumer Futures and now part of Citizens Advice). It states that the organisation must have regard for the interests of consumers that are one or more of the following:

1   disabled or chronically sick individuals;
2   individuals of pensionable age;
3   individuals with low incomes;
4   individuals residing in rural areas

(Consumers, Estate Agents and Redress Act 2007).

It is easy to demonstrate the weakness of such a generalised group-based approach. Are all older people vulnerable? What about personal circumstances such as bereavement, which does not appear on this list and rarely appears on other such lists? Bereavement can put people in a vulnerable position for numerous reasons – for example, the general distress associated with the death or the stress of suddenly having to cope with a plethora of bills or a sudden drop in income. There are many other life events that can induce similar states of vulnerability.

But even a more nuanced and sophisticated understanding of the vulnerabilities induced by circumstances is not adequate. No matter how long the list is it needs to be recognised that consumer vulnerability is not just down to people's circumstances. The market has a major role to play in determining if someone is in a vulnerable position. Personal circumstances mixed with accessibility, affordability and availability are the key ingredients that influence whether people are in vulnerable situations in the market place.

In relation to *accessibility* our essential services sometimes fail consumers. Retail banks paid little attention to the needs of blind or partially sighted people when they installed cash machines which only had a visual screen display. Was the expectation that blind or partially sighted people ask the person next to them in the queue?[1] Another example is the bus company that decided not to let its drivers leave the cab for fear that money might be stolen. What about the wheelchair users who could no longer get on the bus because the driver couldn't put the ramp down? There are many other examples of essential goods and services that are not accessible. Consumers may not be able to get travel insurance because they are deemed to be too old or because they have a chronic illness (Which? 2011).

Affordability is a key issue and is simply a matter of price. The way companies charge for products can determine how affordable they are. For example, some energy suppliers give the best deals to people who apply online and can utilise direct debit. If you are not online and do not have a regular income you may not want to risk using direct debit. Consumers have no choice but to pay more.

The third aspect is *availability*. Shopping around to buy the cheapest goods from different retailers can be time consuming, or, for some, physically impossible. The cheapest transport is invariably the slowest – so relying on a bus to get to work can have a resulting effect on the job you can do. Likewise, living in a rural area with no bus could mean that a car (which can be expensive to run) is the only option. Online shopping may be an option, but only for those with the appropriate access and network connections.

Consumer Futures has summarised these issues in the report *Tackling Consumer Vulnerability: An Action Plan for Empowerment*, where it argued that 'A person is in a vulnerable position when they cannot choose or access essential products and services which are suitable for their needs, or cannot do so without disproportionate effort/cost/time' (Stearn 2012: 11).

Market failure

The central concern of this chapter is the role that the market plays in creating the conditions that lead to consumer vulnerability, and in particular how, for those living in disadvantaged circumstances, the market is not working for them. One particular concern is the poverty premium – where people on low incomes pay more for essential goods and services. The poverty premium is not new – it was nearly fifty years ago that American sociologist and consumer advocate David Caplovitz coined the phrase – but it is still with us.

A research study for Consumer Futures, *Addressing the Poverty Premium*, by the Joseph Rowntree Foundation (JRF) (Hirsch 2013), found people on low incomes in the UK can pay 10p in the pound (£) more for essential goods and services, particularly utilities and credit (Hirsch 2013). This study identified four categories of poverty premium:

- Paying higher than average utility tariffs for a given amount of consumption, either because of the payment method (such as quarterly billing or prepayment) or because of being on a 'sub-optimal' deal.
- Paying more per unit of consumption because of being a low user. This is especially an issue in telecommunications, where tariffs are increasingly structured around inclusive packages, and it has become harder for people with restricted incomes to meet basic needs at much below the average price.
- Paying more because of limited financial and communications capabilities. People on low incomes often have limited choices.

- Paying high interest on consumer credit. In purchasing essential goods on credit, some low-income consumers end up with much higher bills because of high effective interest rates

(Hirsch 2013: 7).

The report points out that for the market to work, privatisation of essential utilities requires householders to become more active as consumers, seeking deals and switching benefits on a regular basis. This is why, to develop competition, regulators provide information to consumers and try to encourage them to switch. But this is not working well. Looking at the telecommunications sector, the regulator Ofcom reports that switching rates are declining – broadband switching went down from 18 per cent to 6 per cent between 2008 and 2014. In the same period those switching electricity and gas suppliers are down from 18 per cent in 2008 to around 12 per cent (2013/2014), with only 3 per cent switching their bank account (Ofcom 2014: 175). Of those who do switch, Ofcom claims the two main reasons are: 'a) cost – another provider offering a cheaper service; and b) poor service – the previous service not meeting requirements' (Ofcom 2013: 133). Ofcom suggests that there is a link between ease of switching and the percentage switching, drawing comparisons with the car insurance market, where there are very high levels of annual switching (around 33 per cent in 2014), mainly attributed to ease of switching. This contrasts with switching levels for bank accounts, estimated at 4 per cent by Ofcom, linked to the perceived difficulty of switching associated with this sector.

The poverty premium

Switching may have hit a ceiling, and in any case it is not the most effective way to deal with the poverty premium. *Addressing the Poverty Premium* (Hirsch 2013) points out that limited financial capability is often linked to limited choices of how to buy goods and services. Active consumers on low incomes may be excluded from the best deals because they do not have internet access or the funds in their bank account to pay by direct debit. As Hirsch (2013: 15) states, credit and a wider range of payment options can 'bring substantial costs to those on low incomes, either because they face additional transaction charges or because they pay large amounts for credit'. On the availability of credit, the report suggests: 'The evidence shows that this premium can be much greater than is justifiable by the additional risk of lending to them' (Hirsch 2013: 8). Hirsch (2013: 15) goes on to point out that there are some fundamental problems and 'a market [like those for essential goods and services] where prices are only competitive for a minority of buyers, cannot be said to be working well'.

Regulators

In order to make sure that people on the lowest incomes and in vulnerable positions can get access to affordable essential goods and services we need action from regulators. *Addressing the Poverty Premium* has a particular focus on the role of regulators – a good starting point when looking at what can and should be done to tackle market failings and consumer vulnerability. In addition to providing information and encouraging people to switch, the report points out that regulators, working with governments, need to intervene to make markets fairer and/or target support packages to make sure everyone can have affordable access to the essentials of life. The model for regulators is discussed in detail in the Consumer Futures report (Hirsch 2013), and Figure 6.1 shows the three main types of intervention proposed.

From this diagram there are three main forms of intervention. First, at the top of the diagram we have initiatives which embody the everyday role of the regulator – that is, activities aimed at the enforcement of fair trading and competition. The second category relates to interventions of the supply chain, mainly concerned with the regulation of price structures and product structures. This category is often treated more carefully by regulators since they do not want to appear to be over-regulating the market, which may lead to possible negative repercussions in relation to market innovations. Finally, the lower-right category relates to steps aimed at helping low-income households or households in vulnerable situations, in the form of subsidies or social tariffs. This tends to fall under the responsibility of government rather than regulators, who may be more involved in the implementation of such initiatives.

Figure 6.1 Three main types of intervention

Regulators sometimes suggest restricted powers limit their actions and potential interventions. Consumer Futures ran a series of roundtable discussions with the regulators of energy (Ofgem), water (Ofwat), financial services (FCA) and communications (Ofcom) in 2013/14 and commissioned research from the University of Leicester to interpret and implement their powers to tackle consumer vulnerability. Ofcom, Ofgem and Ofwat have legal duties to take account of groups of consumers who are assumed to be 'vulnerable'. The FCA does not have a similar duty but may consider the ease with which consumers can access services. Many important powers and duties derive from EU frameworks (e.g. Ofcom and Ofgem). Regulators are either producing strategies or investigating particular areas of consumer vulnerability, an example of which is the energy regulator Ofgem's recent consumer vulnerability strategy (Ofgem 2013). From this report, Ofgem seems to accept that the market and the behaviour of companies have a key role to play in consumer vulnerability. But Ofgem also observes:

> Our work on vulnerability is shaped by our remit and powers as a regulator, with a recognition that some matters are for us and others are for Government. Much of Ofgem's focus is facilitating access to services and choice in the market, whereas Government can, for example, establish price support for certain consumers. But to leave it just to the regulators would move the spotlight away from the companies that are providing, and making a profit from providing, essential goods and services.
>
> (Ofgem 2013: 10)

The next section places the spotlight on some of those companies that are providing, and making a profit from providing, essential goods and services.

Companies

Although essential goods and services are needed by everyone, the tendency is for companies to appeal to those consumers who are in the least vulnerable situations – those who can afford to utilise direct debit and have good credit ratings, for example. In the context of consumer vulnerability, the challenge is how to get the companies to look beyond middle-income consumers and those who are not in vulnerable positions and recognise the need to provide services that are inclusive. To flip our definition of consumer vulnerability (from Stearn 2012: 11), perhaps a more meaningful definition would be to 'create a situation where people can choose and access essential products and services which are suitable for their needs, and can do so without disproportionate effort/cost/time'.

What has been outlined above suggests the need for a more hands-on and interventionist approach from regulators. But it is in the interests of companies themselves to become inclusive in their provision of essential goods and services. If companies are going to be sustainable they need to become more inclusive. The Consumer Focus report *Tackling Consumer Vulnerability: An Action*

Plan for Empowerment (Stearn 2012) draws on examples where companies, such as British Gas, have, at least partially, realised the benefits of a more inclusive approach to consumers in debt and vulnerable positions (Cummins and Nolan 2011).

In Britain, the 2006 Companies Act introduced a requirement for public companies to report on social and environmental matters. Environmental and social impacts are now regularly reported on by 90 per cent of the top UK companies, in addition to financial performance. Numerous companies may provide some financial support for charities or, for example, encourage staff to volunteer. But there are few examples we could find of companies that appear to go beyond this 'first level' of engagement and work an understanding of consumers in vulnerable positions into the company's DNA.

In an attempt to encourage companies to be more inclusive and to encourage business to develop more inclusive practices, Consumer Futures, Citizens Advice and other organisations worked with BSI to produce British Standard 18477 'Inclusive service provision: requirements for identifying and responding to consumer vulnerability'. This British Standard gives organisations clear guidance on how to recognise consumers who could be in vulnerable situations; how they should, could and can provide inclusive services so they are able to meet the needs of all consumers. It also means they are in a stronger position to comply with the Unfair Commercial Practices Directive, the Consumer Protection from Unfair Trading Regulations (2008) and other pertinent legislation, such as the Disability Discrimination Act and equality and human rights laws.

However, although British Standard 18477 came out in November 2010, very few organisations have used the standard to benchmark their services. The Financial Ombudsman Service has been the first organisation to do so, and in 2014, Western Power Distribution became the first company in the UK to achieve this benchmark status (Citizens Advice 2015). In 2013, the BSI produced a white paper for service providers, promoting the adoption of BS18477, and showcasing the adoption of the standard by the Financial Ombudsman Service as a way of ensuring more inclusive service delivery.

Civil society

Civil society may help speed things up. In 2012 Consumer Futures (at that time Consumer Focus) commissioned some research with the National Council of Voluntary Organisations (NCVO) to look at the way civil society was getting involved in the market (Jochum, 2013). What emerged was that boundaries were blurring in different sectors. Parts of the voluntary and community sector or more generally civil society (community organisations, social enterprises, co-operatives and mutual) are recognising that markets may not be equally benefiting all groups of consumers. Some civil society organisations are acting as intermediaries to encourage companies to recognise how they exclude certain consumers. A good example of this is the Royal National Institute of Blind People's (RNIB) talking cash machine campaign (http://www.rnib.org.uk/campaigning-latest-campaigns/talking-atms). Some organisations are directly providing goods and services to include and empower the consumers that are ignored or getting a poor deal from commercial organisations. For example, Ebico (https://www.ebico.org.uk/) is a not-for-profit energy supplier that charges everyone fairly and at the same rate, with no additional payments for pre-pay or quarterly payment of bills. These and thousands of other actions by civil society organisations – including housing associations – are based on an understanding of people who are in vulnerable positions. But this engagement with the market does not receive the level of recognition or analysis that is necessary for this model to grow.

Government

The role of government in promoting a wider sense of responsibility among organisations providing services to consumers in vulnerable situations has gained some traction in recent years. The UK government seems to be aware of the benefits to companies of thinking beyond simply corporate social responsibility. In 2010, Cameron launched Every Business Commits, which set out a responsibility deal between the government and business to help build the Big Society. In the deal, the government committed to creating a stable economy, with lower taxation and less regulation. In return, the government wanted a commitment from business to invest in skills and jobs, reduce carbon usage, improve well-being and support communities and enterprise. However, from our analysis of the regulatory context, this may be problematic. The work with JRF on the poverty premium indicated the need for *more involvement and more intervention* from regulators but companies and government are arguing for less.

Consumer vulnerability is starting to gain some interest at a European level. The Third Energy Package (European Commission 2007) focused on improving the operation of retail markets to yield real benefits for both electricity and gas consumers. The European Commission established the Citizens' Energy Forum in 2007, the aim of the Forum being the implementation of competitive, energy-efficient and fair retail markets for consumers. Several working groups were established to focus on issues raised in the Forum, covering topics such as 'vulnerable consumers', price transparency and consumers as energy market agents. The European Commission's DG Sanco[2] is also looking more closely at consumer vulnerability. It has asked VVA Europe, together with London Economics and IPSOS, to carry out a study on consumer vulnerability. The objective of the study is to identify both marketing practices that are especially problematic for consumers and good practice measures employed in member states to mitigate consumer vulnerability (BEREC 2013).

Consumers

It may seem odd to leave consumers to the end, but starting with consumers could have meant the focus was on the individual's situation and not on companies, regulators and government, all key players in this market who have a role to play in addressing the issues around consumer vulnerability.

Accessing empowerment

Research for *Tackling Consumer Vulnerability: An Action Plan for Empowerment* (Stearn 2012) found some empowered action by consumers in vulnerable positions – for example, switching suppliers. People recognise that their loyalty is of value to companies, and can be leveraged to secure better service and/or tariffs. However, switching is not always an easy option for consumers, as discussed earlier. Consumers from our research often felt that the information encouraging switching was not aimed at them but at new customers that companies were trying to attract. This raises questions about the switching-centric view that regulators have of competition. More attention needs to be paid to loyalty, and how to support customers to use their loyalty as a way to get a better deal from their supplier.

As things are, much could be achieved for consumers through information which is particularly focused on the needs of individuals. This could mean the voluntary sector becoming trusted intermediaries, sharing information on the market, and on how and where to get the best deals. This, in addition to the more traditional 'know your rights'-based approach, has the potential to empower consumers in vulnerable situations and put them on the same footing as other consumers.

There is also potential to empower vulnerable consumers through collective purchasing of goods and services. For example, a group of residents in Maidstone, Kent banded together to bulk buy groceries for the local community at discount prices. Supported by the Social Innovation Lab for Kent, The R Shop was set up in response to one mother who had extreme difficulty managing the weekly shop with a small child and no car (http://enginegroup.co.uk/work/kcc-social-innovation-lab).

Collective switching also has potential to increase engagement in energy markets and ensure consumers get a fair deal. Collective switching is already well established in Belgium and the Netherlands and pioneering initiatives have started to emerge in the British energy market. However, participation among pre-pay energy users remains low and addressing the reasons for this will be a key challenge. Bristol Switch & Save was one scheme, developed and run by the Centre for Sustainable Energy (CSE) in Bristol in partnership with the city council, Bristol Credit Union and Bristol Pound (a local currency). Over 5,000 people signed up. There were 1,242 switches and average savings of £105 per household. However, many of the big energy companies were unwilling to offer prepayment customers a decent deal, so CSE chose to use its own scheme finance to offer cash-back to this group if they switched to any other supplier. CSE's chief executive Simon Roberts noted: 'Despite their protestations to the contrary, energy companies are not interested in this group of people who are poorer, more prone to energy debt and more expensive to service. Bristol

Switch & Save has exposed this and we will be pursuing the issue further with DECC and Ofgem' (Energise 2013: 4).

Conclusion

Developments, such as mobile phone banking, smart metering, data matching and 'data dialogues' with companies, could help empower people in vulnerable positions and help tackle the imbalance in the market place. However, much still depends on regulators and government to tackle the current failings in the market. Companies must recognise that they should be inclusive and meet the needs of all consumers. Alongside regulators and government, civil society is becoming an active and trusted intermediary between the market and consumers who may be in vulnerable positions.

Notes

1 Thanks to a campaign by RNIB, all the banks have now agreed to introduce talking ATMs. See http://www.rnib.org.uk/getinvolved/campaign/yourmoney/cashmachine/Pages/ATM_Latestnews.aspx
2 Responsibility for Consumer Affairs has just moved from DG Sanco to DG Justice.

References

BEREC (2013) *Stakeholder Consultation Concerning the Study on Consumer Vulnerability across Key Markets in the European Union.* Online at: http://berec.europa.eu/eng/document_register/subject_matter/berec/others/4471-stakeholder-consultation-concerning-the-study-on-consumer-vulnerability-across-key-markets-in-the-european-union [accessed 13 Jan 2015]

BIS (2011) *Better Choices: Better Deals Business Innovation and Skills.* Online at: http://www.bis.gov.uk/assets/biscore/consumer-issues/docs/b/11-749-better-choices-better-deals-consumers-powering-growth.pdf [accessed 13 Jan 2015]

Citizens Advice (2015) 'Treating consumers fairly: flexible and inclusive services for all'. Online at: www.citizensadvice.org.uk/global/migrated_doucments/corporate/treating-consumers-fairly.pdf

Consumers, Estate Agents and Redress Act (2007). London: Her Majesty's Stationery Office. Online at: http://www.legislation.gov.uk/ukpga/2007/17/section/6 [accessed 13 Jan 2015]

Cummins, J. and Nolan, A. (2011) *Reaction to presentation, Too Many Hurdles: Information and Advice Barriers in Energy Services.* 20 July, National Council for Voluntary Organisations, London

Energise (2013) News From the Centre for Sustainable Energy. Spring. Online at: http://www.cse.org.uk/downloads/file/energise_spring_2013_A4.pdf [accessed 13 Jan 2015]

European Commission (2007) *Single Market for Gas and Electricity.* Online at: http://ec.europa.eu/energy/gas_electricity/legislation/third_legislative_package_en.htm [accessed 13 Jan 2015]

Hirsch, D. (2013) *Addressing the Poverty Premium: Approaches to Regulation*, JRF for Consumer Futures, London. Online at: http://www.consumerfutures.org.uk/files/2013/06/Addressing-the-poverty-premium.pdf [accessed 13 Jan 2015]

http://enginegroup.co.uk/work/kcc-social-innovation-lab [accessed 13 Jan 2015]

http://www2.le.ac.uk/departments/law/research/cces/too-many-hurdles-information-and-advice-barriers-in-energy-services [accessed 13 Jan 2015]

http://www.rnib.org.uk/campaigning-latest-campaigns/talking-atms [accessed 13 Jan 2015]

http://www.which.co.uk/news/2011/05/older-consumers-face-travel-insurance-problems-254174/ [accessed 13 Jan 2015]

https://www.ebico.org.uk/ [accessed 13 Jan 2015]

Jochum, V. (2013) 'Tackling consumer vulnerability: the role of civil society'. Online at: http://blogs.ncvo.org.uk/2013/01/24/tackling-consumer-vulnerability-the-role-of-civil-society/ [accessed 13 Jan 2015]

Ofcom (2013) *The Consumer Experience 2013*. Ofcom's annual report into the consumer experience of the fixed and mobile, internet, digital broadcasting and postal markets. Online at: http://stakeholders.ofcom.org.uk/market-data-research/market-data/consumer-experience-reports/consumer-experience/ [accessed 13 Jan 2015]

Ofgem (2013) Consumer Vulnerability Strategy. Online at: https://www.ofgem.gov.uk/ofgem-publications/75550/consumer-vulnerability-strategy.pdf [accessed 13 Jan 2015]

Stearn, J. (2012) Tackling consumer vulnerability: An action plan for empowerment. Online at: http://www.consumerfutures.org.uk/files/2013/05/Tackling-consumer-vulnerability.pdf [accessed 13 Jan 2015]

Which? (2011) Older consumers face travel insurance problems: Upper age limits cause angst for older travellers. 21 May

Part II

Consumer vulnerability and key life stages

7 Children as vulnerable consumers

Agnes Nairn

Introduction

This chapter presents some of the most recent research on children as vulnerable consumers. This is a highly contentious and hotly debated area for researchers and policy makers alike and there are still many unanswered questions. It is hoped that the chapter will stimulate interest in taking this field of research forward.

Perhaps a good place to begin is with the United Nations Convention on the Rights of the Child, which was drawn up in 1989 with the express intention of recognising children as potentially vulnerable citizens and according them special rights. One hundred and ninety-three countries are party to the Convention, including all members of the United Nations except South Sudan, Somalia and the United States of America. It is thus enshrined in the legislation of most nations and these rights are usually the starting point for the work of children's charities.

The interpretation of children's rights in the commercial world poses an interesting challenge as two parts of the convention accord children rights which could be seen as conflicting. Article 3 accords all those under the age of 18 the right to be protected, while at the same time Article 12 accords them the right to be heard. Many advertisers and commercial researchers claim under Article 12 that children have the right to be fully involved in the commercial world and thus to see and hear advertising messages, to participate in market research studies and to be active consumers in their own right as well as influencers of family purchases. On the other hand, campaigners and, indeed, many governments, wish to restrict children's involvement with commerce on the grounds that they have a right to be protected from the negative effects of being targeted with consumer goods or food and drink that might be bad for them or with commercial messages the implications of which they may not fully understand. We can already see that how we conceptualise the vulnerability of the child consumer is highly contested.

This chapter focuses on the ways in which children may be vulnerable to consumer culture and materialistic values in general and to TV advertising in particular. As these are now inextricably enmeshed within children's everyday lives we need a clearer understanding of how these phenomena interact and how they are related to children's well-being.

Watching, wanting and well-being

Studies by Juliet Shor (2004) in the USA and by Nairn, Ormrod and Bottomley (2007) in the UK have identified what has come to be called the "watching, wanting and well-being" dynamic – in other words the links between three phenomena: first, the level of children's exposure to TV advertising; second, the extent of their adoption of materialistic values and third, their levels of self-esteem, self-satisfaction and general happiness. Research now concurs that more hours of watching TV in general and advertising in particular is correlated with higher levels of materialism, which in turn correlates negatively with a range of well-being indicators. The discovery of this dynamic clearly flags up a potential issue for protecting the interests of the child consumer, yet these links are far from simple and the direction of the correlations is not necessarily obvious.

Even defining materialism has posed problems. Consumer researchers originally defined materialism as a collection of personality traits comprising possessiveness, non-generosity and envy (e.g. Belk, 1984), but it is now usually understood as a set of personally held values. The most widely used definition is that proposed by Richins and Dawson over 20 years ago: "a set of centrally held beliefs about the importance of possessions in one's life" (1992, p. 308). For materialistic individuals the acquisition of money and possessions is assumed to be: (i) *central* to life giving it meaning and guiding behaviour, (ii) important for life satisfaction and *happiness*, and (iii) crucial for judging *success* of oneself and others. Items measuring these three components make up Richins and Dawson's (1992) Material Values Scale, which is the measure that has been most widely used in adult research over the past 15 years. The Richins and Dawson tri-partite scale (1992) has been adapted for use with children with a number of slightly different scales available (e.g. Achenreiner, 1997; Goldberg et al., 2003; Kasser, 2005; Schor, 2004; Chaplin and John, 2007; Bottomley et al., 2010).

Link between advertising and materialism

Turning now to the links, let us begin with the one between materialism and advertising. Ten years ago a large-scale review of a range of studies over a number of years (Buijzen and Valkenburg, 2003a) highlighted a consistently positive correlation between exposure to TV advertising and youth materialism. Work since then has reinforced this finding (e.g. Goldberg et al., 2003; Shor, 2004; Nairn, Ormrod and Bottomley, 2007). However, the key question is: does advertising make children materialistic or is it the case that materialistic children simply seek out more adverts to inform their interest in buying things? All the evidence so far points to the former and, indeed, Buijzen and Valkenburg (2003a) concluded that "analysis clearly suggests that exposure to advertising stimulates materialistic values in children" (p. 451). Longitudinal and experimental studies support this claim. For example at the macro-level, a longitudinal study of 300,000 17/18-year-old Americans across three generations (1976 to 2007) showed that advertising spend (as a proportion of GDP) has both contemporaneous and lagged positive associations with materialism (Twenge and Kasser, 2013). At the micro-level four studies have also established a causal or quasi-causal connection between advertising exposure and child materialism. Goldberg and Gorn (1978) found that 4–5-year olds exposed to a toy commercial would subsequently rather play with this toy than their friends; Moschis and Moore (1982) established that heavy TV viewing by 12–18 year olds predicted high materialism one year later; and Greenberg and Brand (1993) showed that 15–16-year olds who were exposed to the classroom commercial TV station "Channel One" were more materialistic than those who were not. The most recent longitudinal study by Opree et al. (2014) with Dutch 8–11-year olds found that greater exposure to advertising dense TV programmes was associated one year later with increased product desire for the advertised brands which in turn was associated with increased materialism more generally. These authors propose that cultivation theory (Shrum et al., 2011, Sirgy et al., 2012) allows us to conjecture that the children in this sample who watched a lot of TV advertising came to believe that an unrealistic proportion of people own desirable brands and that this augments their happiness and life satisfaction. Opree et al. (2014) go on to demonstrate that the relationship between advertising exposure and materialism is fully mediated by advertised product desire. The supposition is that watching a lot of advertising changes not only children's perceptions but also their desire to buy specific advertised products and that this leads to materialistic values. Thus, while more longitudinal research is required it certainly seems that advertising does "cause" children to associate the acquisition of consumer goods with status, happiness and a viable lifestyle.

Link between materialism and low well-being

The second link – between materialism and low well-being – is arguably the more important in a consideration of children as vulnerable consumers for if materialism "causes" children psychological distress then it clearly triggers an undesirable state. Over two decades of research have resulted in extremely consistent findings relating to the negative relationship between materialism and a wide range of measures of child well-being such as a qualitative parent assessment of child happiness (e.g. Goldberg et al., 2003); scales measuring life satisfaction (e.g. Ahuvia and Wong, 2002) and life dissatisfaction (e.g. Buijzen and Valkenburg, 2003b); self-esteem (Nairn et al., 2007; Chaplin and John, 2007, 2010) and various measures from standardised psychologists' scales screening for anxiety, depression and psychosomatic symptoms (Schor, 2004). There seems little question that materialism and well-being are closely linked. However, although the existence of this link is well documented, the directionality is much less well understood. There has traditionally been an assumption that materialism leads to low well-being, nurtured no doubt by the historical legacy of the term itself, which was coined in negative contrast to "higher-order" spiritual beliefs (Berkeley, 1988) and bears the traces of greed – one of the seven deadly sins. Thus – at least in Western cultures – we have come implicitly to expect that harbouring materialistic values will be intrinsically damaging.

In line with this, a number of hypotheses have been put forward to account for the negative effects of materialism. In relation to children the theory that has gained most traction is the *displacement hypothesis* (e.g. Kasser and Ryan, 1993; Nairn and Ipsos MORI, 2011), which posits that obsession with material possessions acts to displace the human relationships with family and friends that children need for healthy social development. Of relevance is also the *escalation hypothesis* or *hedonic adaptation hypothesis*, which suggests that centring one's life on the acquisition of consumer goods in the twenty-first century is destined to disappoint, as no sooner is the latest fashion in shoes or the most advanced version of phone acquired than trends and technologies have moved on, necessitating the purchase of the next newest thing (Lyubomisky, 2011).

However, it is also possible and just as feasible, that children who find themselves in unhappy situations will turn to material objects for comfort and to compensate for other things that are missing in their lives. Indeed, a growing body of research on what has come to be referred to as *compensatory consumption* concurs that the need to consume can be propelled by a range of threats to the self (Rucker & Galinsky, 2013; Mandel et al., 2013; Vignoles et al., 2006). These may be fundamental threats to our existence – for example *terror management* research in adults has shown that priming individuals with thoughts of their death before completing the Material Values Scale results in higher materialism scores (Maheswaran and Agarawal, 2004). But these threats may also be to other needs such as that for self-esteem, power or belonging (Mandel et al., 2013). Recent experimental and longitudinal research with young people appears to support a trajectory from low well-being to materialism and thus the possibility of the relevance of the compensatory consumption theory to children.

In a first attempt to test this theory, Chaplin and John (2010) showed in an experiment that priming high self-esteem could reduce materialism in children in the short term. However, due to its design this study was unable to show any longer-term effects of low self-esteem on materialism. Important new longitudinal research, however, has been able to do this. In 2012 the Dutch research team referred to above (Opree et al. 2012) released the results of their first longitudinal study with 8–11-year olds which measured children's materialism and well-being at two points in time, one year apart. They found that children who were more materialistic at time 0 did not have lower life satisfaction at time 1 but that, on the contrary, those who had low life satisfaction at time 0 went on to become more materialistic at time 1. While this supports the compensatory consumption hypothesis, there is an important caveat. Only those children who had been exposed to a lot of advertising-dense TV compensated for their low well-being by turning to material possessions. The authors conclude that, *"it is plausible that the material values portrayed in advertising teach children that material possessions are a way to cope with decreased life satisfaction"* (Opree et al., 2012, p. e486).

Meanwhile a rather more complex three-wave longitudinal study with over 2,000 8–15-year olds in the UK (Wright et al. 2011) also showed, in line with the compensatory consumption theory, that, for the whole sample of children, low life satisfaction at time 0 predicted materialism at time 1. Beyond this the team also made another important discovery, namely that high materialism at time 1 also predicted low well-being at time 2 – another eight months into the future – implying that the link between materialism and well-being may be bi-directional or, indeed, cumulative and cyclical. The empirical evidence we have so far thus points to a dynamic whereby children at their most vulnerable are most susceptible to the appealing claims of advertising, but that attempts to compensate for unhappiness by buying the right stuff not only do not succeed but bring more unhappiness in their wake.

If childhood materialism is initially triggered by a need to compensate for some kind of self-threat then the next question is, what kind of catalyst drives advertising-fed materialism? What can render children particularly vulnerable consumers? Recent research proposes four drivers of childhood compensatory consumption: first, biological changes associated with puberty; second, peer rejection; third, low socio-economic status; and fourth, family disharmony. I will deal with each of these in turn below.

Drivers of childhood compensatory consumption

Puberty. In the priming experiment referred to above where boosting young people's self-esteem led to a decrease in materialism, Chaplin and John (2010) explained variations in self-esteem levels as a biological age-related function of puberty. Through a survey administered to three age groups of young people they showed that self-esteem was relative high amongst 8–12-year olds, dipped for 13–15-year olds and was restored again by 16–18, whilst materialism rose and then fell concomitantly. They concluded that 13–15-year-olds are particularly vulnerable to the appeals of consumer culture as adverting tends to offer products that will make you look better and feel better about yourself. This age-related dip in self-esteem – particularly for girls – has been borne out across many studies, including the international Health Behaviour of School Age Children Survey (http://www.hbsc.org/), which has been conducted across 43 countries for 30 years. Thus, whilst we perhaps tend to think of the very youngest children as the most in need of protection, it seems that teenagers are possibly the most vulnerable group when it comes to the appeals of advertising for products that promise to raise self-esteem.

Peer Rejection. Puberty, however, cannot account for all psychological and emotional turbulence in youth and a second identified driver of childhood compensatory consumption is peer rejection – something not necessarily experienced by all young people. A recent survey (Benton, 2011) highlighted the potential harm done to young people when they do experience bullying through "being left out". They noted that this type of bullying is more strongly associated with poor emotional well-being than any other type, including more explicit forms such as physical or verbal abuse. The three-wave study carried out in the UK referred to above (Wright et al. 2011) specifically explored being left out as a catalyst for materialism. Through 60 in-depth interviews the team discovered that overall children's motives for materialism were overwhelmingly both extrinsic and social in nature. In other words, materialistic values were driven by the need to own the "right" or "cool" things in order to bolster status within their peer group, in particular to "be popular", "fit in" and "look good." At time 0 they used socio-metrics to identify a group of children rejected by their peers. This group showed the lowest well-being across the sample and therefore unsurprisingly this group showed a significant rise in consumer culture orientation at time 1. However, the study also found that the attempts by this group of children to use consumer goods to look good, gain popularity and fit in failed miserably as they not only remained rejected at time 2 but levels of depression among this group increased significantly between time 0 and time 2. Thus, materialism triggered by peer rejection seems to be both highly likely and particularly harmful.

Low socio-economic status. While at the micro level small groups of children in a class use consumption in an attempt to gain peer acceptance, at a macro level children also appear to be attracted to consumer culture as compensation for their low socio-economic status. Shor (2004) and Nairn, Ormrod and Bottomley (2007) for example found that 9–13-year olds from lower socio-economic groups were dramatically more materialistic than their better-off counterparts. While these studies were not designed to explore causality, qualitative work again suggests a compensatory motivation. A study by the young people's group Amplify (2011) for the UK Children's Commissioner found that when young people were asked why they felt under pressure to buy expensive brands, common replies included, "Because everyone else seems to have them and none of us wants to look poor", and "Anything to prove you've got money" (15-year-old girls). Here anxiety about fitting in is compounded by concern over socio-economic status. This concern is in evidence among not only children but also their parents. Qualitative research amongst parents in the UK (Bailey, 2011) highlighted pressure felt by parents to buy specific consumer goods and brands to stop their children being bullied or left out. As one parent put it, "My eldest's school shoes and coat were bought out of us worrying that he may be bullied if it wasn't the right look." The "right look", it turns out, is an "expensive" look. Research for UNICEF UK (Nairn and Ipsos MORI, 2011) found a similar discourse amongst UK parents. As one low-income mother reported in relation to the coat bought for her toddler, "I got it because it didn't look cheap … it looked expensive."

Family disharmony. The UNICEF UK study (Nairn and Ipsos MORI, 2011) referred to above included qualitative research with over 200 children aged 8–14 across the UK, Spain and Sweden. In discussions with children in schools the most common spontaneous response to the question "What makes a good day?" was "Time with my family", while the most common response to the question "What makes a bad day?" was "Arguments with my family". These responses were constant across all countries, socio-economic backgrounds and ages, confirming that children can be vulnerable if their family relationships are disrupted. Of interest to this chapter is whether the unhappiness caused by family arguments is a catalyst for compensatory consumption in the same way as peer rejection, socio-economic status and puberty appear to be. And what role might advertising play in this? It turns out that these family dynamics are both more complex and less well understood than the three other drivers we have considered. This is an area that urgently requires more research, particularly as we have no experimental or longitudinal data yet.

Correlational studies by Buijzen and Valkenburg (2003b), Shor (2004) and Nairn, Ormrod and Bottomley (2007) all found that children's levels of materialism were highly correlated with family conflict – more materialistic children argued more with their parents. The assumption behind the findings in all of these studies, however, was that materialism was the cause of the conflict rather than the other way round. This is primarily because of the other correlational paths within the models built to analyse the data. For example Buijzen and Valkenburg (2003b) also showed a correlation between advertising exposure and purchase requests – or "pester power" – and another link between purchase requests and both family arguments and disappointment/dissatisfaction. Their assumption was that children who watched more advertising more often nagged their parents to buy what they had seen on the television. In turn, children who pestered their parents more often, argued with their parents more often and also experienced greater levels of disappointment (presumably as many if not most purchase requests were refused). This proposed pattern of events is in fact extremely familiar to parents and children. Research for a UK government (Bailey, 2011) found that nearly a third (32 per cent) of UK children say that if they really want something and know their parents do not want them to buy it, they will *always* keep on asking until their parents give in. More than half (52 per cent) say they *sometimes* do this and only 15 per cent said they *never* do. It seems intuitive that constant nagging like this will cause family disputes and indeed other research shows that advertising is linked to rows between parents about purchasing priorities (Flouri, 2004). However, what we do not yet know is whether these disputes drive children to crave compensatory objects even more.

Conclusion

This chapter has considered in some detail the watching, wanting and well-being dynamic and has shown both that it is highly complex but also that we are beginning to understand how the interplay between advertising, materialism and children's well-being can create vulnerabilities for children in general and for some groups in particular. Advertising clearly creates desires in children. These desires can be particularly strong for children who feel inadequate because of biological changes, peer rejection or low socio-economic status. It seems that these vulnerable groups come to believe that advertised cool stuff can compensate for their low well-being. Yet, we now know that not only do the products fail to deliver popularity, acceptance and high self-esteem but that aspiring to solve status issues through consumer goods creates increased unhappiness. We also know that advertising and materialism are strongly bound up with family conflict but we do not yet know how this dynamic plays out over time. Does advertising-induced materialism create family conflict or do children hope that cool stuff will alleviate the ill effects of an unhappy home life?

Areas for further research

As all serious researchers know, correlations are not the same as causations and it is highly dangerous to conflate the two. While "proving" the relationship between two phenomena in social research is always fraught with difficulty, longitudinal and experimental research provides a more accurate picture of cause and effect than cross-sectional research that is a snapshot in time. We need more of this type of research to explore how vulnerabilities that are particular to childhood may be exacerbated by consumerism. Studies on family dynamics are needed particularly urgently and I hope this chapter may spur on researchers to take up this challenge.

References

Achenreiner, G.B. (1997). Materialistic values and susceptibility to influence in children. In M. Brucks and D.J. MacInnis (eds), *Advances in Consumer Research*, 24: 82–88.

Ahuvia, A.C. and Wong, N.Y. (2002). Personality and value-based materialism: Their relationship and origins. *Journal of Consumer Psychology*, 12/4: 389–402.

Amplify (2011). *Children, Young People and the Commercial World*. Children's Commissioner, London.

Bailey, R. (2011). *Letting Children Be Children: Report of an Independent Review of the Commercialisation and Sexualisation of Children*. London: Department for Education.

Belk, R.W. (1984). Three scales to measure constructs related to materialism: Reliability, validity and relationships to measures of happiness. In T. Kinnear (ed.), *Advances in Consumer Research*, 11: 291–297.

Benton, T. (2011). 'Sticks and stones may break my bones, but being left on my own is worse': An analysis of reported bullying at school within NFER attitude surveys. NFER, Slough.

Berkeley, G. (1988). *Principles of Human Knowledge/Three Dialogues*. London: Penguin Books.

Bottomley, P., Nairn, A., Kasser, T., Ferguson, Y. and Ormrod, J. (2010). Measuring childhood materialism: Refining and validating Schor's consumer involvement scale. *Psychology and Marketing*, 27/7: 717–740.

Buijzen, M. and Valkenburg, P.M. (2003a). The impact of television advertising on materialism, parent-child conflict, and unhappiness: A review of the research. *Journal of Applied Developmental Psychology*, 24/4: 437–456.

Buijzen, M. and Valkenburg, P. (2003b). The unintended effects of television advertising: A parent-child survey, *Communication Research*, 30/5: 483–503.

Chaplin, L.N. and John, D.R. (2007). Growing up in a material world: Age differences in materialism in children and adolescents. *Journal of Consumer Research*, 34/4: 480–493.

Chaplin, L.N. and John, D.R. (2010). Interpersonal influences on adolescent materialism: A new look at the role of parents and peers. *Journal of Consumer Psychology*, 20/2: 176–184.

Flouri, I. (2004). Exploring the relationship between mothers' and fathers' parenting practices and children's materialistic values, *Journal of Economic Psychology*, 25/6: 743–752.

Goldberg, M.E. and Gorn, G.J. (1978). Some unintended consequences of TV advertising to children. *Journal of Consumer Research*, 5/1: 22–29.

Goldberg, M.E., Gorn, G.J., Peracchio, L.A. and Bamossy, G. (2003). Understanding materialism among youth. *Journal of Consumer Psychology*, 13/3: 278–288.

Greenberg, B.S. and Brand, J.E. (1993). Television news and advertising in schools: The 'Channel One' controversy. *Journal of Communication* 43/1: 143–151.

Kasser, T. (2005). Frugality, generosity and materialism in children and adolescents. In K.A. Moore and L. Lippman (eds), *What do Children Need to Flourish? Conceptualizing and Measuring Indicators of Positive Development*. New York: Springer Science: 357–374.

Kasser, T. and Ryan, R.M. (1993). A dark side of the American dream: Correlates of financial success as a central life aspiration. *Journal of Personality and Social Psychology*, 65, 410–422.

Lyubomisky, S. (2011). Hedonic adaptation to positive and negative experiences. In S. Folkman (ed.), *The Oxford Handbook of Stress, Health and Coping*. New York: Oxford University Press: 200–224.

Maheswaran, D. and Agrawal, N. (2004). Motivational and cultural variations in mortality salience effects: Contemplations on terror management theory and consumer behavior. *Journal of Consumer Psychology*, 14/3: 213–218.

Mandel, N., Rucker, D.D., Levav, J. and Galinsky, A.D. (2013). Compensatory consumption: How it fills psychological voids and needs. Working paper, Arizona State University.

Moschis, G.P. and Moore, R.L. (1982). A longitudinal study of television advertising effects. *Journal of Consumer Research* 9/3: 279–286.

Nairn, A. and Ipsos MORI (2011). Children's well-being in Sweden, Spain and UK: The role of materialism and inequality. UNICEF UK. Retrieved from: http://www.unicef.org.uk/Documents/Publications/IPSOS_UNICEF_ChildWellBeingreport.pdf (accessed 13 January 2015).

Nairn, A., Ormrod, J. and Bottomley, P. (2007) *Watching, Wanting and Well-being: Exploring the Links. A study of 9–13 year-olds in England and Wales*. London: National Consumer Council.

Opree, S., Buijzen, M. and Valkenburg, P.M. (2012). Lower life satisfaction related to materialism in children frequently exposed to advertising. *Pediatrics*, 130/3: e486–e489.

Opree, S.J., Buijzen, M., Van Reijmersdal, E.A. and Valkenburg, P.M. (2014). Children's advertising exposure, advertised product desire and materialism: A longitudinal study. *Communication Research*. 41/5: 717–735.

Richins, M.L. and Dawson, S. (1992). A consumer values orientation for materialism and its measurement: Scale development and validation. *Journal of Consumer Research*, 19 (Dec): 303–316.

Rucker, D.D. and Galinsky, A.D. (2013). Conspicuous consumption. In Russell Belk and Ayalla R. Ruvio (eds), *The Routledge Companion to Identity and Consumption*. New York: Routledge, 207–215.

Schor, J.B. (2004). *Born to Buy: The Commericalized Child and the New Consumer Culture*. New York: Scribner.

Shrum, L.J., Lee, J., Burroughs, J.E and Rindfleisch, A. (2011). An online process model of second-order cultivation effects: How television cultivates materialism and its consequences for life satisfaction. *Human Communication Research*, 37/1: 34–57.

Sirgy, M.J., Gurel-Atay, E., Webb, D., Cicic, M., Husic, M., Ekici, A., Herrmann, A., Hegazy, I., Lee, D.J. and Johar, J.S. (2012). Linking advertising, materialism and life satisfaction. *Social Indicators Research*, 107 (March): 79–101.

Twenge, J. and Kasser, T. (2013). Generational changes in materialism and work centrality, 1976–2007: Associations with temporal changes in societal insecurity and materialistic role modelling. *Personality and Social Psychology Bulletin*, 39: 883–897.

Vignoles, V.L., Regalia, C., Manzi, C., Golledge, J. and Scabini, E. (2006). Beyond self-esteem: Influence of multiple motives on identity construction. *Journal of Personality and Social Psychology*, 90/2: 308–333.

Wright, M.L., Dittmar, H. and Banerjee, R. (2011). Consumer culture ideals and motives: Links with well-being in childhood and adolescence. Paper presented at the British Psychological Society Social Psychology Section Annual Conference, Cambridge, UK, 6–8 Sept. Oxford: Wiley: 95–131.

8 Consuming childhood grief

Stephanie O'Donohoe

Introduction

Within the literature in childhood studies and marketing/consumer research there is much debate around the vulnerability of children in their dealings with the market (Marshall 2010; Buckingham et al. 2009). There is little doubt, however, that in general bereaved children are vulnerable. Even for adults, bereavement is a devastating, disorienting and traumatic life event; the loss of beloved family members or friends brings in its wake ruptures in social routines and social networks, as well as destroying the assumptive world that sustains our daily lives (Parkes 2010). For children in particular, bereavement poses distinctive risks to mental health, social integration and academic performance (Nguyen and Scott 2013; Penny and Stubbs 2015).

Bereaved children do not exist outside consumer culture, so in that sense they are vulnerable consumers, with their experience of vulnerability shaped by 'the interaction of individual states, individual characteristics, and external conditions' (Baker et al. 2005, p. 134). Like any children, they are exposed to a range of marketing practices and messages. It is not clear, however, that their particular experience of consumer vulnerability is best characterised as 'a state of powerlessness that arises from an imbalance in marketplace interactions or from the consumption of marketing messages and products' (Baker et al. 2005: 134).

This chapter, then, does not engage with debates about children as vulnerable to particular marketing practices or unscrupulous marketers; these important issues are addressed elsewhere in this book. Instead, the focus here is on how bereaved children's vulnerability is played out through consumption and in consumer culture – how what they have and use helps shape their experiences and relationships at this particularly difficult time in their lives. The chapter begins by outlining distinctive aspects of childhood grief, particularly among very young children. Taking a case study approach, it then examines a detailed account of one bereaved toddler's grief through the lens of consumption, and considers the implications for parents and others seeking to support young children through grief.

Childhood grief

While grief is universal and may be experienced throughout the lifecourse, it has a particular inflection among children. The extent to which contemporary Western society is death-denying is debatable (Walter 1999), but even if death features prominently in news reports, films, and electronic games, it tends to be an unfamiliar, invisible presence in children's immediate surroundings. Children's direct encounters with death and dying are limited by factors including lower mortality rates, geographic distance between extended family members, the removal of the elderly and seriously ill to hospitals or nursing homes, and the desire to preserve childhood innocence (Walter 1999).

The urge to protect children from exposure to death is understandable. Complex, shocking and disorientating as it often is for adults, it can be especially difficult for children. This may be their first experience of overwhelming negative emotions such as anger, guilt, and fear, and the first time they see grown-ups cry or realise that they are not invincible (Stokes 2004; et al. 2009). The transition from survival mode to processing the loss can be particularly challenging for children, and their behaviour may deteriorate or regress as a result (Gilbert 2014). They may also experience somatic symptoms such as headaches, loss of appetite, insomnia, restlessness, and fatigue (Penny and Stubbs 2015). There may be major changes to their daily routines, and grieving parents or carers may have less time, energy or patience to devote to their children (Wolchik et al. 2008). Others may treat grieving children differently; they may be kind and offer comfort, say thoughtless or hurtful things, or fail to acknowledge their loss at all (Corr et al. 2009; Gilbert 2014).

Children may deal with their loss intermittently, creating respite from difficult thoughts and feelings by playing or immersing themselves in aspects of 'normal' life. As Van Horn (2006) notes, resilience in the face of bereavement involves growth as well as grieving, and even bereaved children have much to explore, enjoy and accomplish. Unfortunately, this can lead to their grief being misunderstood or disenfranchised (Walter and McCoyd 2009).

Many factors shape a child's response to bereavement, including the nature of the death and the child's particular relationship with the person who died; the character of individual children; their social support; their cultural, religious and family norms; and their developmental stage (Corr et al. 2009; Penny and Stubbs 2015). The relationship between bereavement and children's development is complex: bereavement disrupts children's developmental processes (Gilbert 2014), and their response to loss reflects their developmental stage. Focusing on the content and organisation of memories, for example, Buschbaum (1996: 114) compares the 'fragmented, egocentric, and often contradictory images of the pre-schooler' with the 'consolidated, objective, and multidimensional recollections of the adolescent'.

Experiences at the youngest end of the age range are less well understood (Bugge et al. 2014), although the enormity of parental loss experienced by infants, toddlers and pre-schoolers is evoked by Van Horn (2006: 971–2):

Children discover who they are in the ways in which their parents look at them, hold them, soothe them, talk to them, and play with them. When parents die, children lose their mirror into their own souls and lose a piece of themselves.

This loss may be experienced even before they understand the finality, irreversibility, inevitability and causality of death. Very young children may also struggle to verbalise their feelings or questions, and thus may be considered unaware of the death or 'too young to remember' (Wolchik et al. 2008), although preschoolers seem to understand more than traditional theories of child development allow (Corr et al. 2009; Wolchik et al. 2008). This suggests that careful attention needs to be paid to their nonverbal responses: bereaved Norwegian preschoolers struggled to sleep, or to sleep in their own bed; had nightmares; and frequently checked surviving family members for signs of illness (Bugge et al. 2014).

Various scholars and bereavement professionals have highlighted the importance of play in coping with grief, particularly among young children (Webb 2000). Indeed, 'play, fantasies, and any other references to the deceased parent should be accepted as part of the work of mourning' (Buschbaum 1996: 123). The parents interviewed by Bugge et al. (2014: 41) described how their children wanted to look at pictures and videos of their dead parent or sibling, talked about them, asked to visit their grave, and included them in games and family rituals.

Between the ages of eight and 12, children tend to develop a more sophisticated understanding of death, and to respond to loss with existential as well as practical concerns, although they may also regress to younger behaviours or ways of thinking (Corr et al. 2009). Adolescents' grief may be compounded by their general struggle to become independent and autonomous; they may not feel able to share their grief within the family or want to seem different from their peers (Corr et al. 2009; Gilbert 2014). Silverman and Nickman (1996a) traced the grief responses of 6–17-year-old parentally bereaved children over two years, noting that, regardless of age, they were actively involved in making sense of their loss and 'finding a way of carrying the deceased parent with them' (p. 71). Particular objects often played a role in these children's sense-making: in some cases they treasured particular things that their dead parents had given them; in other cases they took or were given something of theirs after the death. Over time, such objects often shifted from highly visible transitional objects to keepsakes, displayed and used less prominently (Normand et al. 1996). The importance of ritual – often involving objects such as candles, balloons, and memory boxes – has also been highlighted in scholarly and practitioner literature on child bereavement (Stokes 2004; Rolls 2008).

Several studies highlight the importance of parents and carers in supporting children's grief (Bugge et al. 2014; Silverman and Nickman 1996b). This demands a great deal of grieving adults, however, who may also be facing changes in financial circumstances, roles and relationships (Wolchik et al. 2008). They may have less time, energy or patience for their children, even as they worry about being 'good enough' grieving parents (Bugge et al. 2014). Although the bereaved Norwegian parents underestimated the influence of their own moods and actions on their preschoolers, they valued their children's concern for them, appreciating that 'sleeping together, sitting closer and giving each other hugs filled both parent's and children's needs' (p. 39).

Overall, it appears that children of all ages are deeply engaged in ongoing processes of sense-making and renegotiating family relationships and practices in the aftermath of a death in the family, although less is known about the experiences of very young children. Previous studies also allude to the role of particular objects and consumption practices in children's response to loss, although there has been little elaboration on this theme. The remainder of this chapter, then, explores the role of consumption in the bereavement experiences of one very young child.

Consumption and consumer culture in a grieving toddler's life

Thirty-three-year-old Desreen Brooks was killed by a car mounting the pavement as she, her husband Ben and their two-year-old son Jackson left their friends' London home one November evening in 2012. *It's Not Raining Daddy, It's Happy* (Brooks-Dutton 2014) is Ben's account of the year following her death. The book emerged from his influential and award-winning blog, *Life as a widower*, which he began just two months after Desreen's death. Frustrated by the lack of peer support available to young widowers, his blog offered regular dispatches from the alien territory he inhabited as a newly bereaved husband and father.

As Durrant (2014) notes, Ben's writing hit a nerve not only because of its honesty but also for its 'detailed anger, humility and self-scrutiny, his challenge to the common edict to "be strong"'. For the purposes of this chapter, his book is invaluable for its detailed account of a newly bereaved parent committed to understanding and supporting his toddler son through their grief; indeed, he resolved that

> I would never brush his loss under the carpet nor tell myself that his sea of grief was any shallower than mine just because of his age. Instead I would teach myself to better interpret his and I would become the person he could trust to share it without judgement, reservation or limits.
>
> (p. 151)

Throughout the book's harrowing account of his own loss, Ben's commitment to understanding, respecting and supporting Jackson's grief is evident. He offers detailed observations of Jackson's response to his mother's absence, and he does not gloss over occasions where he saw his own response to Jackson as inadequate. He also 'read books ... scoured the internet ... spoke to child bereavement charities and ... soaked up any advice I could get' (p. 148).

The remainder of this chapter outlines Ben's insights into the general contours and challenges of toddler grief, and the role of consumption in Jackson's response to his mother's death. It concludes with some tentative implications and suggested resources for anyone seeking to support bereaved children, as well as a brief reflection on research methods.

Experiencing grief

Ben's close observation of Jackson following his mother's sudden, continued absence captures the concrete nature of his loss and disorientation; physical objects were intertwined with his psychological upheaval. The night of the accident, Jackson was put to bed in their friends' house while the paramedics treated his mother, and after she was pronounced dead Ben and Jackson were driven home in a police car:

> I had to wake my son from a strange bed to put him into what should have been the car of his dreams, a car that says Nee nor! Except he didn't look excited, he looked confused and exhausted ... .
>
> (p.13)

Jackson awoke the next morning cross and confused; as Ben notes, '[h]is three favourite things in the world had gone missing during the chaos: his mother, his scooter and Thomas the Tank Engine' (p. 29). Furthermore, the house was filled with people who had recently been around celebrating his second birthday.

> Everyone he knew well was in the room except for his mum. How could we be having a party again so soon, but this time without her? Why was everyone crying? Where was the cake?
>
> (p. 29)

One challenging aspect of baby or toddler grief is that 'by the time they are articulate enough to be able to tell you how they once felt, they almost certainly can't remember' (p. 148). Toddlers not only struggle to articulate their loss; death is too complex a concept for very young children to understand (Corr et al. 2009). Indeed, at the time of Desreen's death, Jackson could not even make sense of its dimensions; he 'didn't know the geographical difference between paradise and the local park' and was 'arguably too young to know for sure whether it had been a day or a fortnight since he last saw his mummy' (p. 29). After her death, he would 'often squeal with excitement when he heard a key in the door' (p. 77), but didn't display signs of missing her for several weeks. Jackson's apparent ability to take his mother's absence in his stride led Ben to worry that he was forgetting her already. About a month after Desreen's death, however, it became clear that this was not the case; all of a sudden, Jackson erupted:

'Where's Mummy? Where's Mummy? Where's Mummy gone? Where's Mummy gone? Want Mummy. Want Mummy. Want Muuuuuummmmmmmyyyyy!' he cried over and over again.

(pp. 78–9)

Once Jackson had begun to ask about his mother, Ben explained that she had to go, even though she didn't want to because she loved him so much. He also reassured his son that he would look after him, '[a]nd I know how … because Mummy taught me' (p. 81). Jackson seemed to accept this without becoming upset, even repeating some of what he had been told. Although Ben did not assume that this meant he had taken it all in, 'Where's Mummy?' soon became 'Want Mummy', and a few months later, Ben overheard him tell a playmate, 'She's gone away in the sky, far away. She can't come back' (p. 83). Hope, desire and imagination co-existed with this understanding, however; eight months after she had died, Jackson announced 'Mummy's coming to Grandma's house tonight, Daddy … . She's coming in an aeroplane' (p. 303).

Just as realism and fantasy jostled around in Jackson's experience, so did mixed emotions and inconsistent reactions; as Ben notes, '[s]omething that he responded to positively one day might leave him reeling the next' (p. 149), and dancing and singing could be followed by outpourings of upset or anger. Two key triggers for anger and frustration were seeing other children with their mothers, and when things he wanted couldn't be found or were taken away from him; missing Lego pieces, or having the lid of a saucepan or a scooter he was going too fast on taken away would leave him incensed and lashing out:

Had each outburst not ended in him exhaustedly crying out or whimpering for his mummy, I might even have accepted that, as everyone was keen to reassure me, he was just throwing paddies, like any other kid his age … to me it went without saying that his loss had affected his behaviour and ability to feel sure that those around him wouldn't suddenly disappear, too.

(p. 328)

Although it was not always easy to distinguish between 'normal tantrums' and 'toddler grief', Ben resolved to give him the benefit of the doubt, and to comfort rather than punish him after outbursts. Such comfort often took the form of 'a nice lie-down and a cuddle'. Reflecting his emotional upheaval, Jackson would lie beside his father combining smiles and angry roars. For a while he became hostile to women, especially those resembling Desreen somehow. A general sense of malaise was also evident at times; one day, he suddenly announced 'It hurts, Daddy', and when asked what hurt, he said 'Jackson' (p. 309).

As Buschbaum (1996) notes, children are always changing, and as Jackson's language and understanding developed, he needed to know more about his mother's absence. One day, as well as repeating what he had been told about his mother's absence and saying how much he missed her, he added "Mummy wanted to go away", which prompted Ben to explain that she was hit by a car. Jackson gradually absorbed this new information, and could become very agitated by speeding cars. Again however, reality and fantasy were juxtaposed in his sense-making: questions clarifying what had actually happened ("Did Mummy bang her head, Daddy?") could be followed by imaginative solutions ("'Don't worry, Daddy!" he squealed enthusiastically. "I'll make it better"' (p. 339)).

Expressing grief

In the early days following Desreen's death, even before being told what had happened, Jackson's unease was articulated in his protective attitude towards her things:

> [H]e grew increasingly irritable about certain things that concerned her. One day … I started throwing things into one of her holdalls, just because it was the closest thing to hand.
> 'Don't touch it, Daddy!' he yelled. 'It Mummy's!'
>
> (p. 59)

As mentioned above, his loss was sometimes played out through anger and tantrums. One weekend, things came to a head when they passed a bus shelter and he saw a woman who reminded him of Desreen:

> He started kicking the shutters on a shop window … . I let his infant size fives give the shutters a good whack to help release his frustration, knowing that he was too small to do any damage to himself or to the shop. Then I gave him a hug and together we went and bought him his first ever croissant. He wasn't himself for the rest of the day – he was quiet and short-tempered – but at least he had been able to show me how he felt, even if he couldn't put it into words.
>
> (pp. 121–2)

Ben's sensitivity to how Jackson treated toys and things was heightened by advice from a play therapist. Playing trains with his son, on Jackson's terms, became an important part of their routine:

> Being the leader in our games allowed my son to more freely express his own feelings. Sometimes this meant he got angry and I would have to duck when carriages flew at my head. Other times, however, he would show nothing but love.
>
> (p. 223)

One day, at a toddler football class, Jackson was more interested in using the gym floor's markings as tracks for his train. At some point the calm was disrupted:

He picked up the ball and threw it at the wall over and over. He was in a mini-rage. I joined in and we took out our pent-up aggression on an innocent pile of bricks and released some of our at-the-surface-grief-induced anger. Then we carried on playing with the trains as if nothing had happened.

(p. 180)

Playing together also created opportunities for conversations about Desreen to develop, especially as Jackson's understanding matured. Playing with things also created space for playing with ideas. On one occasion, for example, Ben and Jackson were playing with modelling clay:

Chatting as we went, I brought up Mummy and explained once more what had happened. 'Mummy gone!' he confirmed. 'Not come back!' he went on. 'Mummy!' he shouted towards the hall, a direction that would once have been met with a certain reply. 'Not coming!' he reaffirmed with a shrug. And so we continued to play and chat.

(pp. 180–1)

In the spring after Desreen's death, when Ben praised some butterflies he had made from the clay, Jackson remarked, 'Mummy would be very proud of me' (p. 224). The use of the conditional here is striking, and not only as evidence of a toddler's linguistic development; articulating how his mother *would* react suggests that Jackson, like the older children in Silverman and Nickman's (1996a) study, was 'finding a way of carrying the deceased parent with them'; he appears to be extrapolating from his memories and knowledge of Desreen to imagine how she would feel about something she could not see him do.

Escaping grief

Immediately after Desreen's death, Jackson's train collection grew considerably as visitors came to the house bearing gifts. The book refers to many occasions where things and consumption experiences were used – with varying degrees of success – to obtain some brief respite from grief. There was for example the miserable experience of joining friends on holiday three months after Desreen had died; putting himself in Jackson's shoes, Ben reflects:

So there we were, sharing a sun lounger, recently bereaved of the one person who meant most to us in the whole wide world and you reckon a swimming pool and a scoop of ice cream is going to sort it out. Did it make you feel any better? That's what I thought.

(p. 159)

Shortly before her death, Jackson's love for Thomas the Tank Engine had led Desreen to book a family outing to a Thomas theme park. The date she had chosen fell a week after the accident, and Ben felt compelled to honour her plan. Unfortunately, Jackson fell asleep before they arrived, leaving Ben to endure the spectacle of happy families and Christmas scenes alone.

> Eventually I decided I could take no more. I positioned him in front of his favourite train … and gave him a nudge. He pulled a grumpy face and slowly opened one eye. In a split second both were wide open and he leapt from his pushchair, elated.
>
> (p. 58)

Another family outing planned before Desreen's death was to Crystal Palace Park. When Ben eventually took Jackson there, they both enjoyed Jackson's first experience of various childhood treats:

> soft ice cream in a cone from an old-school ice cream van; building sand-castles despite not being on a beach; sculptures of prehistoric creatures; and his first joyous jump on a bouncy castle.
>
> (p. 270)

Similarly, when Jackson turned three, '… he filled his face with birthday treats and reached dizzy new heights of locomotive bliss. We played and he was happy' (p. 353). Seeing Jackson's pleasure in the moment, Ben dropped his plans for an action-packed day, realising that spending time playing with his son mattered infinitely more than 'showering a child with material things and overblown gestures' (p. 353). It is easy for parents, bereaved or otherwise, to forget the value of giving their children time rather than things. Following a major loss, parents may resort to 'retail therapy', seeking to brighten certain days or moments for their grieving children. Treats, gifts, and the care they represent may make a difference, but as Ben highlights, spending time rather than money may matter much more.

Sharing grief

Although Ben initially tried to hide his grief from his son, Jackson picked up on the sadness and distress around him. More fundamentally, Ben began to ask himself

> what kind of husband and father would I look like to him if I showed no signs of hurt about his mother's sudden disappearance from our little world? … [W]as I protecting my child by not showing emotion around him, or teaching him that feelings are best hidden?
>
> (p. 169)

It soon became clear that Jackson was watching out for his father as well as observing him closely. A few weeks after the accident, he was playing trains when he noticed Ben crying on the sofa.

He weighed up all the people in the room ... to try to establish whether any of them had upset me, gave them all a dirty look just in case, and then tenderly wiped my eyes with his soft little hands.

(p. 168)

Other attempts at consoling his father involved sharing the things that mattered to him.

'Want dummy, Daddy?' he asked, offering his favourite form of comfort to me freely. 'Take Thomas, Daddy', he also commanded, thrusting his beloved toy into my hands.

(p. 182)

Jackson's care and concern for his father resonates with the accounts provided by adolescents in Gilbert's (2014) study of 'parenting the surviving parent'. Reflecting the mercurial nature of toddlers, however, there were other times where seeing Ben cry led him to throw himself around the room in mock despair, saying 'oh boo hoo hoo Daddy', and wiping away pretend tears. While this sometimes made Ben feel even worse, he also saw it as Jackson's attempt to cheer him up; essentially, they were 'two guys trying to make each other feel better – one of us two years old and the other thirty-three' (p. 115).

Continuing bonds

Over the past two decades, 'new wave' theories of bereavement have focused on how death changes rather than ends relationships between the living and the dead (Klass et al. 1996; Walter, 1999). Bereaved children as well as adults have been found to proceed in this way; various patterns of ongoing relationships have been identified among 6–17-year olds (Silverman and Nickman 1996b; Normand et al. 1996), while preschool children included dead parents and siblings in conversations, games and family rituals (Bugge et al. 2014).

Ben offers a detailed insight into the energy that even a toddler can invest in continuing bonds. Of course, he modelled and nurtured such behaviour, talking about Desreen every day, having many photographs of her on display in the house, and even changing his and Jackson's last name from Dutton to Brooks-Dutton to highlight her ongoing role in their lives and identities. Nonetheless, it was clear that Jackson himself saw the bond with his mother as persisting beyond death. Some, but not all of this could be attributed to a toddler's limited understanding of death's finality.

Examples of Jackson's sense of an ongoing relationship with his mother included his announcement that 'Mummy likes this one [a shirt bought after her death]. She's coming to see me later' (p. 304). Eight months after Desreen's death, when a nursery worker asked who his best friend was, he replied 'Mummy' (p. 304), and even a year on, whenever Jackson was hurt or upset, he would still call out for her first. Photographs played a role in his ongoing relationship with Desreen. For example, one day he pointed at family pictures on the wall and was lifted up to take one down.

> [H]e brought the picture to his face and kissed it, saying 'Kiss Mummy!'. He wasn't letting go so I let him keep it and we stuck it to his little play kitchen station in the living room … . As we turned out the lights and left the living room for bed, he said 'Night night, Mummy'. He knew she wasn't in the living room but her memory was. The two of us went up to bed and he began to sing the few words he knew from Alicia Keys' hit '*No One*' [one of Desreen's favourites, played at her funeral].
>
> (p. 122)

On a train journey, he and Ben started chatting to some women.

> He picked up my iPhone and showed them the picture of Desreen I had as my screensaver.
> 'That's my mummy!' he shrieked adoringly, out of nowhere.
> And that's my boy, I thought, my breath taken away by the pride he confidently showed in the parent he had not seen for seven and a half months, the parent he was starting to understand that he would never see again.
>
> (p. 298)

Conclusions

> If a life ends then everyone, regardless of their age, has the right to mourn.
> (Stokes, 2004, p. 12)

Brooks-Dutton (2014) bears witness to how his toddler son exercised that right. Jackson experienced, expressed, escaped and shared his grief in ways that were meaningful to him, and he was actively engaged in continuing bonds with his mother. His improvised grief responses transcended language, incorporating a wide range of material objects and consumption experiences: toy trains, dummies, photographs, footballs and even saucepan lids or shutters on shop windows were drawn upon, helping others to understand, acknowledge and support his response to loss.

By drawing attention to a range of toddler-led, materially mediated responses to grief, this chapter seeks to further the book's agenda of exploring the varied conditions, contexts and characteristics of consumer vulnerability. Just as experiences of consumer vulnerability are often overlooked in marketing literature, very young children's experiences of loss are underrepresented in the bereavement literature. Jackson's story suggests that bereaved toddlers are also vulnerable consumers, actively engaged in vital meaning-making. Given their developmental stage, it is hardly surprising that they may voice their grief by showing as well as telling. Play therapists have long incorporated toys and creative arts into their work with bereaved children (Webb 2000), and many charities, such as those listed at the end of this chapter, emphasise the value of rituals, transitional objects and creative therapies to children who are grieving (Rolls 2008; Stokes 2004). Several charities have developed materials, such as Winston's Wish's memory boxes and Grief Encounter's sand bottle kits and Forever Journals, to harness children's creativity in the process of meaning-making. Recognising the decline in formal mourning rituals in the UK, they seek to create time and space for children and young people to build their life stories, incorporating missing family members into their past, present and future (Gilbert 2014).

Jackson's story suggests that paying careful attention to children's use of things more generally may also help adults to understand and support bereaved children. Sometimes, toys and things may simply provide children with a temporary escape from their grief, building their resilience through 'engagement in the pleasures that the world has to offer' (Van Horn 2006: 975). Rather than thinking this means young children have forgotten the dead or are unaffected by their absence, adults could perhaps try to accept even fleeting moments of pleasure themselves as they watch or join a child absorbed in play; indeed, such moments could be seen as part of the dead person's 'legacy of love and laughter' (Brooks-Dutton 2014: 153).

A key principle of child bereavement practice is that 'children must be seen, and can best be helped, embedded in their families' (Van Horn 2006: 974). As Brooks-Dutton (2014) notes, although the British national health service offers significant post-natal family services, it provides no parallel 'post-fatal' support for families. Brooks-Dutton felt this lack keenly, despite having a strong network of family and friends and the educational and professional resources to access specialist advice from books, articles and experts. Policy makers may learn something from his frustration that bereaved parents rely on individual GPs with varying degrees of empathy and knowledge, rather than receiving dedicated guidance and support from the health service. Indeed, in the UK there are no official statistics on the number of bereaved children, and child bereavement support is unevenly distributed across the country and largely undertaken by voluntary organisations (Penny and Stubbs 2015).

Clearly, this chapter is based on one toddler's response to grief, as interpreted by his grieving father, and there is considerable need for further research on bereavement experiences among young children, including the role of consumption in those experiences. Despite the limitations of a single case study, there are important benefits to be gained from examining detailed accounts of bereavement or other experiences that may increase consumer vulnerability. In such contexts, as Turley and O'Donohoe (2013) note, references to goods and consumption experiences are not evoked in response to specific questions posed by consumer researchers; rather, they emerge organically as part of a story being told for other purposes, highlighting the seamless and salient nature of consumption in vulnerable people's lives.

Acknowledgement

I am extremely grateful to Dr Shelley Gilbert, founder and CEO of Grief Encounter, for taking the time to provide rich insights and invaluable expert feedback on this work.

References

Baker, S. W., Gentry, J. W. and Rittenburg, T. L. (2005) 'Building understanding of the domain of consumer vulnerability', *Journal of Macromarketing*, 25/2: 128–139

Brooks-Dutton, B. (2014) *It's Not Raining Daddy, It's Happy*, London: Hodder & Staughton

Buchsbaum, B. (1996) 'Remembering a parent who has died: a developmental perspective', in D. Klass, P. Silverman and S. Nickman (eds), *Continuing Bonds: New Understandings of Grief*, Washington, DC: Taylor & Francis: 113–124

Buckingham, D. et al. (2009) *The Impact Of The Commercial World On Children's Wellbeing: Report of an Independent Assessment*, Nottingham: DCSF Publications

Bugge, K., Darbyshire, P., Røkholt, E., Sulheim Haugstvedt, K., and Helseth, S. (2014) 'Young children's grief: parents' understanding and coping', *Death Studies*, 38: 36–43

Corr, C., Nabe, C. and Corr, D. (2009) *Death & Dying, Life and Living*, Belmont, CA: Wadsworth

Durant, S. (2014) 'A young widower's tale continued …', *The Guardian*, May 3, online at: http://www.theguardian.com/lifeandstyle/2014/may/03/young-widowers-tale-continued-benjamin-brooks-dutton

Gilbert, S. (2014) 'Insights into the grief of parentally bereaved young people: a grounded theory study exploring young people's psychological and emotional experiences following the death of a parent', unpublished PhD thesis, Middlesex University

Klass, D., Silverman, P. and S. Nickman (eds) (1996) *Continuing Bonds: new understandings of grief*, Washington, DC: Taylor & Francis, 113–124

Marshall, D. (ed.) (2010) *Understanding Children as Consumers*, London: Sage

Nguyen, H. and Scott, A. (2013) 'Self-concept and depression among children who experienced the death of a family member', *Death Studies*, 37/3: 197–211

Normand, C., Silverman, P. and Nickman, S. (1996) 'Bereaved children's changing relationships with the deceased', in D. Klass, P. Silverman and S. Nickman (eds), *Continuing Bonds: New Understandings of Grief*, Washington, DC: Taylor & Francis, 87–111

Parkes, C. (2010) *Bereavement: Studies of Grief in Adult Life*, 4th ed., London: Penguin

Penny, A. and Stubbs, D. (2015) *Bereavement in Childhood: What Do We Know in 2015?*, London: National Children's Bureau/Child Bereavement Network, online at: www.childhoodbereavementnetwork.org.uk

Rolls, L. (2008) 'The ritual work of UK childhood bereavement services', in S. Earle, C. Komaromy and C. Bartholomew (eds), *Death and Dying: A Reader*, Sage/Open University: London/Milton Keynes: 175–183

Silverman, P. and Nickman, S. (1996a) 'Bereaved children', in D. Klass, P. Silverman, and S. Nickman (eds), *Continuing Bonds: New Understandings of Grief*, Washington, DC: Taylor & Francis: 71–72

Silverman, P. and Nickman, S. (1996b) 'Children's construction of their dead parents', in D. Klass, P. Silverman and S. Nickman (eds), *Continuing Bonds: New Understandings of Grief*, Washington, DC: Taylor & Francis, 73–86

Stokes, J. (2004) *Then, Now and Always: Supporting Children as they Journey Through Grief: A Guide for Practitioners*, Cheltenham: Winston's Wish

Turley, D. and O'Donohoe, S. (2013) 'The sadness of lives and the comfort of things: goods as evocative objects in bereavement', *Journal of Marketing Management*, 28: 11–12, 1331–1352

Van Horn, P. (2006) 'A review of "*The River of Grief: Helping Children Cross to the Other Side*"', *Death Studies*, 3/10: 971–975

Walter, T. (1999) *On Bereavement: The Culture of Grief*, Buckingham: Open University Press

Walter, C. and McCoyd, J. (2009) *Grief and Loss Across the Lifespan: A Biopsychosocial Perspective*, New York: Springer

Webb, N. (2000) 'Play therapy to help bereaved children', in K. Doka (ed.), *Children, Adolescents, and Loss: Living with Grief*, New York: Routledge, 139–152

Wolchik, S., Ma, Y., Tien, J., Sandler, I. and Ayers, T. (2008) 'Parentally bereaved children's grief: self-system beliefs as mediators of the relations between grief and stressors and caregiver-child relationship quality', *Death Studies*, 32: 597–620

Useful links

Care for the Family: http://www.careforthefamily.org.uk/family-life/bereavement-support
Childhood Bereavement Network: www.childhoodbereavementnetwork.org.uk
Grief Encounter: www.griefencounter.org.uk
Winston's Wish: www.winstonswish.org.uk

9 An adolescent-centric approach to consumer vulnerability

New implications for public policy

Wided Batat

Introduction

The concept of consumer vulnerability has been defined in various ways by authors in consumer research and other human science disciplines. Although different conceptualizations of consumer vulnerability have been offered (Shultz and Holbrook, 2009; Baker, 2009; Baker, Gentry and Rittenberg, 2005) and other recent studies on disadvantaged consumers (Garrett and Toumanoff, 2010; Commuri and Ekici, 2008) have contributed to the clarification of the concept, these research studies have not focused on the interesting but potentially problematic group, namely young consumers and including both younger children and adolescents. Specifically, there is a lack of research focused on exploring adolescents' perceptions of vulnerability within their youth consumption culture.

   The objective of this chapter is thus to provide a comprehensive overview of adolescent vulnerability within youth consumption culture. Using an adolescent-centric approach to consumer vulnerability leads us to a deeper understanding through a bottom-up approach of the domains and dimensions of consumer vulnerability as defined by adolescents aged 11–15. This chapter first presents the existing literature on consumer vulnerability in youth and details the key studies in consumer research. It then addresses the particularities of adolescent consumer vulnerability through an ethnographic research based on an *emic* adolescent-centric approach. Details regarding the method and specifications of the data analysis are presented in this part. The last part of the chapter expands on consumer vulnerability research by integrating an adolescent-centric perception of consumer vulnerability, since it provides a useful guide to the evolution observed in adolescent education and offers indications about future changes to public policy.

Youth consumer vulnerability in the literature

Among the existing studies focusing on youth vulnerabilities within the market-place and consumer society, Pechmann et al. (2005) have identified three adolescent vulnerabilities: 1) impulsivity, 2) self-consciousness and self-doubt, and 3) an elevated risk from product use for both alcohol and tobacco. According to Pechmann and colleagues, these factors enhance adolescent vulnerabilities to marketplace and marketer discourses. Most consumption studies on or related to youth risky behaviour provide evidence of the fact that young consumers are viewed as a vulnerable group of consumers.

Prior research studies have looked at youth consumption vulnerabilities such as impulsivity (Pechmann et al. 2005), sexting (Soster and Drenten, 2011), obesity (Grier and Davis, 2013), smoking and alcohol (Zhao and Pechmann, 2007; Kelly, Slater, and Karan, 2002), video games and internet addiction (Kuss and Griffiths, 2012), drugs (Carpenter and Pechmann, 2011), and advertising influence (Martin, James, and Hill, 1999), but did not explore the way adolescents perceive and define consumer vulnerability from their own perspective anchored within an adolescent consumption culture. Recent work published in the Transformative Consumer Research (TCR) special issue of *Journal of Public Policy & Marketing* recommended a focus in future research on the "dark side" of adolescent behaviour by incorporating limitations acting on youths related to his/her "inaccurate perception of invulnerability" (Pechmann et al., 2011). Furthermore, Mason and colleagues (2013) suggested that future research on adolescent risky behaviors should explore youth vulnerabilities through a bottom-up approach by shifting the focus away from adult perspectives to an adolescent perspective.

Certainly, individuals and groups have different viewpoints when they tend to evaluate their potential in terms of consumption. Some of them may see themselves in relation to their skills and strengths, while others may focus on their limitations and weaknesses (Pechmann et al., 2011). Thus, risk taking is inherently higher for adolescents than adults due to differences in growth, brain development, psychology, etc. Besides, adolescents do not constantly behave in ways that serve their own interest. In some situations, adolescents underestimate risks and engage in risky behaviours such as binge-drinking, smoking, drugs, consumption of unhealthy food, etc. because of their perception of invulnerability. Since the adolescence stage is characterized by strong pubescent urges and inaccurate risk perceptions, adolescents are more likely to experience vulnerability by engaging in risky behaviours than adults or even children (Steinberg, 2008). Despite this, consumer researchers have not explicitly defined consumer vulnerability from the adolescent perspective. This has allowed the term of vulnerability to be used in different ways according to the adult perception and with a direct inadequate application to the youth consumption culture.

Therefore, there is a need for research exploring the gap existing between self-perceptions versus external perceptions of what consumer vulnerability means for adolescents. This will help social marketing and policy makers to set up educational campaigns based on adolescent self-perceptions of risk or vulnerability by distinguishing two sides: the "dark side" and the "light side" of the adolescent behaviour (Pechmann et al., 2005). In contrast to the "light side", which is characterized by adolescents' cognitive, psychological, and physiological limits, the "dark side" is linked to adolescents' inaccurate perception of vulnerability that leads them to overestimate their own skills and underestimate the risks. In the light of the above-mentioned reasons, a comprehensive framework of the perception of vulnerability within adolescent consumption culture appears to be an urgent issue to be taken into consideration.

Exploring adolescent consumer vulnerability through an ethnographic approach

Using an ethnographic adolescent-centric approach to consumer vulnerability in this study leads the researcher to explore through a bottom-up approach the domains and the dimensions of consumer vulnerability as defined by adolescents aged 11–15. A sample of 10 adolescents aged 11–15 years (six girls and four boys) was obtained and our initial observations and interactions suggested that there were new factors emerging, which caused us to seek additional informants through a snowball sampling technique.

Using this process, initial informants provided names of friends for the researcher to contact. In total, an additional four girls and six boys were obtained in this manner. Thus, the total sample comprised 20 informants aged 11–15 (10 boys and 10 girls). The criteria respected in this study were: socio-professional profiles of families involved in the study, geographic zones (rural vs. urban), and family structures (nuclear, single parents, etc.). We were given authorization from the head of school to recruit a sample of adolescents aged 11 to 15 years in a private middle school in southwest France.

To investigate the dimensions related to adolescent vulnerability within the consumption context, we conducted a longitudinal ethnographic research study (Wolcott, 1994) for six months with a group of 20 adolescents. Informed written consent was obtained from each participant and his/her parent/guardian before inclusion in the study. Following this ethnographic framework, we sampled the cultural frame of adolescents. We began by immersing ourselves in adolescent consumption culture, participating in adolescents' conversations and practices, observing their behaviors and reactions, and informally interviewing as many adolescents as possible.

Our strategy for getting 'close' to the adolescents included informal means of addressing one another, proposing subjects that interested them (television series, celebrity gossip, reality TV, fashion, first loves, music, technology, films, video games, etc.). The different meetings with the middle-schoolers took place over 48 sessions at a pace of two sessions per week (Monday and Friday from 2 p.m. to 3 p.m.) for six months. The mixed-gender group of 18 adolescents participated in all the sessions and everyone was systematically filmed. The study also required a large capacity for empathy, putting oneself in the adolescent's shoes, with all their preoccupations, and trying to think like them.

As we became more involved and adolescents started to trust us and consider us as a member of the group sharing the same interests and not as an adult and/or researcher, interviewing became more systematic and easier to conduct. The downsides to our immersive and familiar strategy were related to the informal conversions that led adolescents to feel confident with the researcher and thus provide more personal information instead of focusing on the vulnerability issues within their consumption experiences. This led the researcher to focus more on the research object and reorient the informants towards the main topic linked to their vulnerabilities as consumers.

Qualitative data have been collected using mixed methods, which included participant and non-participant observations, informal conversations and formal interviews, document reviews, photographs, and drawings. Initially we were interested in exploring adolescents' perceptions of consumption incompetency and vulnerabilities as well as discussing with them their shopping habits, their consumption behaviors, and the socialization agents – such as peers, family, and internet – involved within their consumption experiences.

A grounded theory approach (Strauss and Corbin, 1990; Glaser and Strauss, 1967) was used to analyse the data collected from in-depth interviews, followed by Wolcott's (1994) ethnographic conventions to interpret the data emerging from specifics transcripts, artefacts, and observations. The first approach, based on grounded theory, led the researcher to define themes, concepts and behaviors, that were indicative of adolescent consumer vulnerability. The second method, with respect to analysis and interpretation as defined by Wolcott's framework, was used to develop patterned regularities in the data on adolescents' perceptions of consumer vulnerability and their risky behaviors.

The meanings of consumer vulnerability from an adolescent perspective

The adolescent definition of consumer vulnerability appears to be more reflexive and irrational than the adult definition. Consequently, the conceptualization of consumer vulnerability should incorporate a distinction between adults and youths and provide a comprehensive framework of vulnerability from an adolescent perspective. The results of this research suggest that researchers should study adolescent consumer vulnerability according to two categories: (1) imposed and (2) deliberate vulnerability (see Figure 9.1).

Figure 9.1 captures the multiplicity of meanings adolescents associate with consumer vulnerability according to their consumption culture. The adolescent-centric approach to consumer vulnerability framework identifies adolescent perceptions of consumer vulnerability as a component of adolescent consumption culture shaped by a consumer society where adults, marketers, researchers and policy makers are supposed to be the guardians and the principal socialization agents involved in educating and empowering young consumers.

In this framework, consumer vulnerability appears to be based on a personal definition that is tied to the dark side of adolescent consumption culture characterized by self-esteem and self-concept, socialization and symbolic consumption, transgression, cyberspace, and *bricolage* (Batat, 2008). This comprehensive framework contributes to a better understanding of imposed and deliberate adolescent vulnerability within the consumption context. The dimensions composing each category are explained in the next section.

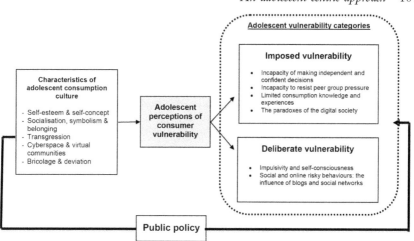

Figure 9.1 Adolescent-centric approach to consumer vulnerability framework

Adolescent imposed consumer vulnerability

The first category, "imposed vulnerability", refers to consumption situations where adolescents feel obliged to adopt risky behaviors to fit in with their peer group norms. Adolescents experience imposed vulnerability because they are powerless and unable to resist peer-group pressure. Adolescents have referred to this situation as a vulnerable state, especially those who belong to families with a low income who mentioned different feelings such as guilt, remorse and shame towards their parents. Imposed vulnerability might be explained by four dimensions: incapacity of making independent and confident decisions, incapacity to resist peer group pressure, lack of knowledge and consumption experiences, and the paradoxes of the digital society.

a) Incapacity of making independent and confident decisions

One of the key features adolescents associate with being a vulnerable consumer is engaging in behaviors that lead to bad, or unsatisfying, decisions. Although adolescents associate dependency with vulnerability, they also indicate that as young consumers they do not have the ability, or perhaps the confidence, to make decisions on their own. Therefore, adolescents' purchase decision-making is mainly driven by or dependent on others' advice. This means that they are incapable of evaluating the advice according to their needs and thus can't make independent and confident purchase decisions. For adolescents, two aspects of decision-making are considered to be challenging in the decision-making process. First, adolescents found it difficult to make independent decisions since their purchases are often determined or at least influenced by what others tell them to buy. This was perceived as both frustrating and paralyzing for adolescents, who feel dependent and powerless.

Second, adolescents' incapacity for making independent and confident decisions has direct consequences for the way they deal with market actors, especially salespeople. Adolescents consider that dealing with salespeople is stressful and makes them feel uncomfortable and anxious. As shown in this quote:

> I don't feel comfortable when dealing with salespeople particularly when I'm alone, it's very difficult to resist their pressure, they start by asking you if you need any help and then they propose you an item and they try to convince you that it will fit with your need even you are not interested. I can't resist the salespeople pressure, so I purchase the item then when I get home I'm always very angry against myself because I did not control the situation and I was vulnerable … it's not funny.
>
> (male, 15)

This discomfort appears to be related to youth lack of self-confidence with respect to making independent decisions and being satisfied and happy with their decisions. Thus, inexperienced, unknowledgeable and unconfident adolescents may lack self-belief to such a degree that they suppress their better judgment regarding product quality when faced with strong opposing opinions from others or predictive extrinsic cues.

b) Incapacity to resist peer group pressure

Adolescents' susceptibility to peer influence has been documented previously (Bachmann et al. 1993). As indicated by researchers who studied the socialization process of children and adolescents (Roedder-John, 1999), peer group influence is a factor that affects decision-making among adolescents. In their struggle, adolescents form a personal identity and fit in socially with peers. According to Erikson (1968), the primary developmental task of adolescence is the struggle to formulate an identity that is independent of parents, a struggle that typically lasts until late adolescence or early adulthood. Adolescents often turn to peers to help them forge identities that are independent of those of their parents and more suited to their youth culture. In adolescence, the amount of uncontrolled time spent with peers increases drastically, with a decrease in the time spent with parents or other adults (Larson and Richards, 1991). Furthermore, adolescents are more likely than children to adopt prosocial behavior and identify peers as their most important role models (Brown, 1990). As mentioned by our informant:

> I don't feel comfortable with my mates if I'm not dressed like all the rest of my group, I mean wearing famous brands such as Comptoir des Cotonniers is very important to get involved within the group, in addition it allows you to be respected by all the members.
>
> (female, 13)

Adolescence is a time when peers play a crucial role. Peer groups may exert influence by providing information in ambiguous situations and/or enhancing an adolescent's self-image; furthermore, peers can help adolescents explore their identity, feel accepted, and develop a sense of belongingness. Conversely, peer influence is more complex than our stereotype of the negative influence of friends. Peer influence can be both positive and negative. The results show that as adolescents approach adulthood, they become uncertain about their self, and as a consequence the need to belong and to find one's unique identity as a person becomes very important. In fact, conformity to peer pressure is considered to be one of the hallmarks of adolescents who are struggling to determine their social role and status within their peer group. In order to meet this objective, some of the older adolescents might try out risky and/or forbidden behaviors to impress their peers and show them that they are not afraid and that they deserve their respect.

c) Lack of consumption knowledge and experience

The findings emphasize a strong relationship between adolescents' vulnerability and their limited consumption knowledge. Adolescents reported feeling not in possession of sufficient facts within the marketplace when they compare themselves to their parents or other adults. Adolescents mentioned that their parents have already experienced different consumption fields and this makes them more knowledgeable. As shown in this quote:

> [H]onestly, I can't answer the question whether I'm competent or vulnerable consumer because I'm too young and I don't have enough experience in terms of purchasing. However, I can say that I'm incompetent consumer because of my low consumption experience ... I did not buy a car, I have an account secured by my parents, I don't have to deal with banks, or even search for a house or something like that. I think that we can get empowered through our experiences even the worst.
>
> (male, 13)

Adolescents refer to themselves as inexperienced and therefore vulnerable consumers, lacking the relevant knowledge and skills to optimize their purchases as their parents do. This suggests that there is some sort of normative prescription – at least in their minds – of the gap between them and adults in terms of consumption. Thus, limited consumption knowledge also means that adolescents did not experience vulnerability in the fields that have already been explored by adults, such as buying a car or a house, paying bills, debt problems, etc.

a) The paradoxes of the digital society

Adolescents' relationship to technology – and specifically the internet – has a paradoxical character. The findings show an interesting dimension linked to the paradoxes of adolescents' internet usage within their consumption experiences. These paradoxes are considered to be the main factor enhancing youth vulnerability within the marketplace. The perspectives of studies focusing on the role of technology in postmodern society are numerous and the conclusions vary according to each author's perspective.

Some authors argue that technology provides freedom, control, and efficiencies, while others view it as a tool that degrades the environment, usurps human competence, and encourage human dependence and passivity. Considering the existence of opposite visions of technology in the consumer society, Handy (1995) argues that the only viable response is to accept the paradoxes of technology and develop coping mechanisms and strategies. In their work, Mick and Fournier (1998) defined the paradoxes of technological products according to eight dimensions: control/chaos, freedom/enslavement, new/obsolete, competence/incompetence, efficiency/inefficiency, fulfils/creates needs, engaging/disengaging, and assimilation/isolation. Based on the theoretical framework of the paradoxes of technology offered by Mick and Fournier (1998), two categories linked to adolescent vulnerability in using technology and the internet have been identified in this study.

The first category refers to efficiency/inefficiency and the second to the paradox of freedom/enslavement. In relation to efficiency/ inefficiency, technology can both facilitate *less* effort or time being spent on certain activities and lead to *more* effort or time on certain activities. Our findings underline this idea by showing that adolescents' use of the internet and other online sources can be efficient, but at the same time it can lead to misinformation because of online info-abundance and info-pollution. Certainly, the profusion of information on professional websites, personal blogs and informal forums where people exchange information about consumption items and bargains is considered a source of confusion because adolescents feel unable to sort out the relevant offers and/or information. Hence, adolescents perceive themselves as vulnerable consumers because they feel completely lost within both non-digital information and the information provided by online consumers and company websites.

The second category of technology paradoxes revealed by our study is freedom/enslavement. Technology can facilitate independence or fewer restrictions, and at the same time it can lead to dependence or more restrictions. This generation lives in-between a real world (family, school, peers) and a virtual world (Facebook, Twitter, blogs, Second Life). Adolescents mentioned that they couldn't imagine themselves living without an online connection. As shown in this quote:

> We are a lucky generation because of the Internet and all the digital equipment. We can gain a lot of time when working, and use this time to socialize, to go out and to play of course. If I have homework to do, the first thing I think about is to check out information on the Internet and sometimes I can find the solution of my homework so I don't need to prepare the work but just print it out and give it to my professor ... the life and the work are very cool with Internet thanks God and obviously scientists! However,

if I can't get access to the Internet during the exam in the classroom, it's very hard to find a solution, I feel that the Internet is an integral part of my life and I cannot live without it.

(male, 12)

This emphasizes the fact that the majority of adolescents interviewed felt that they were vulnerable because they are entirely dependent on the internet for their homework and their social activity.

Adolescent deliberate consumer vulnerability

Deliberate vulnerability refers to the fact that risky behaviors such as surfing porn websites, smoking and taking drugs are activities that adolescents consider desirable and would like to experience. For adolescents, the main purpose of this practice is to transgress the rules established by adults by experiencing what is considered socially unacceptable. For example, adolescents consider smoking a means of departing from implied standards and not simply an end in itself. This makes it an invulnerable behavior, and it is considered the easiest way to appear grown-up, show independence, receive recognition and have fun. The findings revealed two categories related to adolescents' deliberate vulnerability within adolescent consumption culture. The first category is composed of two dimensions: impulsivity and self-consciousness. The second category encompasses social and online risky behaviors.

a) Impulsivity and self-consciousness

Impulsivity within youth consumption culture is enhanced by heightened suscept-ibility to self-consciousness. In contrast to younger children (under 11) and adults, adolescents are more likely to experience self-consciousness and social anxiety (Inhelder and Piaget, 1958) since they are focused on their physical appearance, their image, and how others –especially their peers – perceive them (Pine, Cohen, and Brook 2001).

Adolescents' impulsive behavior due to self-consciousness might be explained by two main factors: adolescent's self-esteem and consumption symbols. In early and late adolescence, self-esteem exhibits a strong age-related pattern. Self-esteem often declines around age 12 or 13 (Erikson, 1963; Harter, 1986; Rosenberg, 1986) and rebounds by middle to late adolescence (McCarthy and Hoge, 1982). This vulnerability is deliberate because adolescents are aware of their impulsive behavior but do not consider it as part of a vulnerable state because they pretend to control their purchase behaviors. As mentioned by one informant:

For me, even it's a very expensive brand, I have to buy it and sometimes my mother is against that because we don't have enough money to buy this kind of brand but she does understand the importance of such a brand for me. You know, I feel like I'm vulnerable and I can't cope when I'm really forced to involve my parents and push them to buy me stuff even though I know that we can't afford it because we're poor, so yes in these situations I feel very bad and sad at the same time.

(female, 14)

Therefore, the impulse buying related to adolescent low self-esteem, "I shop, therefore I am", has become the stereotype of modern consumerism, in which consumption items play an unceasingly stronger psychological role in today's adolescents' lives.

b) Social and online risky behaviors: virtual communities and blogs
as reliable sources of information

Teenagers learn to be consumers while having online interactions. The results show that adolescents experience the internet as a physical and social space, allowing them to talk, form relationships, discuss issues and work, play games, train, and perform many of the social tasks normally performed in the physical environment (Damer, 1997). Internet and virtual communities constitute an integral part of adolescent social life and therefore potentially are strong socialization agents. They give adolescents more freedom in and control over their lives.

Adolescents stated that online practices are the only way to ask questions about taboos such as sexuality or drugs without requiring adult advice. Virtual communities may also give adolescents a feeling of empowerment and the confidence to overcome boundaries and adopt risky behaviors. Adolescents use virtual communities and online social networks to try out risky and even illegal behaviors such as the illegal downloading of music, movies and games. This statement shows that the postmodern philosophy of these adolescents abounds with ideas of contravening various socio-cultural boundaries.

Consequently, any reflection on a boundary presupposes the possibility of crossing it. Moreover, transgression is a crucial part of an adolescent's personal and social identity building process. However, because of the psycho-sociological traits of adolescence such as lack of self-confidence and low self-esteem, adolescents appear more eager to trust their internet contacts and follow the advice of possibly unsafe online actors and communities.

Observations revealed that virtual communities and websites based on themes such as pornography, suicide and anorexia are very popular among both male and female adolescents aged 11–15. These communities have a huge impact on and strong prescriptive power among adolescents who are struggling to build their identity or those who feel depressed. Besides, risky online communities contribute to isolating adolescents from their families and therefore from society. An online community allows an adolescent to feel like a member of a big family with the same interests – for example, Proana, an online community with a focus on extreme diet and anorexia – which understands without making judgments. As mentioned by one adolescent in the group:

One day, I started a diet when I was chatting with a girl on her blog, she was giving advice regarding the diet and the way we should do it. In her website, she shows her photo before and after her magical diet … . I was convinced and I said to myself why not test this diet and keep in touch with the girl. Of course it's very important to share this with the same people online rather than talking with our parents, they don't understand. When I feel sad, I prefer talking with people online who are in the same state as me and in addition, they don't know me and they don't judge me.

(female, 15)

To sum up, the results of this study show that consumer vulnerability is a social construction embedded in an adolescent consumption culture where its meanings are grounded. The adolescent-centric approach revealed the dimensions of consumer vulnerability in the eyes and voices of adolescents who define it according to their own norms, codes, and consumption culture. Thus, the experience of consumer vulnerability within the adolescent consumption culture might be either "deliberate" or "imposed". The meanings of consumer vulnerability are not limited to the factors identified by Baker, Gentry, and Rittenburg (2005) and applied to adults. Indeed, what adults might consider a dangerous situation involving risky behaviors, adolescents would view as fun, "cool", and a way to socialize and be recognized by peers.

Public policy implications

This research contributes to the comprehension of explicit and implicit dimensions of adolescent vulnerability within the consumption context. The framework based on an adolescent-centric approach to consumer vulnerability might change the way researchers are studying at-risk groups such as young consumers and have several implications for public policy. An adolescent-centric approach to consumer vulnerability (see Figure 9.1) identifies a communication campaign based on youth culture, norms, values and language.

This communication reflects a deeper understanding of adolescents' definition of their vulnerabilities. Using messages that demonize the consumption of illicit drugs or tobacco can have a negative impact on adolescents since it pushes them to transgress, to smash the rules. For adolescents, the use of drugs is valuable, being viewed as "cool" behavior amongst their peer group. Consequently, targeting adolescents using authoritarian or persuasive messages that are relevant for adults but considered nonsense by adolescents will push them to adopt risky behavior to show their anti-adult culture. Thus, an effective educational communication strategy targeting adolescents should avoid warning messages and use the "cool" dimension. Humoristic discourse can be memorized easily and its content is more likely to be accepted by adolescents as they will feel less manipulated.

Furthermore, understanding peer group influence (positive/negative) within youth consumption culture can help public policy makers adapt their policy to the youth target by using peer groups as a communication medium and tool to empower young consumers through a bottom-up approach based on adolescent consumption cultures.

Conclusion

The present chapter aimed to illustrate the domains and behaviors related to consumer vulnerability from an adolescent perspective. The results revealed two kinds of consumer vulnerability: deliberate and imposed. This research contributes to the comprehension of explicit and implicit dimensions of adolescent vulnerability within the consumption context. By focusing on the dark side, policy makers would be better able to understand the attractiveness of risk for adolescents and then protect them from themselves. In contrast, the "light side" would help social marketers and other stakeholders to develop educational actions based on youth strengths – such as the use of sports and clubs to discourage youths from smoking or eating unhealthy food (Davis and Pechmann, 2010).

References

Bachmann, G. R., John, D., and Rao, A. R. (1993). Children's susceptibility to peer group purchase influence: An exploratory investigation. In Leigh McAlister and Michael L. Rothschild (eds), *Advances in Consumer Research*, Provo, UT: Association for Consumer Research, 20, 463–468.

Baker, S. M., Gentry, J. W., and Rittenburg, T. L. (2005). Building understanding of the domain of consumer vulnerability. *Journal of Macromarketing*, 25(2), 128–139.

Baker, S. M. (2009). Vulnerability and resilience in natural disasters: A marketing and public policy perspective. *Journal of Public Policy & Marketing*, 28(1), 114–123.

Batat, W. (2008). Exploring adolescent development skills through internet usage: A study of French 11–15-year-olds. *International Journal of Consumer Studies*, 32(4), 379–381.

Brown, B. (1990). Peer groups and peer cultures. In S. S. Feldman and G. R. Elliot (eds), *At the Threshold: The Developing Adolescent*, Cambridge, MA: Harvard University Press, 171–196

Carpenter, C. S. and Pechmann, C. (2011). Exposure to the above the influence anti-drug advertisements and adolescent marijuana use in the United States, 2006–2008. *American Journal of Public Health*, 101(5), 948–954.

Commuri, S. and Ekici, A. (2008). An enlargement of the notion of consumer vulnerability. *Journal of Macromarketing*, 28(June), 183–186.

Damer, B. (1997). *Avatars! Exploring and Building Virtual Worlds on the Internet*, New York: Peachpit Press.

Davis, B. and Pechmann, C. (2010). Structured group activity, proximity to fast food, and unhealthy consumption. Unpublished manuscript, Baylor University, Waco, TX.

Erikson, E. H. (1963). *Childhood and Society* (2nd ed.). New York: W. W. Norton & Company.

Erikson, E. H. (1968). *Identity: Youth and Crisis*. New York: W. W. Norton & Company.

Garrett, D. and Toumanoff, P. (2010). Are consumers disadvantaged or vulnerable? An examination of consumer complaints to the Better Business Bureau. *Journal of Consumer Affairs*, 44(1), 3–23.

Glaser, B. and Strauss, A. (1967). *The Discovery of Grounded Theory*. Chicago: Aldine.

Grier, S. and Davis, B. (2013). Are all proximity effects created equal? Fast food near schools and body weight among diverse adolescents. *Journal of Public Policy & Marketing*, 32(1), 116–128.

Handy, C. (1995). *The Age of Paradox*, Boston, MA: Harvard Business School Press.

Harter, S. (1986). Processes underlying the construction, maintenance, and enhancement of the self-concept in children. In J. Suls and A. G. Greenwald (eds), *Psychological Perspectives on the Self*, Hillsdale, NJ: Erlbaum, 137–181.

Inhelder, B. and Piaget, J. (1958). *The Growth of Logical Thinking from Childhood to Adolescence*. New York, NY: Basic Books.

Kelly, K. J., Slater, M., and Karan, D. (2002). Image advertisements' influence on adolescents' perceptions of the desirability of beer and cigarettes, *Journal of Public Policy & Marketing*, 21(2), 295–304.

Kuss, D. J., and Griffiths, M. D. (2012). Online gaming addiction in adolescence: A literature review of empirical research. *Journal of Behavioural Addiction*, 1(1), 3–22.

Larson, R. W. and Richards, M. H. (1991). Boredom in the middle school years: Blaming schools versus blaming students. *American Journal of Education*, 99(4), 418–443.

Martin, M.C., James, W., and Hill, R. P. (1999). The beauty myth and the persuasiveness of advertising: A look at adolescent girls and boys. In M. Carole Macklin and Les Carlson (eds), *Advertising to Children: Concepts and Controversies*, Thousand Oaks, CA: Sage Publications, 165–187.

Mason, M. J., Tanner, J. F., Piacentini, M., Freeman, D., Anastasia, T., Batat, W., Boland, W., Canbulut, M., Drenten, J., Hamby, A., Rangan, P. and Yang, Z. (2013). Advancing a participatory approach for youth risk behavior: Foundations, distinctions, and research. *Journal of Business Research*, 66(8), 1235–1241.

McCarthy, J. D. and Hoge, D. R. (1982). Analysis of age effects in longitudinal studies of adolescent self-esteem. *Developmental Psychology*, 18(3), 372–379.

Mick, D. G. and Fournier, S. (1998). Paradoxes of technology: Consumer cognizance, emotions, and coping strategies. *Journal of Consumer Research*, 25(2), 123–143.

Pechmann, C., Levine, L., Loughlin, S., and Leslie, E. (2005). Impulsive and self-conscious: Adolescents' vulnerability to advertising and promotion. *Journal of Public Policy & Marketing*, 24(2), 202–221.

Pechmann, C., Moore, E. S., Andreasen A. R. Connell P. M., Freeman, D., Gardner, M. P., Heisley, D., Lefebvre, R. C., Pirouz, D. M., and Soster, R. L. (2011). Navigating the central tensions in research on consumers who are at risk: Challenges and opportunities, *Journal of Public Policy and Marketing*, 30(1), 23–30.

Pine, D. S., Cohen, P., and Brook, J. S. (2001). Emotional reactivity and risk for psychopathology among adolescents. *CNS Spectrum,* 6(1), 27–35.

Roedder-John, D. (1999). Consumer socialization of children: A retrospective look at twenty-five years of research. *Journal of Consumer Research*, 26(3), 183–213.

Rosenberg, M. (1986). Self-concept from middle childhood through adolescence. In J. Suls and A. C. Greenwald (eds), *Psychological Perspectives on the Self*, Hillsdale, NJ: Lawrence Erlbaum, 107–136.

Shultz, C. J., II and Holbrook, M. B. (1999). Marketing and the tragedy of the commons: A synthesis, commentary, and analysis for action. *Journal of Public Policy & Marketing*, 18(2), 218–229.

Soster, R. L. and Drenten, J. M. (2011). Flirting with technology: Understanding the motivations for and consequences of adolescent sexting. Marketing and Public Policy Conference, Washington, DC.

Steinberg, L. (2008). A social neuroscience perspective on adolescent risk-taking. *Developmental Review*, 28(1), 78–106.

Strauss, A. and Corbin, J. (1990). *Basics of Qualitative Research: Grounded Theory Procedures and Techniques*. Thousand Oaks, CA: Sage Publications.

Wolcott, H. F. (1994). *Transforming Qualitative Data: Description, Analysis and Interpretation*. Thousand Oaks, CA: Sage Publications.

Zhao, G. and Pechmann, C. (2007). The impact of regulatory focus on adolescents' response to antismoking advertising campaigns. *Journal of Marketing Research*, 44 (November), 671–687.

10 Care leavers' transitions to adulthood

Challenges to self in adapting to new consumer roles

Sally Hibbert, Maria Piacentini and Margaret K. Hogg

Introduction

Life transitions are important stages for identity formation, since people strive to achieve a desired self-identity and demonstrate their value and worth as a person in domains of life that are relevant to their new roles and status (Crocker and Wolfe, 2001). The movements between life stages represent a time of disruption and uncertainty, especially as new social roles and responsibilities are navigated (Wheaton, 1990). For people who face difficult life circumstances, transitions can be salient periods because risk factors associated with other aspects of their situation (e.g. poverty, ill health) often come to the fore as they confront challenges to the self during periods of change (Murphy et al., 1988). The transition from childhood to adulthood is a particularly significant period as it is a formative stage when self-identity is not well established. The risk of poor performance in new social roles heightens individuals' sense of vulnerability, threatens their self-worth and adversely affects their ability to adjust to adult roles. In this chapter we focus specifically on experiences of transition to adulthood amongst young people who have been fostered or in care[1] during their childhood. These young people typically face the transition to adult roles much earlier than their peers, without the same level of support (Jones, 2002), and are exposed to multiple risk factors associated with life chances, which interact to affect their experiences of assuming new consumer roles and attempting to coalesce a desired adult identity.

Life transitions: changing social roles and self identity

Over their life course, people undergo a number of socially significant transitions that bring change to their status and social roles (George, 1993). Pertinent transitions are age and family-related, including the move from child to adult, single to co-habiting, childless to parent, married to divorced, and married to widowed, but transitions such as healthy to unwell, companion to carer, student to worker, employed to unemployed (and vice versa) also involve considerable adjustment. Consumption experiences are integral to broader adaptations to new roles and responsibilities (Fellerman and Debevec, 1993; Gentry et al., 1995) and there is now a reasonable body of consumer research into life transitions (e.g. Andreasen, 1984; McAlexander, 1991; Young, 1991; Bates and Gentry, 1994; Gentry, Baker and Kraft, 1995; Gentry et al., 1995; Gentry, 1997; Price et al., 2000). Life transitions are recognised as processes rather than step changes (Hogg, Curasi and Maclaran, 2004) and are characterised by 'liminality': the experience that one is between stages and roles (Murphy et al., 1988; Gentry et al., 1995).

Life transitions are important stages for identity formation. Experiences related to role entry and exit can augment or threaten individuals' self-view. However, not all experiences during transition are equally important; the saliency of an experience depends on the importance of that context for creating a desired self-identity relevant to a new role or status, with implications for self-worth. Crocker and Wolfe (2001) have expressed this in terms of the notion of contingencies of self-worth, defined as the domains of life where people seek to demonstrate their value and worth as a person. Contingencies of self-worth are shaped by individual and collective experiences throughout life, from early attachment relationships with caregivers, to interactions with the family, neighbourhood, school, community and culture, all of which make that person feel valuable and worthwhile (Crocker and Park 2004).

Contingencies of self-worth vary across individuals and life stages according to normative social influences. Many situations relevant to forming new identities correspond with entry into and exit from social roles. For instance, in the transition from work to retirement, people face adjustments, from detachment from their occupational status and attachments (Kim and Moen, 2002) to new or expanded roles in domains such as leisure, volunteering, household, friendships and care (Carter and Cook, 1995). People strive to achieve in domains in which their goals are linked to self-worth, which can incur costs (as well as benefits) for the individual, and the possibility of failure and setbacks is a feature of their experience (Crocker et al., 2003). Whereas positive events relevant to domains of contingency are associated with increases in self-worth, negative events lower self-worth, especially when the satisfaction of contingencies depends on other people's approval or validation. The likelihood that people will face setbacks and experience negative events is heightened when their transitions are non-normative (at a different time and sequence than is the norm) or at odds with supportive social structures, or when they lack appropriate resources (Carter and Cook, 1995). Threats to self-identity formation are also intensified when people encounter prejudice due to social stigma and biased judgements of their potential to perform roles in salient domains (Desmette and Gaillard, 2008). Research has demonstrated that when stigma is activated there are detrimental effects on an individual's performance in roles and tasks (e.g. Croizet and Claire, 1998; Quinn, Kahn and Crocker, 2004). Studies of consumption similarly identify social stigma as a threat to consumers' identities (Hamilton, 2012) and thus their sense of self-worth (Baker, Gentry and Rittenburg, 2005), although there is evidence that some of the effects can be mitigated when an individual is able to deploy their resources in various coping strategies (Adkins and Ozanne, 2005).

Transition to adulthood

The transition from childhood to adulthood is a particularly important period for identity formation. The situations relevant to forming new adult identities correspond with the key tests of adulthood (George, 1993): starting family life/ entering parenthood, setting up home/becoming an effective consumer and establishing a foothold in the world of work. Consumption activities are inherent to a range of adult roles which play a vital role in addressing ambiguous, incongruous and unsatisfactory aspects of the self-concept, and in helping to achieve greater coherence in the emergent identity as people undergo the liminal phase of transition to adulthood (Schouten, 1991). Although this period brings an array of opportunities for self-development, the task of configuring a coherent identity that provides the basis for a person to commit to these pillars of adult life often creates a psychological burden and some young people require external help or guidance (Schwartz et al., 2005). The cultural environment in Western countries has become less normatively structured (Bauman, 2001) and there is more variability in the timing and sequence of life transitions. Yet social structures and expectations continue to reflect certain norms, which can make the period of emerging adulthood particularly challenging for young people who are out of kilter with their peers and/or who are not well supported through the process. Amongst the research that has examined young adult-hood, most studies concentrate on privileged groups of consumers (e.g. college students, see Schwartz, Cote and Arnett, 2005) and assume that they are embedded within functioning and supportive families. However, research is sorely needed to understand the experience of transition to adulthood, and its implications for self-worth, for people growing up in less conventional family circumstances.

Young people in care often leave education at or before the minimum age and are often unable to be self-supporting due of factors such as unemployment, insecure or low-paid work or early family formation (Social Exclusion Unit, 2005). Moreover, they face a high risk of involvement in 'problematic' social behaviours including drug and alcohol abuse or criminal offending (Rogers, 2011). This by no means applies to all individuals who have been in care and there are many who benefit from successful placements and adjust well to adulthood. Nevertheless these characteristics are prominent among this group. The implications tend to be regarded by various public bodies, and the public too, in terms of the problems that young people pose to society. However, to address the welfare issues that they face during emerging adulthood it is necessary to recognise 'the very real problems that society, and social policies, present to young people' (Jones, 2002: 39).

When young people leave their care placements, they are expected to transition directly from childhood dependence to adult self-sufficiency (Propp,

Ortega and NewHeart, 2003). Yet they often face their early transitions to adulthood with insufficient socialisation for adult roles and a lack of social support during the transition. Institutionalised lifestyles during childhood and adolescence also contribute to deficits in key skills required to navigate consumer roles, with important implications for their developing self. The social stigma of being in care is an additional problem for young care leavers. State intervention in family life can bring a sense of disqualification or stigma for the parents and children alike (Scholte et al., 1999). The backdrop to intervention by child welfare services can involve death of a parent(s)/carer, illness, drugs, alcoholism, violence, breakdown of family relationships, and special needs. All too often, others in society ignore the background to and causes of families facing difficulties and regard them as 'problem families'; the children, by association, as 'problem children'. Evidence from the UK suggests that attitudes towards young people who have been in care are improving, but most young people leaving care still expect to experience prejudice during their adult life (Cathcart, 2004). In addition, children in care approaching adulthood face threats to their identity from other negative labels attached to them through social categorisation and stereotyping (e.g. 'teenage mother', people 'on-benefit', 'druggies' and 'trouble causers'), which may affect them across a range of social exchanges in their neighbourhoods, at college and work, with service providers and in their social networks more broadly.

The transition to adulthood is an important process for these young people and the challenges that they face pose particular threats as they shape an adult identity (Hiles et al., 2014). While social policy research has explored a range of issues that inhibit the smooth transition to adulthood, there is a lack of research that examines their attempts to perform consumer roles, despite the importance of these for meeting basic needs and gaining and maintaining access to crucial services.

In this chapter, we adopt an emic perspective on vulnerability (Spiers, 2000; Runquist and Reed, 2007) in relation to transition and, as such, we are concerned with individuals' lived experience of the challenge of adapting to new consumer roles. A primary assumption of this approach is that vulnerability is defined by a person's self-identity and his or her perceptions of the challenges to self and the resources available to cope with the challenges (Spiers, 2000). Therefore, we seek individual perspectives on contexts (cultural, society and institutional) and social relations and their efforts to integrate and manage the challenges that they face. This stance avoids the reductionism of identifying individual causes of vulnerability during transition and acknowledges that there are inter- and intra-individual differences in the way that people feel the effects of the same factor (Wisner and Luce, 1993). It also recognises that vulnerability can afford opportunities for increased resilience – for individuals and groups – and for social change (Delor and Hubert, 2000). From this perspective of vulnerability, our purpose with this study is to gain insights into care leavers' experience of adapting to new consumer roles in key domains of adult life.

Research method

We adopted a qualitative research approach to gain an in-depth understanding of the complex experiences of care leavers' transitions to adulthood. Data were collected over an eight-month period through focus groups and individual interviews with 16 participants.

We conducted two focus groups for the first stage of the study. Through a national children's charity, we recruited four male and five female participants to take part in single-sex discussion groups. Participants were aged between 16 and 21, and had either left care to live independently or were preparing to do so. The focus group discussions were held in an environment familiar to the participants, and lasted between 60 and 90 minutes. We followed the focus groups with individual in-depth interviews (with seven women and two men), mainly with new informants, and again recruited via a national children's charity and by a local authority leaving-care team. This facilitated the inclusion of participants with a range of characteristics that have been shown to affect the life experiences of cared-for children (see Barn, Andrew and Mantovani, 2005). Two interviews were with young men from the original focus group, which provided a further opportunity to explore their personal stories. The interviews, lasting 60–90 minutes, were conducted in a range of settings familiar to the participants, and took place over a two-month period. Intratextual and inter-textual interpretive analyses were used in order to derive an evolving conceptual framework (Adkins and Ozanne, 2005). The focus groups and interviews were transcribed in full and read independently by all three researchers, and detailed memos were written. Analysis was undertaken independently by the researchers, who moved between deductive and inductive approaches and compared and re-interpreted data to reach an agreed understanding of the key stories and themes. We moved back and forth between the literature and the integrated thematic analyses to enrich interpretation of the findings (Thompson, 1996).

Findings

In our informants' stories of their transition to adulthood, consumer roles and responsibilities are mainly associated with two key contingencies of self-worth deemed central to this transition: (1) setting up home/becoming an effective consumer, and (2) starting family life/entering parenthood. The overview of our findings provides insights into their experience of consumption, how they manage the multiple challenges they face in their marketplace interactions, and the effects on their emergent adult identities.

Setting up home and becoming an effective consumer

The challenges associated with consumer roles and responsibilities emerged as a common feature of the young people's stories. They referred to a wide range of roles relating to household consumption and production: finding rental accommodation or negotiating the allocation of public housing, budgeting and keeping up with bill payments, organising credit, arranging the supply of utilities and telecommunications contracts, acquiring various categories of goods (groceries, clothes, furniture, consumer electronics and white goods), preparing meals, keeping the home clean and tidy, home maintenance/improvement, etc. Among their accounts of performing these roles are examples of experiences that contribute positively and negatively as a test of adulthood. The more positive experiences relate to situations in which the young people feel that they can deploy their existing resources and strategies (e.g. knowledge of consumer rights) to achieve positive outcomes (e.g. value-for-money purchases/ deals, achieving or maintaining access to services) or can develop and successfully deploy new resources (e.g. cooking skills, negotiating with financial services personnel) to meet needs and achieve other valued outcomes in the domain of adult life. These experiences create positive emotions and constructive developments to self-identity:

> I got six months discount and I was surprised and dead chuffed. On the odd occasion I can get people to do what I want.
>
> (Chantal, 20)

It is reasonably common to acquire goods from non-market sources (such as second-hand goods), but this can create ambivalence. The young people recognise that it helps them to meet their needs, and when they actively find cheap goods that they like, they report that they feel like a 'smart shopper'. However, one informant gives an account of someone giving her hand-me-down clothes, about which she has mixed feelings; she is heartened that someone is concerned about her welfare but sensitive to the idea that others consider her to be in need of charity:

> I felt uncomfortable, 'cos she'd say, 'I've got something for you' ... I'd feel like, 'Oh, I'm getting clothes given. Is it because I'm a tramp?' or something like that. But she was like, 'Oh no,' she said, 'my cousin's giving you them'. In one way I was embarrassed, but then I thought it was nice that she was thinking about me.
>
> (Veronica, 19)

The informants told us about situations where they struggle to grasp what they need to do to enact particular consumer roles effectively or how to coalesce appropriate resources or deploy effective strategies, which can be costly, and potentially increases their vulnerability:

> I didn't realise that if you keep turning it [the heating] on and off it was costing you more money.
>
> (Georgia, 18)

However, by far the most common negative experiences they report in relation to setting up home are in service interactions. Informants complain of a lack of respect for young people and express frustration and upset when prejudicial views create barriers even when they are able to perform consumer roles:

> [P]eople think we've got nowt and we don't know anything. They think you don't know what you're talking about … and you can't get people to listen to you.
>
> (Gwyneth, 17)

In public sector organisations, where their 'cared for' status is revealed in records, and especially when they have a record of failing to conform to contractual conditions (e.g. falling into arrears with payments, causing damage to/ not keeping the property in good condition), they feel frustrated by and angry at the negative and inflexible reactions they encounter and lack of empathy from front-line staff and their own sense of powerlessness to influence the service interaction or outcomes.

> If I've got problems with my rent or something, if I build up a few arrears and get an eviction notice, he [Matt, support worker] will come through with us. Otherwise I'd probably end up losing my flat. And he'll advise us what to do and say and things like that … if it wasn't a major problem he'd just tell us what to do and what to say. I could probably do it myself, but I'd be there longer. With Matt there we just get in, sort it out, get out … I start getting frustrated. They say, 'You owe three hundred and odd pounds' and I start losing my temper, I just think 'F★★★in' hell, I can't pay that'. But if Matt comes with me, I can start paying off two pound a month or something.
>
> (Andrew, 20)

The quote from Andrew illustrates that such experiences undermine (rather than build) the young people's confidence that they can manage service interaction (sometimes crucial to avoid getting into further difficulties), create negative feelings and sometimes produce maladaptive strategies (swearing and screaming at front-line staff). They are also aware that their own influence in these contexts is limited by comparison to that of other adults and many report instances of a support worker or another adult being able to resolve a problem with little difficulty.

Starting family life and entering parenthood

Family life and parenting represent an important domain of self-worth for participants who had children or were pregnant (half of our sample). A number of consumer roles linked to their efforts to establish themselves as parents and build a family life interface with their role as householders (e.g. grocery shopping, acquiring clothes, finding suitable accommodation, etc). In particular, they focused on being able to protect the welfare of children and/or developing a relationship with a partner. Organising parties and gift-giving are additional consumer responsibilities that informants highlight as important for parenting contingencies of self-worth. Indeed, many positive experiences of progressing in this domain of adulthood feature in stories of symbolic consumption in which celebrations, gifts and possessions signify movement towards perceived norms of good parenting (providing positive childhood experiences) and distance them from a low-income identity:

> We had a big party at Fun Factory on the promenade. She [Megan] got quite a lot of money. She got £40 off my mum, she got £40 off my sister, Theresa bought her a new suit, all my mum's friends they bought her toys and dolls and that. Me and Martin, we bought her like a book that reads the story. Got her loads of new clothes, she got everything. She had a really good time. Me and Martin wanted a party for her, 'cos Theresa only had a tea party for Annalise, but I thought it would be nice to have a party for Megan, so we'd a big party for her.
>
> (Veronica, 19)

Our informants indicate that they experience a sense of satisfaction at prioritising a child's needs:

> [I] just get something every couple of months. But I don't mind 'cos I've got a daughter now and she needs more than I need.
>
> (Veronica, 19)

Conversely, they report high stress levels when struggling to meet basic needs for their children, compared to when they had only themselves to worry about. This is exacerbated considerably when their parenting is subject to scrutiny and others judge their abilities:

> I've worked in a nursery and she [Christine] sees a different side to us and people are saying that I'm not going to be able to cope when I have the baby but she says, 'You haven't seen the way she is with children, she will cope.'
>
> (Georgia, 18)

> [People] who haven't been in care, judge people and they don't realise how hard it is. It hurts … we don't get any chances, like the kid can be taken off you. Like if your house is dirty or filthy or stuff like that … . But it's extra pressure 'cos you've got to be a really good mum, and make sure that she eats well and stuff.
>
> (Theresa, 20)

Georgia's sense of self is partly protected by her social worker's confidence that she will be able to adapt to this adult role. By contrast Theresa, who explains the importance of being able to keep her home clean as a signifier that she is taking good care of her baby, emphasises the hurtfulness of being considered incapable because she herself was in care.

Discussion and conclusion

During emerging adulthood young people have opportunities to explore potential identities as they trial adult roles and extend their sphere of experience (Cote, 2000). Consumption activities are an integral part of this (Gentry, Baker and Kraft, 1995) and help people to achieve greater consistency in their identity as they move between life stages (Schouten 1991). For many young people in Western cultures, emerging adulthood has become a protracted process (Arnett, 2007) marked by a gradual increase in autonomy and decreasing dependency on family. Typically, family, friends and social structures prepare young people for greater independence and provide fairly steady and continuous support throughout the transition process, including a general 'safety net' when things do not go as planned. Financial, physical and social/psychological support for young people leaving home encourages them in their new roles, in order that they become capable and confident to live independently (Morrow and Richards, 1996) and enjoy a smooth transition to adulthood. However, for young people who have grown up in care, sometimes within an institutional setting, the transition typically happens much earlier, and is condensed and often disruptive (Rogers, 2011; Jones, 2002). They tend to be less well prepared for adult roles, enjoy less social support than their peers, and the consequences of setbacks and failures in demonstrating their capability to cope in key domains of adulthood can be harsh.

Our study of young people leaving care illustrates that their attempts to assume consumer roles relevant to two key domains of adulthood – setting up home and establishing a family – constitute important transitional experiences that contribute positively and negatively to their emerging adult identities. The atypical circumstances of their transition to adulthood are clearly felt because of perceived normative expectations of adult roles. These are strongly reinforced by pervasive consumption cultures and consumer narratives (Rafferty, 2011) when expressed in social interactions (including those with service personnel) and when codified in service providers' systems and terms and conditions.

In the face of these perceived norms, the young people are sensitive to the (mis)alignment between the apparent demands of new adult roles and the resources (e.g. money, knowledge, skills, social support, social status, emotional resilience) that they are able to draw upon and combine to facilitate coping strategies (e.g. conduct research to be informed of consumer/citizen rights prior to interactions with service personal, assert a viable limit for debt repayment, amass records of payments/notifications/complaints, symbolic consumption).

When care leavers judge that they are doing well, they express joy at their mastery of adult consumer roles and their confidence grows, reinforcing elements of their adult identity that remain ambiguous. Within their stories many positive experiences relate to events when they feel they successfully engage in symbolic consumption or conform to a positively framed consumer narrative (e.g. 'the smart shopper', 'the effective complainer'). Their experiences are also positive when social interactions with others, usually a close social tie (e.g. support/ social worker, grandparent), reveal empathy, admiration or respect for them as they adapt to adult responsibilities.

When care leavers feel that they are struggling, they sometimes regard their experience as part of a learning process. But they often express anxiety about new roles, especially when they are unable to gain control over time, suffer repeated setbacks, and when their situation is precarious (e.g. losing their home, not having enough to eat, facing fines or legal action). Stories of struggles and setbacks often link to situations in which they get more direct and explicit reactions from others and experiences of interacting with service organisations, including front-line staff and administrative processes (e.g. penalties, threats to cut off service access), are particularly prominent. Care leavers feel frustrated when service terms and conditions are incompatible with their circumstances, either because they reflect norms geared to more privileged social groups or because they have restricted access and encounter less favourable and flexible conditions (e.g. pay-as-you-go gas meters) than other market segments (Hill, Ramp and Silver, 1998). In addition, they are highly sensitised to others' evaluations of their efforts to perform adult consumer roles and to social stigma (related to their cared-for status or other features such as being a young single parent or unemployed). They feel upset, anger and fear when they detect such prejudice and vigorously resist it using a variety of strategies including learning about/taking advice on consumer and citizen rights or contingent service scripts. However, even the most resourceful of our informants struggle to use these strategies effectively when service providers are insensitive to their situation and inflexible. The fact that their situations can often be rectified when a representative (e.g. support worker, Citizens Advice Bureau) intervenes simply reinforces their disempowerment in these adult consumer domains.

The study extends prior research that demonstrates that consumption-related activities are associated with life transitions and vulnerability (Mason and Pavia, 2006; Gentry et al., 2005). Specifically, it introduces contingencies of self-worth (Crocker and Wolfe, 2001) as a concept that explains why changes in social roles (entry and exit) during life transitions are especially important for self-identity and highlights the influence of perceived norms around social roles in creating challenges to the self, especially for people who undergo non-normative transitions. Prior consumer research shows that people who cannot fully participate in the pervasive consumer cultures of Western societies, and those who encounter unfairness and lack control in the marketplace activity, struggle to meet basic needs and feel vulnerable (Hill and Stamey, 1990; Gentry et al., 1995), although there is evidence of high levels of resilience and creative coping strategies by which consumers resist unfavourable conditions. Our findings highlight that these aspects of consumer experience are commonplace for care leavers, as a group of young people facing the transition to adulthood with restricted resources, and emphasises that study of transitions to adulthood should encompass consumer perspectives because they are critical to understanding vulnerability and emergent adult identity. From a practical perspective, our findings that service interactions are common among the negative experiences that affect care leavers' transitions to adulthood highlight the importance of responsible service management and the need for specific policies and practices to protect the well-being of these consumers.

Note

1 Being 'fostered' (US) or 'in care' (UK) covers a range of circumstances in which children are looked after following intervention of the state into family affairs for a child's welfare.

References

Adkins, Neve Ross and Julie L. Ozanne (2005), 'The low literate consumer', *Journal of Consumer Research*, 32 (June), 93–105.

Andreasen, Alan R. (1984), 'Life status changes and changes in consumer preferences and satisfaction', *Journal of Consumer Research*, 11 (December), 784–794.

Arnett, Jeffrey J. (2007), 'Suffering, selfish, slacker? Myths and reality about emerging adults,' *Journal of Youth and Adolescence*, 36(1), 23–29.

Baker, Stacey M., James W. Gentry and Terri L. Rittenburg (2005), 'Building understanding of the domain of consumer vulnerability', *Journal of Macromarketing*, 25(2), 1–12.

Barn, Ravinder, Linda Andrew and Nadia Mantovani (2005), *Life After Care: The Experiences of Young People from Different Ethnic Backgrounds*, York, UK: York Publishing Services for the Joseph Rowntree Foundation.

Bates, Myra Jo and James W. Gentry (1994), 'Keeping the family together: How we survived the divorce', *Advances in Consumer Research*, 21, Provo, UT: Association for Consumer Research, 30–34.

Bauman, Zygmunt (2001), *The Individualised Society*, Cambridge: Polity.

Carter, Mary A.T. and Kellie Cook (1995), 'Adaptation to retirement: Role changes and psychological resources', *Career Development Quarterly*, 44(1), 67–82.

Cathcart, James (2004), *Looking Beyond the Label: Public Attitudes to People in Care*, The Prince's Trust, London.

Cote, James E. (2000), *Arrested Adulthood: The Changing Nature of Maturity and Identity in the Late Modern World*, New York: New York University Press.

Cote, James E. (2006) 'Emerging adulthood as an institutionalized moratorium: Risks and benefits to identity formation', in J.J Arnett and J.L. Tanner (eds) *Emerging Adults in America: Coming of Age in the Twenty-first Century*, Washington, DC: American Psychological Association, 85–116.

Crocker, Jennifer and Connie T. Wolfe (2001), 'Contingencies of self-worth', *Psychological Review*, 108(3), 593–623.

Crocker, Jennifer and Lora E. Park (2004), 'The costly pursuit of self-esteem,' *Psychological Bulletin*, 130(13), 392–414.

Crocker, Jennifer, Andrew Karpinski, Diane M. Quinn and Sara K. Chase (2003), 'When grades determine self-worth: Consequences of contingent self-worth for male and female engineering and psychology majors', *Journal of Personality and Social Psychology*, 85(3), 507–516.

Croizet, Jean Claude and Theresa Claire (1998), 'Extending the concept of stereo-type threat to social class: The intellectual underperformance of students from low socioeconomic backgrounds', *Personality and Social Psychology Bulletin*, 24(6), 588–594.

Delor, F., and M. Hubert (2000), 'Revisiting the concept of "vulnerability"', *Social Science & Medicine*, 50(11), 1557–1570.

Desmette, Donatienne and Mathieu Gaillard (2008), 'When a "worker" becomes an "older worker": The effects of age-related social identity on attitudes towards retirement and work', *Career Development International*, 13(2), 168–185.

Fellerman, Ritha and Kathleen Debevec (1993), 'Kinship exchange networks and family consumption', *Advances in Consumer Research*, 20, Provo, UT: Association for Consumer Research, 458–462.

Gentry, James W. (1997), 'Life-event transitions and consumer vulnerability', Special Session, *Advances in Consumer Research*, 24, Provo, UT: Association for Consumer Research, 29–31.

Gentry, James W., Stacey M. Baker and Frederic B. Kraft (1995), 'The role of posses-sions in creating, maintaining, and preserving one's identity: Variation over the life course', *Advances in Consumer Research*, 22,Provo, UT: Association for Consumer Research, 413–418.

Gentry, James W., Patricia F. Kennedy, Catherine Paul and Ronald P. Hill (1995), 'Family transitions during grief: Discontinuities in household consumption patterns', *Journal of Business Research*, 34, 67–79.

George, Linda K. (1993), 'Sociological perspectives on life transitions', *Annual Review of Sociology*, 19, 353–373.

Hamilton, Kathy (2012), 'Low-income families and coping through brands: Inclusion or stigma?', *Sociology*, 46(1), 74–90.

Hiles, Dominic, Duncan Moss, Lisa Thorn, John Wright and Rudi Dallos (2014). '"So what am I?" Multiple perspectives on young people's experience of leaving care', *Children and Youth Services Review*, 41(June), 1–15.

Hill, Ronald P. (2001), *Surviving in a Material World: The Lived Experience of People in Poverty*, Notre Dame, IN: University of Notre Dame Press.

Hill, Ronald P. and M. Stamey (1990), 'The homeless in America: An examination of possessions and consumption behaviors', *Journal of Consumer Research*, 303–321.

Hill, Ronald P., David L. Ramp and Linda Silver (1998), 'The rent-to-own industry and pricing disclosure tactics', *Journal of Public Policy & Marketing*, 17(Spring), 3–10.

Hogg, Margaret K., Carolyn F. Curasi and Pauline Maclaran (2004), 'The (re)-configuration of production and consumption in empty nest households/families', *Consumption, Markets and Culture*, 7(3), 239–259.

Jones, Gill (2002), *The Youth Divide: Diverging Paths to Adulthood*, York, UK: York Publishing Services for the Joseph Rowntree Foundation.

Kim, Jungmeen E. and Phyllis Moen (2002), 'Retirement transitions, gender, and psy-chological well-being: A life-course, ecological model', *The Journals of Gerontology Series B: Psychological Sciences and Social Sciences*, 57(3), P212–P222.

Mason, Marlys and Teresa Pavia (2006), 'When the family system includes disability: Adaptation in the marketplace, roles and identity', *Journal of Marketing Management*, 22(9/10), 1009–1030.

McAlexander, James H. (1991), 'Divorce, the disposition of the relationship and everything', *Advances in Consumer Research*, 18, Provo, UT: Association for Consumer Research, 43–48.

Morrow, Virginia and Martin Richards (1996). *Transitions to Adulthood: A Family Matter?*, York, UK: York Publishing Services for the Joseph Rowntree Foundation.

Murphy, Robert F., Jessica Sheer, Yolanda Murphy and Richard Mack (1988), 'Physical disability and social liminality: A study of rituals in adversity', *Social Science and Medicine*, 26(2), 235–242.

Price, Linda L., Eric J. Arnould and Carolyn Folkman Curasi (2000), 'Older consumers' disposition of special possessions', *Journal of Consumer Research*, 27(Sept), 179–201.

Propp, Jane, Debora M. Ortega and Forest NewHeart (2003), 'Independence or interdependence: Rethinking the transition from "Ward of the Court" to adulthood', *Families in Society*, 84(2), 259–266.

Quinn, Diane M., Sang K. Kahn and Jennifer Crocker (2004), 'Discreditable: Stigma effects of revealing a mental illness on test performance', *Personality and Social Psychology Bulletin*, 30(7), 803–815.

Rafferty, Karen (2011), 'Class-based emotions and the allure of fashion consumption', *Journal of Consumer Culture*, 11(2), 239–260.

Rogers, Ruth (2011), '"I remember thinking, why isn't there someone to help me? Why isn't there someone who can help me make sense of what I'm going through?": "Instant adulthood" and the transition of young people out of state care', *Journal of Sociology*, 47(4), 411–426.

Runquist, Jennifer J. and Pamela G. Reed (2007), 'Self-transcendence and well-being in homeless adults', *Journal of Holistic Nursing*, 25(1), 5–13.

Scholte, Evert, Matther Colton, Ferran Casas, Mark Drakeford, Sue Roberts and Margaret Williams (1999), 'Perceptions of stigma and user involvement in child welfare services', *British Journal of Social Work*, 29, 373–391.

Schouten, John W. (1991), 'Personal rites of passage and the reconstruction of self', *Advances in Consumer Research*, 18, Provo, UT: Association for Consumer Research, 49–51.

Schwartz, Seth J., James E. Cote and Jeffrey J. Arnett (2005), 'Identity and agency in emerging adulthood: Two developmental routes in the individualization process', *Youth & Society*, 37(2), 201–229.

Social Exclusion Unit (2005), 'Transitions: Young adults with complex needs', Office of the Deputy Prime Minister, London.

Spiers, Judith (2000), 'New perspectives on vulnerability using emic and etic approaches', *Journal of Advanced Nursing*, 31(3), 715–721.

Thompson, Craig J. (1996), 'Caring consumers: Gendered consumption meanings and the juggling lifestyle', *Journal of Consumer Research*, 22 (March), 388–407.

Young, Melissa M. (1991), 'Disposition of possessions during role transitions', *Advances in Consumer Research*, 18, Provo, UT: Association for Consumer Research, 33–39.

Wheaton, Blair (1990), 'Life transitions, role histories, and mental health', *American Sociological Review*, 55(2), 209–223.

Wisner, Ben and Henry R. Luce (1993), 'Disaster vulnerability: Scale, power and daily life', *GeoJournal*, 30(2), 127–140.

11 Older people

Citizens in a consumer society

Roger Clough

Introduction

This chapter has drawn on an Age UK Lancashire action research project, *Linking Communities*, which examined whether the involvement of older people, and others from local communities, would result in a better match between, on the one hand, people's needs and wants and, on the other, the sorts of facilities and services available to support them in leading fuller lives (Clough et al. 2014). Information was collected in a variety of ways, in particular from two surveys using questionnaires that allowed for open-ended responses with 706 and 190 respondents respectively and from interviews with 90 older people and 45 service providers.

Older people were to be involved as fully as possible in the life of the project:

- as researchers following a seven weeks x half-day training course in research methods;
- as members of local community groups;
- as respondents to a survey;
- as interviewees;
- as members of discussion groups pursuing research themes;
- as collaborators in developing activities for older people.

A review of that activity is a core part of the discussion that follows. However, it is important to embed a discussion of participation in the context of older people in society. Two main themes are developed:

a   *The role of older people in society:* How do people perceive themselves as they age? What are the implications for older people's engagement in their communities?
b   *The mechanics of participation:* What were the ways that were used to promote involvement? What were the results?

A further theme is an examination of the impact of language, in particular of the meanings attached to the words 'consumer' and 'vulnerability'.

Older people in society

In the study, we asked people about their experiences of getting older. Some interesting findings emerged. In spite of worries and failing health, the majority of older people enjoyed their current stage of life, in particular the opportunities to live as they want:

> I can choose what I do, go out, stay in, do my hobbies, read, visit my neighbour on Friday evenings to watch DVDs, take turns in providing snacks, visit my daughter and two grandsons … . She takes me shopping, garden centres, arts and craft centres, cinema, has me to dinner on Sunday if I choose to go.
>
> (Woman, single, aged 84)

> Just retired and therefore enjoying the complete freedom to do as we wish.
> (Man, married, aged between 65 and 69)

> I shall be 85 in a few weeks and I am very happy. My three sons are very good to me and my daughters-in-law are lovely. I am fortunate to be in good health, I read, am computer literate, and have my faith. I consider myself well blessed.
> (Woman, widowed, lives alone, aged 84)

However, many struggle with change to themselves, close family and friends, and the places where they live and, thus, to their sense of community. People described ways that they plan their time to manage such changes and so make life easier and build structure to the day:

> I make myself get going, but have learnt to not fill up my day as much as I used to. I have also asked for help from my neighbours; if appropriate I ask relatives. I've also learnt to say 'No' and am withdrawing from various pointless responsibilities. But I am trying to remain involved.
> (Woman, single, lives alone, aged between 75 and 79)

> I'm getting more infirm and have to drive myself mentally to get up and go. I haven't the energy I used to have and get tired quite quickly.
> (Woman, single, lives alone, aged between 75 and 79)

There is a fine line between getting by and feelings of going under. Several people told us of the very difficult situations with which they had to cope. The most distressing were those where a wife or husband was caring for their spouse and managing their own poor health and exhaustion:

> How does one cope with a husband that has very short-term memory? Is diabetic, needs 24-hour care, aged 82 years. Is incontinent, refuses to take

painkillers. … I am very tired … I only get out for three hours each Thursday afternoon, I pay for this.

> (Woman, married, aged between 80 and 84)

Others reported on their coping strategies:

I cope because my own life contracts more and more. He does have respite care for a week every three months and this is an absolute godsend.

> (Woman, married, aged between 75 and 79)

By keeping strong and facing each challenge with an appetite. Also I have wonderful neighbours from where I lived before whom I can never ever repay for everything they have done (and will do) for me. Aren't I blessed?

> (Woman, widowed, lives alone, aged between 75 and 79)

When faced with family problems one person tried to keep calm by going into the garden.

The interplay of perceptions of older people as vulnerable and as consumers

Older people's own accounts of themselves and the management of their lives should be placed in the context of societal perceptions of ageing. What is expected of people as they age? Will they continue to manage more or less on their own or will they require increased assistance? There are numerous competing discourses on the interaction between older people and society. One of these is built on the use of health and social care resources by older people. In this scenario the premise is that older people 'consume' (that is 'use') a large proportion of health and social care activity. 'What are the ways that such consumption may be reduced?' the discussion continues. The other scenario, typified by the leisure and retail industry, is to view older people as a group who may be persuaded to consume more. The word *vulnerable* has different connotations in each of these discussions. In the first discourse, older people are seen as vulnerable in that circumstances that commonly occur in old age make them liable to being unable to cope without calling on others for support. However, the vulnerability of older people as users of leisure and retail facilities is likely to refer to potential problems in providing goods and services for people who may be seen in some way as at risk. Thus, there might be discussions about people's capacity to understand contracts they are asked to sign, or about what would happen if someone fell ill on holiday.

'Vulnerability' is often used interchangeably with 'risk': people are said to be 'vulnerable to …' or 'at risk from…'. However, 'vulnerability should not be confused with risk' (Australian Government Department of Health and Ageing). Yet too often there is no clarity about what it is that people are thought to be vulnerable to, that is, the nature of what might happen. 'Vulnerability' or 'risk' become loose cannons and, left on their own, serve only to alarm or unhelp-fully label someone. It is better to be specific – for example, writing that there is risk of a fall arising from loose carpets (Barry 2007). In a literature review, Barry notes changes in use of the word. 'Risk originally meant calculating the probabilities of events, both positive and negative, and yet increasingly, in social work at least, [it] has come to be associated with negativity or adversity.' Negative stereotypes of older people contribute to assessments by others of risks to older people, as do 'risk avoidance, cultural perceptions and the need to feel they are "doing the right thing"' (Lindley et al. 2012). A special issue of *Health, Risk and Society* focused on vulnerability and risk across the life course (see Alaszewski 2013 for editorial).

Comments that someone is at risk of abuse or at risk of losing their inde-pendence are of little value for action without further definition. Even worse is a description of someone as 'a vulnerable older person', a label without any clarity. So at the start of this discussion it is essential to express clearly and forcefully that old age in itself is not a vulnerable state: old age is neither an illness nor a problem; it is no more than a life stage. Of course this is not to deny that there are problems that, frequently, are encountered by older people. These may arise from health problems, perhaps because arthritis makes daily life difficult, or from environmental factors such as inadequate housing.

In relation to social care, one risk that is identified is that people may be unable to manage on their own – that is, that something may happen so that the person cannot cope without external intervention. This is sometimes defined as 'being at risk of losing one's independence'. However, there are problems with this use of language in that it assumes independence as an absolute: you either have it or you don't. The reality is that at times any of us may do some things for ourselves and have people to do other things for us, whether cleaning, decorating or gardening. The balance of what we do ourselves and what others do for us may shift, in particular if in later life we find ourselves less physically able. There will be a stage when, if they have sufficient money, people may choose between doing something themselves, perhaps taking a long time and with considerable difficulty, or having someone else to help. A later stage comes when someone can no longer perform the task. To add to the confusion in terminology, many will see themselves as being independent if they continue to be able to direct the way that something is done even though they may not be able to do it themselves.

The interests of social care commissioners are likely to focus on what tips a situation from being one where a person is managing without state support to one where they need such help. It is at this time that there may be a search for the triggers; that is, the events that change a situation that had been managed without external help to one that no longer can be. However, even when defined as precisely as this, there remains difficulty in specifying what is being examined: someone may be surviving in a situation but finding much of what is happening in their lives to be problematic or out of control. An event such as a fall occurs and the situation collapses. The assumption is that the event has changed the capacity of the person to manage their daily life and, therefore, if the fall is prevented, the person will continue to cope. In many circumstances that will be correct. Yet what is seen as a trigger event may have performed a different function: it may have alerted someone to aspects of their lives that they had found intolerable, and made them unwilling to accept these in the future.

It is also vital to recognize that terms such as 'vulnerable' tend to become seen as absolute states, though the word itself carries within its definition the sense of 'liable to'. The complexity that should be recognized is that people fit several categories at the same time, a fact that terminology fails to recognize. Thus people may be competent to manage for much of their lives, but vulnerable on different occasions. So it may be that in some settings or activities someone is more or less vulnerable. Indeed, vulnerability may vary with mundane physical factors, such as whether or not the individual had a good night's sleep or was in a low state of health.

Older people interacting with service providers: what do we call them?

Yet it is also true, as is so frequently asserted, that older people frequently come into contact with health and social care services. Immediately a question emerges as to how to describe the person in relation to their contact with these services. At different times people have been referred to as 'patient', 'client', 'user', 'customer' and 'consumer'. 'Consumer' defines a person in a narrow way in relation to their use of an article or service. It carries with it the importance of giving consumers adequate rights so that they may maintain a reasonable position in negotiations, and stresses the responsibility of an individual to choose between competing options. On the other hand, 'citizen' captures the relationship of an individual to the state or local community.

Such terms rarely emerge from those who are being treated or supported: they are likely to be words chosen by those who provide and commission. In each case they have been selected to capture an element of the relationship that is thought to have been missed with earlier terminology. *Customer* and *consumer* have been chosen to convey similarity to other negotiations with the external world where an individual has choice in the market, not only as to what to purchase but also from whom. In this scenario the individual is to be given more authority and negotiating strength. Both words present oversimplified versions of the relationship between individual and service provider:

- they ignore the differences between the types of service interactions encountered; for example, sorting out arrangements for social care is quite different from the purchase of a washing machine;
- they presume that individual control and choice are the key determinants to ensure high-quality provision and the best arrangement;

- they take little account of capacity of the individual to work out the 'best buy', in particular at times of stress when services are most likely to be required.

Age UK Lancashire conducted this research project, so it is proper to reflect on the words used to describe the relationship between the individual and the organization. Language may be indicative of, or even influence, the way that people are perceived. The Age UK Lancashire website lists the activities provided (http://www.ageuk.org.uk/lancashire/):

> We work across the county to enable older people in Lancashire to make more of their lives, offering services and support as well as campaigning for older people's rights. … We run a range of services, groups and activities for older people across Lancashire. We also supply products aimed at improving older people's lives, like insurance and personal alarms. … If you'd like to help us, we have volunteering and fundraising opportunities, and several charity shops. … We can offer information and advice on a range of issues including community care, housing issues, local services and support and welfare benefits.

Someone who visits an Age UK Lancashire shop is readily described as a customer, though the person serving them might be termed a shop assistant or volunteer. The same may be the case for the person looking for insurance. However, terminology for many of the other activities and services is less obvious. An older person may go to a lunch club or a day centre, participate in an activity such as a health walk, exercise club or trip out, or have someone visit them as part of a befriending scheme or support following a stay in hospital. In each of these latter examples the function may have more facets than the title of the event may suggest. Thus a health walk may provide comradeship as well as exercise, a visit to a day centre may offer relief to someone at home who looks after the individual, an opportunity for a bath or chiropody, or a new activity. To this mix there should be added the variations in capacity of the older person, and in particular the extent to which they deem themselves – or are thought by others – to be in need of support. A further dynamic is that many of the volunteers are themselves older people.

Thus the dominant perception may be of an older person, responsible and in control of their lives, choosing to join a group activity, in the same way as anyone might join a sports or dance club. Alternatively, the dominant perception may be of someone no longer able to manage independently, who needs support and help. The attitude of staff and volunteers to the individual may be influenced by the dominant perception. Thus, different judgements may be made as to the extent to which individuals should be left free to decide for themselves how to manage their lives. For example, how will a staff member react to someone who decides to take a bus home after an activity when the staff member has doubts about whether the person can manage satisfactorily?

These decisions do not differ in kind from those that are made by anyone in any situation in relation to another. We all have to decide whether to offer advice when we think that a friend is putting on weight. Similarly, we may be concerned when a parent seems to be unsafe, perhaps climbing on top of a step-ladder to get to the loft, and have to work out what to do or say. What is important is that the assumptions that are made of an individual's capacity, and the consequent way in which someone may be put into a 'coping' or 'non-coping' category, are likely to influence the behaviour of staff and volunteers to an older person.

One specific example illustrates the impact of language. In the *Linking Communities* study it was found that some older people with dementia and their close family members had few opportunities to do things together outside the home. Support services tended to offer separate opportunities for the person with dementia and the family member. The person with dementia may be offered a visit to a day centre. Alternatively, support may be offered while their partner has time away from the home, with a worker coming into the house to look after the individual with dementia. Such support is likely to be highly valued. However, some people reported that they no longer went out together to public places such as cafés and cinemas because of anxiety about the ability of the person with dementia to manage or the response from members of the public if behaviour was unusual. They wanted to maintain their long-standing relationships. One outcome was to develop a monthly film show at the Dukes Theatre, an independent theatre and cinema in Lancaster. The environment was adapted to be better suited to the person with dementia, with background music turned off, better signage of key places such as lavatories, and improved lighting of exit doors in case people wanted to leave the auditorium during the show. The film shows were open to the public as part of the theatre's regular publicity. There has been sufficient interest for the shows to continue, for the time being supported by external funding. To reinforce the distinctive character of the project, with changed focus and relationships, it was decided not to refer to the *person without dementia* as 'carer' because this classified them solely in relation to their looking after the other person, not their long-standing relationship as wife or husband, daughter or son. So the language used was of a person with dementia and *family member*, and the word 'carer' was avoided.

Similarly the nature of the association between organization and individual had to be examined. When providing day care, Age UK Lancashire ensures that it has details of each person attending, including next of kin and person to inform in case of an accident. What should the nature of the responsibility be at the film shows? Given that the film shows were open events, it would have been unrealistic and inappropriate to expect everyone to give name and contact details. The decision was made to refer to people as 'patrons', to indicate the ordinariness of the event and the interaction, stressing that this event had more in common with an everyday attendance at a film, rather than a special 'social care' support activity. Language does have an impact on assumptions and behaviour.

The mechanics of participation

The aim of the project was that older people should play a central part in the project, not just as informants but also as a part of the team undertaking the research. There were to be opportunities for involvement in different roles, for example as researchers, interviewees, volunteers or commentators on the findings. The research team wanted to maximize opportunities for involvement and so issued invitations through media releases as well as the well-established volunteer network in Age UK Lancashire.

This participatory approach was allied with a commitment to action: one objective was that there should be regular feedback of findings and ideas, and that these, in turn, should influence the next stages of the project. A parallel thrust was that the information would be available for others to use throughout the life of the project.

Several themes may be identified from the research activity. The first is that the research activity should be constructed from dialogue with older people. Second, it became apparent that the participatory approach was, fundamentally, concerned with the processes of engagement and empowerment. A third theme developed with the realisation that such involvement demanded consideration of the ways that older people were perceived as citizens and as members of their communities.

This chapter was written when the project was in its last month, and the team was involved in report writing and dissemination. Age UK Lancashire is working to construct a framework, built on different scaffolding poles, for a continuing dialogue with older people so that they play a bigger part in the life of Age UK Lancashire and in their own communities, with a strengthened voice. These topics will be discussed further at the end of this chapter, but the focus at this stage returns to the mechanics of participation.

Older researchers

The older people who joined the team as researchers reflected on their reasons for participating, stressing the wish to do something interesting, an opportunity to test out former skills or learn new ones, and a wish to be part of a team. There is little doubt that the researchers enjoyed and valued the experience, a finding that is endorsed by many reports on volunteering. There is no doubt either that they made valuable contributions to the research in conducting interviews, helping to devise the interview schedule and in discussing findings.

However, there is a cost to participation. Even though the team was building on a similar course that had been run over a much longer period by one of their group, developing the course was time-consuming (Clough et al. 2006, Leamy and Clough 2006). The format was that two or three members of the team were to be present at the training so that there was a developing team construction of research activity. It was a regular occurrence for individual older researchers to drop in at the office or phone up to discuss their work, a feature that was not surprising since they had been invited to do so. In planning, it had been presumed that there would be a time saving with older people conducting interviews. This was not the case. The paid research staff could have conducted the same number of interviews in the time taken for training and support.

Therefore, at least with a project of this limited scale with comparatively few older researchers, the conclusion is that such participation is justified by the contribution made by the participants and their future involvement in the dialogue about the interests of older people, rather than by time saved. A second message is also important: there should be detailed and thorough development of the programme to cover the mechanics of research. Third, it is essential not to lose the fact that the best social researchers have taken a long time to hone their skills, often with a three-year PhD programme before further research activity. Skills can be learnt, but the process takes time, and it is unreasonable to expect that short courses will result in all members becoming expert.

Interviewees and group participants

Older people often voice their frustration that although they are consulted, asked for their views and give time to contributing, nothing seems to happen. "What use", they ask, "was our input?" The project team attempted to give regular feedback about the research to all participants: interviewers, interviewees, those who attended group discussions and people who participated in other ways:

- findings were published on the website as they were written up;
- large-scale feedback meetings were held at the three project sites, with reports on project developments and an opportunity to discuss the data and so contribute to an understanding of the material;
- an end-of-project celebration event was held, with project findings, a band and a tea dance.

One interviewee who had expressed strong views about the inadequacies of local transport had been invited to a conference on transport in Lancashire, which county council staff were also attending. She later spoke about her experience:

> When people stop paid work, others stop listening to them and that's the thing Age UK Lancashire doesn't do. I think they look at people as a resource, not just a user of services. ... One of the reasons I kept in touch with Age UK after the interview was because they were very punctilious about following up. They kept in contact with me; they fed back to me what other people had said. ... I was pleased that I was included in an extended consultation period because quite often people ring you up and you never hear anything else and you think 'Was I of any use'? AUKL is very good about being reciprocal ... I think the biggest positive for Age

UK Lancashire is that you don't just consult, and you don't just inform; you interact.

The key point in this discussion is that keeping people informed of what has happened should be an integral part of consultation. Consultation that is devoid of such investment is likely to be seen as a waste of time. Indeed, it may turn out to be disempowering rather than giving people a belief that their views matter.

Of course it is pleasurable to record the positive comments, but not everything worked like this. There had been a previous attempt to run local consultative groups in the three areas. They fizzled out after one or two meetings. The groups had been constructed to try and include local older people, those with an interest in that community, and others from health services or the local authority (for example, GPs and library or social care staff). The groups did not develop from an existing organization, and this may be one of the reasons why they failed to cohere. Membership at meetings was sporadic. Perhaps the research team gave up too soon.

There is one other aspect of the mechanics of participation that is worth noting. The project team developed a style of running group discussions that differs from that of many focus groups. Frequently, some people dislike expressing their views in a group and others are content to respond to others' ideas rather than contribute their own. Therefore, an approach was adopted which had several components:

- there was to be a group leader and co-leader in each group, with the co-leader acting as support and note-taker;
- there was training for group leaders in which the following was stressed: a) their role was to elicit information and help people develop their views rather than provide answers to questions; b) the importance of encouraging people to develop their own views, rather than move to convergence; c) the development of techniques to manage the group, such as starting by asking all members to write down their own opinion on a topic and then discuss it with a neighbour; d) their responsibility as leaders to control contributions so that no one person dominated, emphasising that respect for older people did not mean that the leader could not ask someone to give way to another.

Another feature of many group discussions is that much of the content is lost as a record – though of course it may have an impact on individuals. Consequently, there was an attempt to record detail rather than just headlines on a flip chart that have little meaning after the event. Where possible, and with the agreement of members, discussions were recorded. There were no facilities to transcribe these, but they were available to the group rapporteur as a source of direct quotations or to check their memory. The group leader was also asked to write reflective notes.

A continuing dialogue

By the end of the project, the research team, and Age UK Lancashire as the host organization, had come to see one of the enduring features of the research as being the development of a dialogue with older people in the county. This has been an unexpected result. The themes of what will be a continuing conversation have been drawn from different approaches. For example, in thinking about what people value and look for in their community, information was collected from surveys and interviews. In addition, people were invited to take a photo that captured what for them represented community, and to write a paragraph to accompany this. One person took a photo of a sheepfold on Ingleborough and wrote:

> It encapsulates what, for me, is the most important aspect of community; namely that a community is a shelter (a fold) for the vulnerable; it stands between the weakest members of society and the 'elements' (exploitation, discrimination, racism, sexism, ageism). Without community some will survive, but many more are lost.

Someone else wrote about a local garden:

> This garden is used by the community as a peaceful, beautiful place to be. The gardens are also run by the community, as each plot is tended by people of the community. The pleasure the gardens give to residents and visitors alike is paramount. The gardens have great 'smile' appeal.

Age UK Lancashire plans to build on this work to maintain a dialogue with older people, a dialogue in which people are seen as a resource, freed from descriptions that tie them to language that sees them primarily as 'vulnerable', 'a service user', 'a volunteer' or 'a consumer'. All of us have multiple roles, and it is essential that the multiplicity is not lost in old age.

Roger Clough is a former trustee of Age UK Lancashire, and was the research director for the project on which this chapter is based. He has written in a personal capacity, not as a representative of the organization.

References

Alaszewski, Andy (2013) 'Vulnerability and risk across the life course', *Health, Risk & Society* 15(5), 381–389. Similar information may be found in Culo, S. (2011) 'Risk assessment and intervention for vulnerable older adults', *British Columbia Medical Journal*, 53(8).

Australian Government Department of Health and Ageing, *Living Longer, Living Better*, online at: http://livinglongerlivingbetter.gov.au/internet/living/publishing.nsf/Content/ageing-linking-service-toc~02-defining

Barry, M. (2007) *Effective Approaches to Risk Assessment in Social Work: An International Literature Review*, Edinburgh: The Scottish Government.

Clough R., Bidmead, E., Moore, G. and Sidney, I. (2014) *Managing Our Lives: A Dialogue with Older People About What Would Help Them Lead Fuller Lives*, Chorley: Age UK Lancashire.

Clough R., Green B., Hawkes B., Raymond, G. and Bright, L. (2006) *Older People as Researchers: Evaluating a Participative Project*, York: Joseph Rowntree Foundation.

Leamy, M. and Clough, R. (2006) *How Older People Became Researchers: Training, Guidance and Practice in Action*, York: Joseph Rowntree Foundation.

Lindley, E. et al. (2012) *Improving Decision-Making in the Care and Support of Older People*, York: Joseph Rowntree Foundation.

Part III

Consumer vulnerability, health and wellbeing

12 Health shocks, identity and consumer vulnerability

Marlys J. Mason and Teresa Pavia

Introduction

Consumer vulnerability is often thought of demographically (e.g. the poor), situationally (e.g. the bereaved), or as the by-product of an external event (e.g. a flood). Means to reduce vulnerability often focus on psychological, financial, and resource resiliency. However, consumer vulnerability that derives from a failing body (e.g. illness, disability, aging) strikes deeply at the agency and identity of the consumer. Drawing upon existing literature and depth interviews, we develop insights about consumer behavior and identity in this setting. We use three dimensions to focus our findings: what someone must buy, the time horizon that is in their mind, and what this consumption says about who they are. This is an important area for development because the idiosyncratic experience of health-related consumer vulnerability makes broad systematic vulnerability-reduction schemes less likely to be helpful, particularly in the deeply personal realm of identity.

When conceptualizing consumer vulnerability, it is common to define vulnerability as an inability to engage effectively in the marketplace (Baker, Gentry, and Rittenburg 2005; Shultz and Holbrook 2009). In this setting, vulnerability is characterized as a state of overwhelming sense of powerlessness, lack of control, and dependence (Baker and Mason 2012). Such vulnerability can arise from a variety of individual and external factors (Baker, Gentry, and Rittenburg 2005), but daunting health challenges may be a catalyst central to experiencing vulnerability (Mason and Pavia 2006; Pavia and Mason 2014, 2004). Current research has considered how illness/disability interact with structural aspects of the market and interpersonal consumer dynamics, but it has not addressed how illness/disability in oneself or a loved one challenges identity, or how identity transition during this time is linked to the experience of vulnerability.

How consumers use consumption to build and reinforce their identity has been an active part of consumer research for many years (Belk 1988). In addition to building consumer identity in day-to-day situations, scholars have also looked at identity work during times of transition and the role that consumption plays in identity transition (VOICE Group 2010). While some transitions are desired (e.g. birth of a child) and accompanied with fanfare and ritualized consumption activities, some transitions are disconcerting (e.g. cancer diagnosis, birth of a disabled child). Research that has focused on consumption during transitions triggered by illness, disability, advanced age, or loss of a loved one (Baker 2006; Barnhart and Peñaloza 2013; Gentry et al. 1995; Mason and Pavia 2006; Pavia and Mason 2004, 2014) documents significant reevaluation of consumer attitudes and behaviors that occur during such periods.

The way that consumption interacts with identity during any transition is complex, but the transitions that are tied to failures of the body itself are especially nuanced. It is not uncommon for the consumer to be thrust into new markets and purchases (e.g. needing a wheelchair) with little warning, and the consumer is often at a loss as to where to turn to for consumption advice. In addition to buying new products, routine purchases may come under new scrutiny. Take the example of a woman who loves the sun and always has a tan but is diagnosed with melanoma. She is forced to make acquisitions she is neither familiar with nor wants because she is now a *cancer patient*. She reconsiders activities and behaviors because she is now someone who *avoids the sun*. She may have less certainty about the future because she *faced a threat to her life*. Her health is challenged, her identity is challenged, and her behavior as a consumer is in flux. She is unclear about who she is becoming.

The goal of this chapter is to highlight the ways that illness, death, and disability can evoke vulnerability through consumption challenges and identity dissolution. With the loss of identity comes the opportunity for vulnerability, as consumers not only confront barriers in finding products and services that meet their needs, but question their roles, worth, and future within consumption acts. We begin our analysis with the basic questions consumers ask in relation to: "What do I need in this new situation?" After the initial coping just to get by, the consumers begin to ask: "When will this be over, or when will I die, or when will I know?" Persistent uncertainty makes recrystallization of identity difficult and drags out the time that the consumer spends reconstructing his/her/family identity. Together these questions of what and when coalesce into the broader question, "Who am I?" Addressing each of these questions – what, when, and who – presents opportunity for identity change. This time of reevaluation opens the door for vulnerability since it also includes disrupted routine, product search under stress and time constraints, and limited resources and energy for the consumption process.

The scope and nature of health challenges

A staggering number of consumers live with health limitations due to illness, aging, and disability. In the U.S., nearly 27 million persons live with heart disease, 20 million with cancer, 16 million with diabetes, 25 million with asthma, and 52 million with arthritis (CDC 2012). Similarly in the UK, nearly three million adults suffer from heart disease, three million with diabetes, six million with asthma, ten million with arthritis, and five million with lung or liver disease (NHS 2014). In the U.S. the majority of persons over 65 years have at least one chronic condition and 62 percent report having a physical limitation which restricts basic living activities (CDC 2012). Behind such statistics are the difficulties and ongoing uncertainties that millions of consumers with health challenges face in their daily living and well-being (Charmaz 1991; Frank 1995).

Past literature has recognized that serious challenges to health generate a variety of psychosocial threats to personal well-being. Health problems are argued to produce anxiety, stress, and threats to one's sense of coherence (Antonovsky 1979). No longer is it assumed that the world is manageable and things will turn out fine; one's intrinsic sense of control and optimism is shattered. Health concerns also shock one's "taken-for-granted" continuity and significantly disrupt self-identity (Charmaz 1991, 1995, 2000). When experiencing health problems a person's perceived life trajectory becomes unclear; they question the world and their continued place in it. Charmaz (1991) has argued that such questioning of one's identity begins with the acknowledgement of the present self as having illness and limitations. Individuals then contrast this present self with a healthy past identity, which leads to questions about the future self. Who are they in light of this progressing illness or disability? Further, when questioning identity, persons may become overwhelmed by body concerns and fears of dependency or loss.

Uncertainty can also become a central part of the shared illness experience. Individuals experience separation as they transition from a healthy person to a self that they (or others) perceive to be diseased or with significant limitations (Frank 2002). They may confront difficulties in carrying out daily activities and work responsibilities, which can contribute to isolation. Consumers may wonder how their family roles and relationships will change if they can no longer engage in daily routines and consumption activities (Mason and Pavia 2006). Furthermore, illness is often accompanied by an increased dependency on healthcare providers, family members, and friends. This dependency can further evoke concerns about control or autonomy, and damage perceptions of self-efficacy (Bandura 1977; Charmaz 1995, 2000). In short, severe health problems threaten one's sense of control, continuity, and independence, as well as alter family roles and social relationships. Such changes are likely to disrupt core aspects of identity, and ultimately heighten vulnerability.

Methods

Our analysis is the collective result of the thinking that has converged across four studies involving different types of health concern which the authors conducted over several years. The first stage of inquiry looked specifically at individuals with late-stage AIDS who were facing a terminal diagnosis and end of life. The second study involved consumers who had been given a diagnosis of breast cancer but were in the liminal stage following treatment and uncertain of their prognosis. The third study involved consumers, including some loved ones, who had been diagnosed with a serious chronic illness. This illness did not present an immediate life threat but did alter their life significantly. In the fourth study, we pursued a collective focus more specifically and interviewed parents of children with a significant disability, in order to better understand the family perspective. In laying out our studies in this manner, we were able to explore issues related to both a terminal threat and chronic conditions. Both types of challenges involve ongoing adaptation in consumption but differ in the uncertainty and mortality salience experienced. Specific details about our studies can be found in previous writings (Mason and Pavia 2006; Mason and Scammon 2011; Pavia 1993; Pavia and Mason 2004, 2012).

Interviews with 70 consumers conducted face to face inform our data analysis. Each interview began with the general question: When some form of illness or disability overshadows life, how does this affect your identity and consumer behavior (broadly defined)? While the overall guiding interest was similar, it was explored in different illness contexts, and, subsequently, different nuances within the studies emerged. During the interviews we attempted to understand areas such as background to the onset of the illness/disability and initial changes in consumption (defined broadly), and then moved to more specific areas such as goods/services/experiences, marketplace interactions, consumer roles, temporal concerns, and so on. Specific questions were not predetermined but emerged from the course of the conversation and attempted to elicit a deeper, more detailed response from informants in the topic areas. This type of interview enabled us to obtain a phenomenological understanding of participants' complex attitudes and behaviors without imposing a priori categorization, which can restrain the inquiry (Creswell 2012; Fontana and Frey 2000). Each interview lasted between one and two hours and was both audio-recorded and transcribed verbatim.

The transcripts were analyzed within each study in an iterative manner with the researchers exploring what happened, who was involved, and what meaning was ascribed (Glaser 1992). Coding was conducted separately and then shared for thematic convergence and divergence. Ongoing readings and coding of the interviews were conducted to reassess emerging patterns (Strauss and Corbin 1994). Theoretical questions emerging from this analysis were woven into subsequent interviews within the studies, and raised areas to explore in the new contexts.

Also during this time, both authors worked with government and non-profit organizations, engaged in volunteer activities, and were involuntarily thrust into the experience of serious illness. Throughout our interactions with patients, volunteers, health professionals, and others, we heard many concerns that related to consumption and the marketplace. Our research inquiry and analysis continued to evolve through our prolonged engagement as both researchers and participants in the health area. Through our interviews and fieldwork, we attempted to investigate in-depth consumer concerns and vulnerability when faced with overwhelming health challenges. In the following we discuss our emergent themes.

Analysis

Our informants were experiencing a range of serious health issues that threatened their future, their ability to pursue current lifestyles, and their self-perceptions. While some impairments creep into one's life (e.g. progressive arthritis), for our informants there was almost uniformly a clear demarcation point when an accident occurred, a diagnosis was made, or someone's health reached a tipping point when "something had to be done". In many ways the tipping point mirrors the sudden vulnerability that communities face when a natural disaster strikes (Baker, Hunt, and Rittenburg 2007). However, unlike rapid transitions that communities face, health challenges do not usually happen to a natural cohort at the same time. Eventually, others with similar needs may coalesce, but unlike the community response Baker, Hunt, and Rittenburg (2007) document, our respondents often described how alone they felt in their search process, at least initially. When the consumer sits at the cusp of pre- and post-health crisis there are immediate problems such as, where do I buy a wig? Several months down the road though the consumer faces more personal questions that only she can answer, such as, now that I own the wig, should I keep it, just in case? This example shows how a straightforward coping purchase can evolve into a complicated question of what this body means for who I am, the sorts of products I own, what these say about me and my beliefs about my body. Health challenges lead to identity challenges and while support systems and communities are an important part of minimizing consumer vulnerability in any setting, sometimes the ongoing questions that people must face are so personal and idiosyncratic that the identity challenges continue to be negotiated long after the initial event. We now consider specific ways the changing physical and emotional landscape can result in market vulnerabilities.

What: consumption before and after

Consumer culture theory argues that we enact ourselves reflexively through consumption. What we buy displays who we are, and who we are drives what we buy (Arnould and Thompson 2005; Ogle, Tyner, and Schofield-Tomschin 2013). Because there are negative feelings associated with a failing body, there is often shame associated with buying the products this body needs. Buying adult diapers, prostheses, even anti-depressants makes a statement about who one is. Being a parent who requires state support to feed a child with enzyme deficiency calls the parent's otherwise strong sense of self-sufficiency into question. As the following people relate, consumers are thrust into new buying situations, with few market guides, trying to understand what these new needs mean for who they are.

> I remember going to a store to buy bandages after the biopsy. I just became totally poverty stricken. I thought I couldn't even afford Band Aids ... I mean, here is someone who has multiple assets and resources and I was so freaked out.
>
> Elaine (breast cancer)

Clothes. You can't find them. We had everything that Babies R Us had for Preemies ... in fact we're still wearing some of his newborn outfits [at 8 months]. So he may look normal, but his clothes are still 0 to 3 months.

Olivia (mother of premature infant)

We changed our diet, cut out meat, and went natural. Big-time organic. The whole family changed their diet ... . We cooked straight from scratch. We went back to the natural stuff. We didn't even buy ketchup.

Gloria (daughter of mom with ovarian cancer)

Broadly speaking, these informants reveal consumers working to address new needs and to meet the expectations of others (e.g. appearance). Friends and family are swept into the process of meeting new consumption needs, which may strengthen or weaken existing bonds but rarely leaves them unchanged. These changes can lead to the consumer being vulnerable because he/she is often thrown into new buying situations just when finances become stressed, time becomes limited, and energy for the search process is low. Purchases may not only be unsought but actually unwanted. The goods, far from being hedonic, are constant reminders of the change that illness/disability has brought. Goods received as gifts are markers of social ties, but they also reinforce the consumer's changed standing in the world. Other necessities such as food, which were a normal part of the family's lifestyle, now take on new meaning and practices. He is now the parent of a sick child; she is now the person with cancer; we are now a family fighting for better health. In short, the person from "before" has departed and someone new, who needs all these new things, has arrived.

When: what is going to happen in the future?

An individual's experience with illness, and the ensuing threat to self, is idio-syncratically driven in part by internal factors, in part by external factors (e.g. concern about paying for treatment), and in part by the degree of uncertainty surrounding the future. Uncertainty can lead to deep disruption of a person's sense of self, wellness, independence, and self-reliance (Charmaz 1991; Hardey 1998). When an illness/disability has an uncertain trajectory or outcome (e.g. cancer diagnosis), individuals exist in a prolonged limbo. In such cases, mortality salience contributes to identity disruption (Pavia and Mason 2004) and changes the horizon one uses for making decisions. For example, if one may not live, does saving for retirement make sense? With other ailments, the diagnosis may involve a terminal prognosis (e.g. ALS, late-stage cancer). In such cases, a foreshadowed end of life challenges one's identity continuity (Pavia 1993). Other health conditions are chronic (e.g. heart disease, arthritis, spinal cord injury), during which one's future outlook is not shortened, but it is sig-nificantly altered in terms of functioning and limitations (Pavia and Mason 2012). Many of these situations contrast with vulnerability that acts as an initial shock (e.g. a tornado) but, once the trauma is over, leaves the challenge of rebuilding one's life to its former function. In situations where the future is murky and the response is idiosyncratic, the support function becomes less about restoring one to a previous life than one of supporting the individual as he/she moves into an unclear future.

Uncertainty about the future makes good consumer decision making more difficult. Informants wondered whether they should sell their homes and downsize, whether they should make purchases that involve distant consumption (e.g. travel, retirement), or even whether to make purchases at all. Our informants provide a glimpse into the difficult terrain that some consumers live with on a medical level that then leave their day-to-day lives continually disrupted:

> I found myself really not wanting to spend a lot of money on things because at that point I was still thinking, "Well, what's the use of buying things?" You know, who knows how long you're going to be around?
>
> Denise (breast cancer)

> There has not been one doctor in 21 years that has ever looked at him and been able to positively say, "This is the route we're going to go." It's always been, "Oh my gosh. Oh dear. Oh no. Oh, I don't know anything about this. Oh, I don't know what we're going to do. Hmmm, I'm stumped." So there has never been, from the day he was born, a clear path of what we're going to do.
>
> Irene (son with vascular anomalies in leg and eventual amputation)

> It hit me a few years ago. I could hardly get out of bed in the morning. I couldn't stand. I could hardly walk. I could hardly sit … . It's been a long, slow, painful ordeal … . The doctor said, "Well, take it easy." What does "take it easy" mean to me?
>
> Lois (rheumatoid arthritis)

Uncertainty inherently moves the event horizon that a consumer uses when decision making. Is one buying one's child a Christmas present or the last Christmas present they will receive from their father? Should one buy a fun car that loses value quickly or the sensible car that will last ten years? Is it worth going to college or would it be better to travel while feeling well? A shortened event horizon makes impulse purchases more likely and extended comparative shopping less likely. An event horizon that jumps about makes for inconsistent decision making, sometimes increasing stress when the horizon shortens again (e.g. buying a house just before leaving work due to long-term disability). Uncertainty pervades who one is, what one can do, and what sort of goods and services will be needed as one tries to adjust and envision the future.

Who: continuity and alienation between the before and after self

Illness/disability challenges notions of self at many levels. At the most intimate level, what we know of the world is filtered through our senses and our bodies. When these inputs change, our experience of the world changes. What we desire may change, the energy we have to pursue goals changes, how other actors in the market see us changes, and the sorts of products and services that are deemed appropriate for us changes. In short, the entire internal and external landscape may shift. At the same time there is an abiding sense of continuity, of being "more than my body" – the body may have ailments, but the "I" persists as before. There is a similar sense of continuity in relationships – for example, "I may be ill, but I am still your mother."

One of the attributes of illness/disability is that it usually forces someone into a greater degree of interdependency. Physical impairment, fatigue, confusion, and pain impede the individual's self-sufficiency; if the consumer is the parent of an ill child, it reduces family self-sufficiency and independence. This increased reliance increases the opportunity for consumer vulnerability as financial resources shrink, decisions that used to be made alone are now negotiated with others, mobility is reduced, and one's consumption is exposed to more public view. At the same time, most people realize that the circle of supporters that rally round are there out of love or friendship. Thus, the increase in dependence is a double-edged sword: it is emblematic of one's connections, but at the same time it denotes one's loss of autonomy. Janet reveals her struggle with trying to maintain her role as the family's primary shopper and caregiver, and also contribute to family finances, while her illness and body make her dependent on others for carrying out consumption roles:

> I had four hours tops in me each day. That was it. Four hours to do whatever errands, I had nothing left to give. Four hours to do housecleaning, nothing left to give. I'm back totally desperate, totally fatigued, working from home, and I only have one payroll client. I wasn't leaving the house … . My body was crying out for some help.
>
> Janet (Crohn's disease)

Another aspect of illness/disability is the way it expands group affiliation. One becomes part of the "cancer club" or the group of parents with children with autism. As with dependence this is a double-edged sword. One is not alone and perhaps others who share the experience can provide guidance and advice. Simultaneously, one may not want to be identified as someone who uses a wheelchair or needs a transplant. It is quite common for people to cry, "I am so much more than my disease." Yet this cry is accompanied by the desire to be understood and accepted for whatever limitations the body has imposed.

One prominent arena in which identity is particularly stressed is in the realm of productivity. This often plays out in issues related to paid work, but can be as basic as who makes dinner or tends the yard. As Jean (late-stage AIDS) relates: "So to have to find inside who I was, was really difficult. I had to introduce myself as '... this is what I do', and then all of the sudden it was, 'Well, I stay at home.'" Similarly, other informants discussed losing their professional identities and becoming dependent on others, such as a spouse or the government, and the concerns this raises about dependency for their future finances and consumer well-being:

> I was still was sick and couldn't work...and my husband developed his own [health] problems. He had to quit his main occupation and take something not as good paying. I have to be very, very careful about money.
>
> Violet (chronic fatigue)

> My life fell apart after [diagnosis]. I actually became 100 percent disabled. I wasn't able to work ... . My goal is to get off disability benefits ... . This is *my* life and I have to get back to work because I feel it's important to work ... to get my car serviced, pay my rent, to do what it takes to carry on in life.
>
> Diane (Epstein Barr)

With the loss of work and career, not only were individuals uncertain how to define themselves; they were uncertain of what value they provided for others, uncertain of being able to meet their future consumption needs, and concerned about their dependency on others. Their feelings of powerlessness in production and dependency in consumption left them feeling vulnerable in the marketplace.

Conclusion

It is through our bodies, whether healthy or challenged, that we engage in consumption and construct our identities. Much consumer research has established the positive role that consumption and market interactions play in people's lives and identity formation. Sometimes, when identity is threatened, consumption becomes so important that it undermines financial stability. Our informants discussed consumption involving struggle, uncertainty, dependency, and vulnerability, and yet all informants continued to consume, sometimes with very high engagement. Even when it is hard to perform "normal" activities such as grocery shopping or eating out, this behavior is so central to self and group identity that it is deemed worth the effort.

Following the health crisis, despite the prognosis or trajectory of their illness, all informants described experiencing a shock to the self and felt loss and confusion around how to proceed as a consumer. They questioned what this health crisis meant for consumption, when (if ever) the health crisis would pass, and who they were as a consumer now that they must live with an illness or disability. Undesired consumption, dependency, loss in deeply valued roles and activities, and concerns about future productivity and consumption were common themes associated with this transition. No easy solutions to wellness were found; no quick resolutions to identity occurred. As such, informants were vulnerable as they struggled with what being a person living with significant health limitations meant for consumption, and reflexively, what unwanted consumption changes meant for their disrupted identity (Pavia and Mason 2004).

Unlike disruptions that communities experience together, illness tends to be more individual, making community support and community resilience to vulnerability less relevant. Consumer vulnerability may be lessened by naturally forming cohorts (e.g. support groups), but these tend to focus more on problem solving (e.g. finding a wheelchair) than on "Who am I?" Therapeutic interventions can be useful, but they are also private and individual. Consequently, many of the systemic interventions to reduce the vulnerability of health-challenged consumers (such as additional financing, resources guides, support groups, and information search support) address the visible challenge but leave the consumer struggling alone with the inner challenge to his/her identity.

In summary, health is central to how we view ourselves, organize our lives, and consume. Millions of consumers struggle with an illness/disability which threatens the essence of who they are, what the future holds, and how they meet (or even understand) their present and future consumer needs. Future research is needed to further explore the consumer vulnerability and subsequent adaptation that follows a severe health crisis, particularly the effect of the deeply felt and poorly articulated threat to identity.

References

Antonovsky, Aaron (1979), *Health, Stress and Coping*. San Francisco: Jossey-Bass.
Arnould, Eric J. and Craig J. Thompson (2005), "Consumer Culture Theory (CCT): Twenty Years of Research", *Journal of Consumer Research*, 31(4), 868–882.
Baker, Stacey Menzel (2006), "Consumer Normalcy: Understanding the Value of Shopping through Narratives of Consumers with Visual Impairments", *Journal of Retailing*, 82(1), 37–50.
Baker, Stacey Menzel, James Gentry and Terri Rittenburg (2005), "Building Understanding of the Domain of Consumer Vulnerability", *Journal of Macromarketing*, 25(2), 128–139.
Baker, Stacey Menzel and Marlys J. Mason (2012), "Toward a Process Theory of Consumer Vulnerability and Resilience", in D.G. Mick, S. Pettigrew, C. Pechmann, and J.L. Ozanne (eds) *Transformative Consumer Research for Personal and Collective Well-Being*, New York: Routledge, 543–564.
Baker, Stacey Menzel, David M. Hunt, and Terri L. Rittenburg (2007), "Consumer Vulnerability as a Shared Experience: Tornado Recovery Process in Wright, Wyoming", *Journal of Macromarketing*, 26(1), 6–19.
Bandura, Albert (1977), "Self-Efficacy: Toward a Unifying Theory of Behavioral Change", *Psychological Review*, 84(2), 191–215.

Barnhart, Michelle and Lisa Peñaloza (2013), "Who Are You Calling Old? Negotiating Old Age Identity in the Elderly Consumption Ensemble", *Journal of Consumer Research*, 39(6), 1133–1153.

Belk, Russell W. (1988), "Possessions and the Extended Self", *Journal of Consumer Research*, 15(2), 139–168.

CDC (2012), available at: http://www.cdc.gov/chronicdisease/overview/index.htm.

Charmaz, Kathy (1991), *Good Days, Bad Days: The Self in Chronic Illness and Time*. New Brunswick, NJ: Rutgers University Press.

Charmaz, Kathy (1995), "The Body, Identity, and Self", *The Sociological Quarterly*, 36(4), 657–680.

Charmaz, Kathy (2000), "Experiencing Chronic Illness", in G. Albrecht, R. Fitzpatrick and S.C. Scrimshaw (eds) *Handbook of Social Studies and Health and Medicine*, Thousand Oaks, CA: Sage.

Creswell, John W. (2012), *Qualitative Inquiry and Research Design: Choosing Among Five Traditions*, 3rd ed., Thousand Oaks, CA: Sage.

Fontana, Andrea and James H. Frey (2000), "The Interview: From Structured Questions to Negotiated Text", in N.K. Denzin and Y.S. Lincoln (eds) *Handbook of Qualitative Research*, Thousand Oaks, CA: Sage, 645–672.

Frank, Arthur (1995), *The Wounded Storyteller: Body, Illness, and Ethics*, Chicago: University of Chicago Press.

Frank, Arthur (2002), *At the Will of the Body: Reflections on Illness*, New York: Houghton Mifflin.

Gentry, James W., Patricia F. Kennedy, Katherine Paul, and Ronald Paul Hill (1995), "The Vulnerability of Those Grieving the Death of a Loved One: Implications for Public Policy", *Journal of Public Policy & Marketing*, 14 (Spring), 128–142.

Glaser, Barney G. (1992). *Basics of Grounded Theory Analysis*. Mill Valley, CA: Sociology Press.

Hardey, Michael (1998), *The Social Context of Health*, Philadelphia, PA: Open University Press.

Mason, Marlys J. and Teresa M. Pavia (2006), "When the Family System Includes Disability: Adaptation in the Marketplace, Roles and Identity", *Journal of Marketing Management*, 22(9/10), 1009–1030.

Mason, Marlys J. and Debra L. Scammon (2011), "The Unintended Consequences of Health Supplement Information Regulations: The Importance of Recognizing Consumer Motivations", *Journal of Consumer Affairs*, 45(2), 201–223.

NHS (2014), available at: http://www.nhs.uk/Conditions/.

Ogle, Jennifer, Keila Tyner, and Sherry Schofield-Tomschin (2013), "The Role of Maternity Dress Consumption in Shaping the Self and Identity during the Liminal Transition of Pregnancy", *Journal of Consumer Culture*, 13(2), 119–139.

Pavia, Teresa (1993), "Dispossession and Perceptions of Self in Late-Stage HIV Infection", *Advances in Consumer Research*, 20, Provo, UT: Association for Consumer Research, 425–428.

Pavia, Teresa and Marlys Mason (2004), "The Reflexive Relationship Between Consumer Behavior and Adaptive Coping", *Journal of Consumer Research*, 31 (December), 441–454.

Pavia, Teresa and Marlys Mason (2012), "Inclusion, Exclusion and Identity in the Consumption of Families Living with Childhood Disability", *Consumption Markets & Culture*, 15(1), 87–115.

Pavia, Teresa and Marlys Mason (2014), "Vulnerability and Physical, Cognitive and Behavioral Impairment: Model Extensions and Open Questions", *Journal of Macromarketing*, 34(4), 471–485.

Shultz, Clifford J. and Morris B. Holbrook (2009), "The Paradoxical Relationships Between Marketing and Vulnerability", *Journal of Public Policy & Marketing*, 28 (Spring), 124–127.

VOICE Group (2010), "Buying into Motherhood? Problematic Consumption and Ambivalence in Transitional Phases", *Consumption Markets & Culture*, 13(4), 373–397.

13 Social exclusion

A perspective on consumers with disabilities

Carol Kaufman-Scarborough

Introduction

For many years across several disciplines, academics have studied how people make choices as consumers, whether as individuals or as part of households (see for example, Bettman 1979; Bettman, Luce, and Payne 1998; Bitner 1992; Kohli, Devara, and Mahmood 2004; Park et al. 1981). Their studies examined how consumers form attitudes and beliefs about products, brands, and retail stores, predicting their future consumption choices based on their evaluations. While providing the foundation for models of consumer choice, such studies may also hold an implicit assumption that consumers have relatively equal abilities to make their purchases, to travel freely to retail shopping locations, and to access needed information as they please.

As members of a consumer-based society, people quite naturally seek to participate in its consumer culture and many facets of experience. They seek to create their own identities, to examine and compare products, to feel a sense of belonging and welcome, and to experience companionship as they shop (Baker 2006; Baker, Gentry, and Rittenburg 2005; Hamilton 2009). However, biases based on age, disability, gender, ethnicity, income level, perceived status, and other perceived attributes can erect barriers to consumer participation and form the foundation for marketplace exclusion. As a result, some consumers are regularly underserved, ignored, or excluded on a regular basis from the marketplaces that they seek to experience.

Reported disability rates are found to vary dramatically throughout the world, and responsible agencies point out that the problem is exacerbated by nonstandard definitions and measurement across countries (Mont 2007). Even in the United States, where the proportion is approximately 20 percent of the population, persons with disabilities are found to report discomfort, lack of welcome, and disabling conditions that magnify the impact of their disabilities (Baker, Holland, and Kaufman-Scarborough 2007). As Arnould (2001) aptly stated, "North American consumer culture idealizes certain kinds of consumers and marginalizes others who do not perform to specification" (p. 361).

Exclusion from mass market studies

Ironically, such marginalization extends to the recruitment and screening of consumer samples. Few if any academic studies indicate overtly recruiting and including consumers with disabilities in their samples unless the study focus was related to disability. In effect, we may argue that researchers have created and institutionalized an "ableist" approach to consumer behavior. Consumer and public policy scholars have questioned the resulting idealized view of consumer reality since it overlooks various types of "consumer disadvantages" (Baker 2006; Baker, Gentry, and Rittenburg 2005; Piacentini, Hibbert, and Hogg 2013; Woodliffe 2007).

Gleaning information from a lack of inclusion

Consumer exclusion based on racial, age, and wellness stereotypes "prevents some from marketplace interaction, while a more subtle lack of inclusion also has a similar effect if their needs have not been anticipated" (Bennett, Hill, and Oleksiuk 2013). While appearing less deliberate, a lack of inclusion fails to take well-known requirements into account when considering a specific population (Lee and Shrum 2012), such as not anticipating that people with mobility disabilities would attend an event or overlooking the needs for a qualified sign-language interpreter during a public speech.

Consumer exclusion based on ableism, or non-disability, was addressed through civil rights legislation such as the Americans with Disabilities Act of 1990. Legislation has made progress, but there are still disadvantages and limitations that are readily found. Persons who are limited in mobility, sight, hearing, and various types of cognitive processing have been likely to experience both consumer exclusion as well as a lack of inclusion with its more subtle nuances.

This chapter will examine the experiences of persons with mobility, visual, and learning disabilities utilizing the concept of social exclusion as a foundational building block that may enable us to unfold the lack of consumer inclusion in a meaningful way. Rather than continuing to rely on ability qualifications as admissions markers, we deconstruct disability-based exclusion and ability-based inclusion into a matrix of possibilities that can potentially add richness to our theories and reality to our models.

Consumers with abilities and disabilities

Research on consumers with disabilities has taken many approaches across a variety of disciplines, including how to define persons with disabilities, how to capture their experiences, and how to determine the motivation for inclusion or exclusion. However, several basic questions underlie the attempts to examine the experiences of consumers with disabilities. Research in disabilities studies has traditionally examined the ability of persons to participate in society, the cause of their disability, if any, and whether remediation of the person, the situation, or both is possible.

Modelling disabilities in society

For example, the medical model has focused on the disability of the person who is to be rehabilitated, fixed, or made well. The underlying assumption of this approach has viewed disability in a negative light, as non-transitional, and a burden on the individual's family as well as society. Terms utilized reflect this mindset as disabilities are thought to create a "spoiled identity" (Goffman 1963) that needs to be repaired, remedied, or excluded from the mainstream of society (Oliver (1983, 1990). Research basically focused on the characteristics of the disabled person that define their disability and limit the individual, rather than on the abilities that the person has.

In contrast, the social model changes the focus to society's creation of an "enabling" or a "disabling" environment (Humphrey 2000), by designing accessible facilities from the start, by modifying facilities as required, or by taking an ableist approach in anticipating participation only by those who are not disabled. If architectural design considers accessibility as an afterthought, society can potentially disable an individual, especially if they are disabled already. Researchers such as Oliver (1983, 1990) considered the impact of the built environment from this perspective. Society places restrictions and poor design "on top of disability" and thus multiplies the disabling effect (UPIAS 1976). However, if the environment can be fixed, individuals are no longer excluded.

More recent approaches have argued that neither model allows us to adequately capture the realities of the experiences encountered by persons with disabilities (Humphrey 2000; O'Grady et al. 2004). From some perspectives, disabled persons are considered to be "outsiders who need not apply for entry" to the mainstream of normal, everyday life (Hughes, Russell, and Patterson 2005). As these authors charge, marketers, advertisers, and product designers may view the stereotypical attributes of disability as undesirable in appealing to potential consumers. However, while the fashion world attempts to design and sell from the perspective of "youth, vigor, and beauty," young persons with disabilities may also want to seek the same goals as they increasingly take on consumer roles in daily life.

Vulnerability and normalcy: key concepts for inclusion and exclusion

Stacey Baker and her colleagues have published a series of conceptual pieces in which the realities of consumer vulnerability and consumer normalcy were defined, modeled, and discussed in terms of their context and occurrence (Baker 2006; Baker, Gentry, and Rittenburg 2005; Pavia and Mason 2012, 2014). Both are transitory states and may depend upon the conditions and situations encountered in the marketplace at a specific point in time.

Consumer normalcy is distinguished by four major characteristics: 1) participating or being in the marketplace, 2) achieving distinction in the marketplace, 3) demonstrating competence and control, and 4) being perceived as an equal in the marketplace (Baker 2006). It is not surprising that people enjoy shopping when they feel like themselves with their individual preferences taken into account. They enjoy utilizing their skills and feeling competent, equal to all others in the marketplace. In contrast, consumers may not "feel normal" if they are marginalized in some way, whether they have a disability or not. Consumers who are not listened to or are treated as incompetent are likely to have a dissatisfactory experience that is decidedly not normal.

Consumer vulnerability is not simply the opposite of consumer normalcy. Specifically, it is "a state of powerlessness that arises from an imbalance in marketplace interactions or from the consumption of marketing messages and products" (Baker, Gentry, and Rittenburg 2005). Some persons may be more susceptible to potential harm in a transaction because of situations, personal characteristics, marketplace characteristics, or interactions that limit their abilities to perform as capably as possible. For instance, a deaf consumer may feel helpless without some assistance from store employees. Drawing on Bitner's (1992) conceptualization of servicescapes, the dynamic nature of consumer shopping can lead to shopping failures whether or not a person is disabled. Given the uneven and often partial responses to civil rights legislation like the Americans with Disabilities Act, persons with disabilities may more frequently encounter shopping situations that reduce their control and create imbalance in their transactions.

Social inclusion and exclusion

Definitions

Studies of social exclusion have abounded throughout the social sciences and during the last 20 years, and the concept has had a growing presence in the consumer research literature (Piacentini, Hibbert, and Al-Dajani 2001). For the purposes of this chapter, the concept of social exclusion is a foundational building block that describes a restriction from participation, an aloneness or isolation, the state of being banned or ostracized, or a closing out from a particular social situation or environment (Baumeister et al. 2005; Wan, Xu, and Ding 2014). Social exclusion threatens four fundamental human needs: belongingness, self-esteem, control, and meaningful existence (Williams 2001; Zadro et al. 2004). Being ignored is expected to threaten efficacy needs, which in turn will increase conspicuous consumption. In contrast, being rejected is expected to threaten relational needs, which in turn will increase helping and donation behavior. Research has also demonstrated its profound effect on purchase and consumption as "affiliation tools" (Baumeister et al. 2005; Mead et al. 2011). That is, consumers who feel excluded from a particular group or situation may strategize their purchases in order to maximize the likelihood of enhancing belongingness.

Social inclusion instead includes an enabling of participation, a welcoming, or an opportunity to engage in a particular social situation or environment. In academic studies in the workplace, it incorporates dimensions of fairness, membership, belongingness, and social contact that are possible among individuals and groups (Amado et al. 2013). It is thought to occur when individuals from all possible groups in a given social situation or environment are fairly treated, valued for who they are, and included in core decision making, rather than instilling power among popular in-groups (Nishii 2013).

Unfolding the experience of consumer vulnerability

As Woodliffe argued in her research on consumer disadvantage (2007), "not all consumers are equal in the marketplace," and thus may be disadvantaged by inequalities in their abilities to shop, their access to retail stores, and their abilities to gain desired information. "Consumer disadvantage" is thought to fundamentally incorporate lack of access, lack of flexibility in deciding when and how often to shop, and inconvenience when taking a shopping trip (Bromley and Thomas 1993). Other types of exclusion or failure to include are found in faulty store design, lack of employee training, poor website design, and other types of choice in the retail setting.

Persons with disabilities may encounter restrictions if they attempt to shop in certain retail venues that have not complied with existing accessibility legislation. Recently, Hollister, a trendy clothing chain aimed at "young, beautiful consumers with spending power," was the subject of a class action suit due to a store prototype that added a porch with stairs to the enclosed mall storefront. Two side doors were at ground level and, according to the retailer, would allow access by persons with mobility disabilities. However, multi-location observations indicate that the doors were poorly marked and often blocked by merchandise. Since the new Hollister prototype was constructed after the Americans with Disabilities Act was codified, Hollister was ruled to be not in compliance. In August 2013, a Colorado judge ruled that over 200 stores with the porch-and-stairs prototype storefront would be required to either include accessibility in their primary design or eliminate the stairs completely (Greene 2013).

Examining inclusion and exclusion

Consumer inclusion and exclusion can be used as a valuable lens in examining the experiences, suggestions, and public policy implications. Several prior studies on mobility disabilities, vision impairments, and cognitive disabilities will first be described and then used as contexts within which to apply the proposed framework. The discussion below provides summaries of the studies utilized in this analysis.

Mobility disabilities

A set of sequential studies examined the experiences of shoppers with mobility disabilities in two specific ways: 1) Phase 1: groups of undergraduate students simulated disabilities and went on shopping trips, making observations and taking photographs of disabling situations. They were encouraged to use crutches, wheelchairs, and scooters; 2) Phase 2, groups of undergraduate students accompanied one student volunteer with mobility disabilities on a shopping trip (Kaufman-Scarborough 1999, 2001a).

Color vision confusion

When studying consumers with color vision confusion, one thing is perfectly clear: they feel that their consumer welfare is not uniformly considered in the marketplace. The study included depth interviews with color design and vision care professionals. Participants in the study self-identified their color vision type and described their condition and limitations, using depth interviews, surveys, or online surveys (Kaufman-Scarborough 2000, 2001b).

Cognitive disabilities: Attention Deficit Hyperactivity Disorder

Consumers with differently abled cognitive styles were found to encounter challenging marketplace environments. In some cases, the stimuli that were considered appropriate in-store techniques were actually the cause of discomfort, distress, impaired information processing, and eventual store rejection. In cooperation with CHAAD (Children And Adults with ADHD), the study focused on the shopping experience of persons with ADD/ADHD related to their self-reported impulsivity. Informative interviews with clinical psychologists who treated adults with ADHD underscored the much higher likelihood of uncontrolled impulse spending, financial mismanagement, and ruined credit. The study findings are based on surveys completed by 62 respondents (Kaufman-Scarborough and Cohen 2004).

Vision impairments

Assisted by the National Federation for the Blind in the recruitment of participants, the study of online shopping by persons with visual impairments included 45 persons in the sample at different stages of various kinds of blindness. Depth interviews indicated that they shared common concerns related to the perceived usefulness of web designs and ease of use, as well as an enjoyment of websites (Kaufman-Scarborough and Childers 2009).

The Ability/Inclusion Matrix

The Ability/Inclusion Matrix is based on the intersection between the ability/disability continuum and the inclusion/exclusion continuum. The concepts of inclusion/exclusion and ability/disability can be used as the dimensions of an analytical matrix that enables the researcher to examine continuums of each,

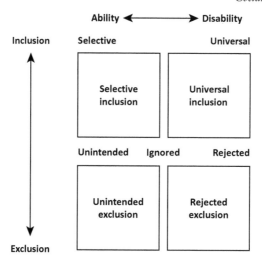

Figure 13.1 Ability/Inclusion Matrix

rather than simple dichotomies. While a disability can be the cause of exclusion, it is also necessary to consider the abilities that are needed for participation and what ranges of ability are assumed for inclusion. That is, there may be certain abilities that qualify a person to become a member of a social situation or environment, and if not present, exclude the individual from participation. In addition, as argued in many of the studies reviewed above, the motivation for inclusion/exclusion can also be considered. For instance, inclusion can be selectively based on certain criteria or can range clear through all persons being universally included, ignored, or rejected.

In this framework, although there are a wide range of conditions that could be plotted along both axes, four quadrants are proposed. They are as follows:

- **Selective inclusion:** The upper left box captures a combination of selectivity and inclusion. That is, rights, admission, access, or membership are based upon criteria established by decision-makers in the social environment. For example, families may join neighbourhood swim clubs, persons with seizures may join a local epilepsy support group, and persons who can sing may join a choir.
- **Unintended exclusion:** Unintended exclusion, on the other hand, will exhibit some form of discrimination based on a well-defined criterion. However, in this quadrant, the motivation for the exclusion is not deliberate and may occur due to a lack of understanding of the needs of persons with disabilities.
- **Universal inclusion:** Universal inclusion is characterized as a situation in which everyone, regardless of ability or disability, is included in the activities of a specific venue.

- **Rejected exclusion:** Finally, rejected exclusion is thought to occur when the marketplace establishes clear criteria for access. Subtly different from selective inclusion, rights, admission, access, or membership are denied based on selected criteria established by decision-makers in the social environment. For example, membership in various groups can be denied on the basis of gender, the ability to walk, or the ability to sing.

In re-examining existing studies with this specific lens, it is apparent that many of the reported experiences were occasions of inclusion or exclusion, although classification in this way was not the original goal. Consistent with Baker's discussion of consumer vulnerability, the participants recounted strategies they developed in order to maximize their inclusion or minimize their exclusion. Not surprisingly, the causality of social exclusion can sometimes be traced to historically based educational norms based on ableism (Johnson and Levin 1985; Rosenthal and Phillips 1997), stereotypes of disabled persons (Goffman 1963), architectural store design based on ableism (Imrie 1999, 2000), popular in-store media use, and online designs that had not incorporated the needs of differently abled consumers (Davis 2003; Kaufman-Scarborough and Childers 2009).

Illustrations and analysis

The findings of each study were reinterpreted along the ability/disability continuum and the inclusion/exclusion continuum. First, the general findings will be presented, followed by their application to the matrix quadrants.

In terms of mobility, the marketplace was found to offer mixed accessibility to shoppers using wheelchairs or motorized carts. Assistive aids were not uniformly available, and employees varied in their degree of training. Merchandise displays and customer services such as fitting rooms were largely inaccessible due to excessive height, crowding, narrow width, and the necessity of using stairs (Kaufman-Scarborough 1999, 2001).

Color vision confusion can occur in both men and women, and while often congenital in males, can be caused by illness, aging, disease, accident, and medication. The respondents indicated that this condition limited consumer behavior in cases when their specific color vision confusion 1) eliminated information, 2) distorted information, 3) inhibited consumer choice, 4) raised concerns with safety, 5) challenged their abilities to make correct purchases, and 6) negatively affected their self-concepts regarding purchases such as décor, clothing, cosmetics, and medicines (Kaufman-Scarborough 2000, 2001).

Persons with ADHD report preferences in terms of the amount and intensity of information they can use comfortably. The study participants criticized the marketplace for being overstimulating, with sounds that are too loud, lights that are too bright, and choices that are overwhelming in number. Basically, information processing was blocked or overloaded by the additional stimuli, resulting in poor consumer choices, repetitive purchasing, and distraction (Kaufman-Scarborough and Cohen 2004).

Finally, persons with visual impairments who used online shopping were found to value independence, control, individualism, and self-expression, desiring to be more self-reliant that store employees might anticipate. They were willing to acquire various assistive aids to use in accessing the web, but could clearly delineate web design flaws that were common across sites. In contrast with bricks-and-mortar stores, which could be unfriendly, full of obstacles, and limited in choice, they viewed online shopping as an opportunity to regain their control and also to create networks of similarly minded persons with whom to share good shopping experiences (Kaufman-Scarborough and Childers 2009).

Findings in these six studies can be classified into quadrants by assessing whether the primary reaction was inclusion or exclusion, whether the criterion used was based on ability or disability, and what the motivation was for applying it.

Selective inclusion

In the mobility studies, all consumers were included for first-floor access but not all could access the second floor of stores in the study. When online shopping is considered, consumers are included as shoppers on certain websites only if they have good vision, the dexterity for typing, and the ability to move their mouse about the screen in a way that maximizes their access to information.

Unintended exclusion

Persons who have problems with color vision indicate that they are excluded from making confident purchases when uninformative names such as "autumn haze" and "summer mist" are used without direct relationships to the standard color palette. Interviewees reported compensating by relying on printed color names as informational cues. Women purchasing cosmetics who have learned to rely on the use of the words *pink, red, or orange* on the label may find themselves experiencing vulnerability in making their purchase if they are unable to access the basic color information they need to choose the right product.

Universal inclusion

In-store investigations identified retailers who planned for accessibility by maintaining adequate aisle width and display height for all shoppers. Those who have color confusions reported perceived inclusion and loyalty to manufacturers and retailers who provided color information in words as well as through actual color cues. Consistent with Elms and Tinson (2012), the respondents felt capable of shopping online as they had the skills needed for shopping successfully.

Rejected exclusion

Consumers may be denied access to transportation to the marketplace, to specific retail stores, to merchandise within accessible stores, or the right to examine or try on merchandise. The mobility studies photographed numerous retailers with broken, dirty, and inoperable accessibility aids such as wheelchairs and scooters that were stuffed into fitting rooms or behind doors. Clearly, there was no intent to provide ready access to customers who needed them. The assistive aids may have been obtained through a half-hearted attempt at compliance with access legislation implying that exclusion is intended.

Discussion

By using the Ability/Inclusion Matrix to re-examine existing research studies on disabilities access to the marketplace, several insights can be reached. Both consumer inclusion and exclusion can result from managerial design choices and motivations. Built environments can increase consumer vulnerability when they make it difficult or impossible for persons with disabilities to engage comfortably and confidently in retail settings. For instance, consumer exclusion can be created by attractive design choices such as porches and spiral staircases. Such features can prevent consumers from participating in the shopping environment by creating unintended barriers.

More fundamental are conscious decisions to create an accessible marketplace and planning ways to include persons with disabilities. Arts venues, for instance, may select certain events for sign language interpretation or warnings about flashing lights and loud noises. A theme park, on the other hand, may control access to certain high-skill attractions, excluding persons with specific disabilities from rock-climbing walls and white water rafting unless their safety can be guaranteed. While legislation may initiate mandatory compliance with accessibility standards, a prudent approach also includes input from the disabled community so that personal feelings are considered. Finally, persons with invisible disabilities may be excluded simply because their needs are not understood. Consumer inclusion can bolster consumer confidence and independence, while exclusion can create or increase inhibition and dependence.

When marketplaces are created based on the principle of universal inclusion, design can take into account a range of abilities and result in design elements that allow for "successful" participation in consumer activities. Rather than worrying about barriers, shoppers with disabilities can feel competent and confident that their purchases represent their actual choices. Such experience of normalcy is likely to occur when participation by persons with disabilities is anticipated, planned for, and encouraged. It is hoped that future use of the Ability/Inclusion Matrix can build awareness of unnecessary social exclusion by consumers with disabilities.

References

Amado, Angela Novak, Roger J. Stancliffe, Mary McCarron, and Philip McCallion (2013), "Social Inclusion and Community Participation of Individuals with Intellectual/ Developmental Disabilities," *Intellectual & Developmental Disabilities*, 51(5), 360–375.

Arnould, E. J. (2001), "Introduction to Special Issue on Ethnography, Consumer Behavior and Marketing: A Sampling of Recent Research," *Journal of Contemporary Ethnography*, 30(4), 359–363.

Baker, Stacey Menzel (2006), "Consumer Normalcy: Understanding the Value of Shopping Through Narratives of Consumers with Visual Impairments," *Journal of Retailing*, 81(1), 37–50.

Baker, Stacey Menzel, James W. Gentry, and Terri L. Rittenburg (2005), "Building Understanding of the Domain of Consumer Vulnerability," *Journal of Macromarketing*, 25(2), 128–139.

Baker, Stacey Menzel, Jonna Holland, and Carol Kaufman-Scarborough (2007), "How Consumers with Disabilities Perceive 'Welcome' in Retail Servicescapes: A Critical Incident Study," *Journal of Services Marketing*, 21(3), 160–173.

Baumeister, Roy F., C. Nathan DeWall, Natalie J. Ciarocco, and Jean M. Twenge (2005), "Social Exclusion Impairs Self-Regulation," *Journal of Personality and Social Psychology*, 88 (April), 589–604.

Bennett, Aronté Marie, Ronald Paul Hill, and Daniel Oleksiuk (2013), "The Impact of Disparate Levels of Marketplace Inclusion on Consumer–Brand Relationships," *Journal of Public Policy & Marketing*, 32 (Spring), 16–31.

Bettman, James R. (1979), *An Information Processing Theory of Consumer Choice*, Boston: Addison-Wesley.

Bettman, James R., Luce, Mary Frances, and John W. Payne (1998), "Constructive Consumer Choice Processes," *Journal of Consumer Research*, 25(3), 187–217.

Bitner, Mary Jo (1992), "Servicescapes: The Impact of Physical Surroundings on Customers and Employees," *Journal of Marketing*, 56 (April), 69–82.

Bromley, R.D.F. and C.J. Thomas (1993), "The Retail Revolution, the Carless Shopper, and Disadvantage," *Transactions of the Institutes of British Geographers*, 18(2), 222–236.

Davis, Joel J. (2003), "The Accessibility Divide: The Visually-Impaired and Access to Online News," *Journal of Broadcasting and Electronic Media*, 47(3), 474–481.

Elms, Jonathan and Julie Tinson (2012), "Consumer Vulnerability and the Transformative Potential of Internet Shopping: An Exploratory Case Study," *Journal of Marketing Management*, 28 (11/12), 1354–1376.

Goffman, E. (1963), *Stigma: Notes on the Management of Spoiled Identity*, New York: Simon and Schuster.

Greene, Susan (2013), "Denver Judge: Abercrombie Brand Hollister Violating Disabilities Act," May 16, *Huffington Post*.

Hamilton, Kathy (2009), "Those Left Behind: Inequality in Consumer Culture," *Irish Marketing Review*, 20(2), 40–54.

Hughes, B., R. Russell and K. Paterson (2005), "Nothing to Be Had 'Off the Peg': Consumption, Identity and the Immobilization of Young Disabled People," *Disability & Society*, 20 (January), 3–17.

Humphrey, J.C. (2000), "Researching Disability Politics, or, Some Problems with the Social Model in Practice," *Disability and Society*, 15, 63–85.

Imrie, Rob (1999), "The Body, Disability and Le Corbusier's Conception of the Radiant Environment," in Ruth Butler and Hester Parr (eds), *Mind and Body Spaces: Geographies of Illness, Impairments and Disability*, New York: Routledge, 25–45.

Imrie, Rob (2000), "Disabling Environments and the Geography of Access Policies and Practices," *Disability & Society*, 15 (January), 5–24.

Johnson, R.D. and I.P. Levin (1985), "More than Meets the Eye: The Effect of Missing Information on Purchase Evaluations," *Journal of Consumer Research*, 12 (September), 169–177.

Kaufman-Scarborough, Carol (1999), "Reasonable Access for Mobility-disabled Persons is More Than Widening the Door," *Journal of Retailing*, 75(4), 479–508.

Kaufman-Scarborough, Carol (2000), "Seeing Through the Eyes of the Color-deficient Shopper: Consumer Issues for Public Policy," *Journal of Consumer Policy*, 23(4), 461–492.

Kaufman-Scarborough, Carol (2001a), "Sharing the Experience of Mobility Disabled Consumers: Building Understanding through the Use of Ethnographic Research Methods," *Journal of Contemporary Ethnography*, 30(4), 430–464.

Kaufman-Scarborough, Carol (2001b), "Accessible Advertising for Visually-disabled Persons: The Case of Color Deficient Consumers," *Journal of Consumer Marketing*, 8(4), 303–316.

Kaufman-Scarborough, Carol and Judy Cohen (2004), "Unfolding Consumption Impulsivity: An Existential-Phenomenological Study of Consumers with Attention Deficit Disorder", *Psychology & Marketing*, 21(8), 637–669.

Kaufman-Scarborough, Carol and Terry L. Childers (2009), "Understanding Markets as Online Public Places: Insights from Consumers with Visual Impairments," *Journal of Public Policy & Marketing*, 28(1), 16–28.

Kohli, Rajiv, Sarv Devaraj, and Adam Mahmood (2004), "Understanding Determinants of Online Consumer Satisfaction: A Decision Process Perspective," *Journal of Management Information Systems*, 21(1), 115–135.

Lee, Jaehoon and L.J. Shrum (2012), "Conspicuous Consumption versus Charitable Behavior in Response to Social Exclusion," *Journal of Consumer Research*, 39(3), 530–544.

Mead, Nicole, Roy F. Baumeister, Tyler F. Stillman, Catherine D. Rawn, and Kathleen D. Vohs (2011), "Social Exclusion Causes People to Spend and Consume Strategically in the Service of Affiliation," *Journal of Consumer Research*, 37(5), 902–919.

Mont, Daniel (2007), "Measuring Disability Prevalence," The World Bank, retrieved online on April 5, 2014, at: http://siteresources.worldbank.org/DISABILITY/Resources/Data/MontPrevalence.pdf.

Nishii, Lisa H. (2013), "The Benefits of Climate for Inclusion for Gender-Diverse Groups," *Academy of Management Journal*, 56(6), 1754–1774.

O'Grady, A., P. Pleasence, N.J. Balmer , A.Buck and H. Genn (2004) "Disability, Social Exclusion and the Consequential Experience of Justiciable Problems," *Disability & Society*, 19(3), 259–272.

Oliver, Michael (1983), *Social Work with Disabled People*, Basingstoke: Macmillan.

Oliver, Michael (1990), *The Politics of Disablement: A Sociological Approach*. New York: St. Martin's Press.

Oliver, Michael (2013), "The Social Model of Disability: Thirty Years On," *Disability & Society*, 28(7), 1024–1026.

Park, C. Whan, Robert W. Hughes, Vinod Thukral, and Roberto Friedmann (1981), "Consumers' Decision Plans and Subsequent Choice Behavior," *Journal of Marketing*, 45(2), 33–47.

Pavia, Teresa M. (2014) "Vulnerability and Physical, Cognitive, and Behavioral Impairment," *Journal of Macromarketing*, 34(4), 471–485.

Pavia, Teresa M. and Marlys J. Mason (2012), "Inclusion, Exclusion and Identity in the Consumption of Families Living with Childhood Disability," *Consumption Markets & Culture*, 15(1), 87–115.

Piacentini, Maria, Sally Hibbert, and Al-Dajani (2001), "Diversity in Deprivation: Exploring the Grocery Shopping Behaviour of Disadvantaged Consumers," *The International Review of Retail, Distribution and Consumer Research*, 11(2), 141–158.

Piacentini, Maria, Sally Hibbert, and Margaret K. Hogg (2013), "Consumer Resource Integration Amongst Vulnerable Consumers: Care Leavers in Transition to Independent Living," *Journal of Marketing Management*, 30(1/2), 201–219.

Rosenthal, O. and R.H. Phillips (1997), *Coping with Color-Blindness*, Garden City Park, NY: Avery Publishing Group.

Wan, Echo Wen, Jing Xu, and Ying Ding (2014), "To Be or Not to Be Unique? The Effect of Social Exclusion on Consumer Choice," *Journal of Consumer Research*, 40(6), 1109–1122.

Williams, Kipling D. (2001), *Ostracism: The Power of Silence*, New York: Guilford.

Williams, Kipling D. (2007), "Ostracism," *Annual Review of Psychology*, 58 (April), 425–452.

Woodliffe, Lucy (2007), "An Empirical Re-evaluation of Consumer Disadvantage," *International Revue of Retail, Consumer, and Distribution Research*, 12(1), 1–21.

UPIAS (1976), *Fundamental Principles of Disability*, London, Union of the Physically Impaired Against Segregation.

Zadro, L., K.D. Williams, and R. Richardson (2004), "How Low Can You Go? Ostracism by a Computer Lowers Belonging, Control, Self-esteem and Meaningful Existence," *Journal of Experimental Social Psychology*, 40, 560–567.

Part IV

Consumer vulnerability, poverty and exclusion

14 Towards an understanding of religion-related vulnerability in consumer society

Aliakbar Jafari

Introduction

Religion is significantly understudied in consumer vulnerability discourses and the limited existing work lacks conceptual clarity and relevance to the broader debates on the status of religious change in contemporary society. This essay is an attempt to address this oversight by (1) delineating how and why discussions of religion relate to the issues of vulnerability in consumer society; (2) problematising the notion of religion-based vulnerability; and (3) setting forth a case towards conceptualising this type of vulnerability. My core argument is that such vulnerability should be understood primarily against the macro environmental factors that impact public perceptions of and engagement with religion and religiosity. I will develop my argument in the following manner: first, I will clarify why religion matters to the subject of consumer vulnerability and set forth some anecdotal evidence to guide the discussion. Next, I will provide an overview of the key theoretical debates on the status of religion and religiosity in society. This should shed light on the prevailing trends in the landscape of religion and their underlying forces. In light of these, I will then discuss how perceptions of and engagement with religion can cause or influence vulnerability. I will conclude by highlighting some areas for further conceptualisation and empirical research.

Religion matters

Taken as either a 'social construction' (Durkheim 1915 [1912]) or a 'transcendental reality' (Polanyi 2001 [1944]), religion matters. It matters not because having or not having one determines a human's destiny in Paradise or Hell in the world hereafter – 'there' – but because people's perceptions of religion influence their very worldly life in the 'here' and now. In everyday life situations (e.g. school, marketplace, work, and family and friends' networks) individuals' religious orientations impact their self-image (Cimino and Smith 2007, 2011), perceptions towards and by others (Baumann 1999), and multiple interactions with the world around them (Beck 2010; Jafari et al. 2014). Religion matters also because having or not having one does not result in a clear-cut divide between the two groups of believers and non-believers or the majority and the minority. The seeds of divide keep multiplying as being and not being a believer become equally problematic in the social reality of life. While those who have one face the questions (and sometimes severe criticisms posed by both non-believers and believers of other religions or sects) of what religion they have, why they have it, and how they practise it (Modood 2005; Kitcher 2011; Jafari and Süerdem 2012), those without one either proactively tend to form their own religion of 'belief in no religion' (Calhoun et al. 2011; Smith 2011) or passively fall prey to the accusations of blasphemy (Luckmann 1967).

Such issues of religious discrepancies are not new: they have historically existed in human societies (see Amarasingam 2010; Sauer 2003). But the increasing presence of such divergences in public debate (Amarasingam 2010; Kitcher 2011; Wheeler 2013) and the new vulnerabilities they may impose on different members of society (Pechmann et al., 2011; Jafari et al., 2014) necessitate systematic examination of religion as a priority in marketing and consumer behaviour research agendas on vulnerability. This is particularly important because consumer vulnerability on the basis of religious orientation, affiliation, perception and experience has remained significantly understudied, both empirically and conceptually.

Even the limited existing studies – e.g. Macchiette and Roy's (1994) reference to advertising in the religious context of the United States; Linh and Bouchon's (2013) discussion of Muslim tourists' food consumption; Broderick et al.'s (2011) mention of religious consumers' vulnerability in multicultural marketplaces – barely clarify the nature of religion-related vulnerability; neither do they explain how and why such vulnerability arises. On the other hand, as generally conceptualised in the broad context of social research, the nexus of religion and at-risk or vulnerable individuals has remained largely at the level of describing group stereotypes and social inclusion/exclusion in multi-ethnic/cultural societies (see Bhargava 2004 for a summary) without documenting how religion-related issues may actually cause or influence consumer vulnerability and how they theoretically sit in the debates on religion and religiosity.

Yet, in the absence of solid empirical investigations, anecdotal evidence indicates that, as members of an 'increasingly dynamic' consumer society (Gauthier and Martikainen 2013), people can experience or report different types of vulnerability in relation to their religious orientations, beliefs and sensibilities. This, however, does not mean that experiencing vulnerability is limited only to those who are religious; various groups of people (e.g. less religious, irreligious and anti-religious) may also be subject to experiencing different forms and degrees of vulnerability. Here I use the term 'experience' deliberately and emphatically because, as I will explain later in this manuscript, religion-related vulnerability should be seen and studied from the perspective of those who experience it. Otherwise, as Karpov (2010) also implies, detachment from the religious experiences of the masses will not lead to the generation of just and progressive knowledge.

In order to clarify my own position as a researcher and in the interest of putting forward a logical proposition and critical analysis, I should emphasise that in this essay I do not intend to defend religion. Religion does not need my defence; the history of religion is as old as human existence and the ongoing heated debate on religion is a strong indicator of the prevailing influence of religion in social life. Neither do I mean to support or justify irreligious and anti-religious ideologies and movements. In this respect, I rather tend to agree with Polanyi (2001 [1944]) that society has the capability to (re)construct itself through creating a balance between different, and sometimes opposing, forces (e.g. secular and religious). Here, my proposition is simply but essentially a step forward towards understanding 'what is actually going on in society that requires empirical and systematic investigations?'

Setting forth the examples

During the past few years, when some churches in Wellington, Leeds and Glasgow (amongst other cities in the UK and the western hemisphere) were converted into bars, restaurants and nightclubs, there was hopeless anger felt by Christian authorities (e.g. the Vatican) (Squires 2009) and some people whose religious sentiments were hurt because a sacred place had been transformed into an entertainment hub. Apart from Christian activists – some of whom stood outside churches converted in this way holding placards with religious mottos – some others (e.g. those who would call themselves 'spiritual' but not religious and those who believed in other religions such as Islam, Judaism and Buddhism) also felt that what was happening was 'disappointing', 'immoral', 'insulting', 'shameful', 'disgusting' and 'hurting the feelings of others' – remembering the exact words of people I have talked to during these years. Hurting feelings, however, as other contributions in this book would indicate, may be seen as a case of experiencing emotional vulnerability.

There are different examples too. The advertising industry generates media contents (e.g. commercial advertisements and images) that are perceived as 'offensive' by different religious groups. For example, in 2013, a court case opened against Indian cricket team captain's (Mahendra Singh Dhoni) 'posing for an advertisement in a business magazine as Lord Vishnu holding several things including a shoe in his hands' (*The Times of India* 2013). In 2011, one of Phones 4U's mobile phone advertisement 'featuring an illustration of Jesus winking and giving a thumbs-up' was banned by the Advertising Standards Authority (ASA) for being 'disrespectful' to the Christian faith (BBC.co.uk 2011). The emphasis of the ASA (2013) and the Committees of Advertising Practice (CAP) (2014) on the sensitivity of organisations to religious issues itself demonstrates the importance of avoiding offence and harm to society. In a different case, in 1997, Nike had to 'recall a range of sports shoes carrying a logo that offended Muslims in America' (Jury 1997). The marketing (pedagogical) literature (e.g. Fam et al. 2004; Mohamed and Daud 2012; Rosenbaum et al. 2013) is also full of instructions and case studies that alert (to-be) marketers on developing appropriate strategies (e.g. communications, packaging, products and services, and distribution) that would take religious issues seriously into consideration. These also testify to the fact that insensitivity to religious issues can have serious negative consequences.

During 2009/10, Domino's Pizza '*halal* only menu' raised criticisms and caused offence to those who did not want to eat *halal* food and wanted their peperoni back (Wilkes 2009; *The Telegraph* 2010). In 2012, Lord Ahmet's (a Muslim British member of parliament) request for *halal* meat at Westminster Palace's restaurant was rejected because 'many of his non-Muslim colleagues' would see the *halal* process (slitting an animal's throat without first stunning it) as offensive (Hastings 2012). In 2014, a British tourist was arrested for 'hurting others' religious feelings' with her Buddha tattoo and deported from Sri Lanka. For the readers of this essay it is also really worth spending some time to browse the Boycott Halal (2014) website (www.boycotthalal.com), where a host of videos, images and narratives echo anti-Islamic views. This website is probably the most tangible justification for my rationale in this paper: under-standing religion-related behaviours and experiences (including vulnerability) needs a deep understanding of the macro dynamics that shape not only such behaviours but also the overall status of religion itself.

Towards a conceptualisation

In all the above-mentioned scenarios, where there are indicators of vulner-ability it is difficult to differentiate between the offender and the offended or determine who is and who is not vulnerable. Seen from different perspectives, there is a thin, or no, line between the two sides of the argument. The rationale of those who claim that they have been offended may be seen as illogical or even offensive by those who are perceived as offender(s), and vice-versa. These examples, which often dominate the public domain (e.g. media), need to be systematically investigated in consumer society. Investigation of such experiences or perceptions of vulnerability, however, needs an in-depth understanding of various movements (i.e. religious, irreligious and anti-religious) that either already exist or are emerging in contemporary society, together with their theoretical explanations.

Religion in contemporary society

Discussions about religion predominantly centre on whether religion is declining, resurging or expanding in society. There are many dimensions to this debate, but a review of the extant literature reveals three main theoretical camps. What is important is the relevance of these debates to the 'forces' that influence the status of religion and religiosity in society. Given the space constraints of this short manuscript, I should stress that what follows is only a customised over-view of these discussions to serve the purpose of the essay and is not by any means intended to represent an exhaustive analysis of the sociological accounts of religion.

The secularisation thesis

The secularisation thesis is not uniform as it encompasses a number of different opinions (see Casanova 1994; Berger 1999; Norris and Inglehart 2004). How-ever, it generally asserts that religiosity is declining and that there is a universal shift from religious to non-religious values. The origins of this thesis are to be found in the work of the early social theorists (e.g. Karl Marx, Max Weber and Emile Durkheim) who argued that as modernisation progresses, the degree of religiosity decreases in society. Karpov (2010, p. 239) summarises Casanova's (1994) 'influential view of secularization as inclusive of three *unintegrated* (emphasis added) processes: differentiation of societal institutions from religious norms, decline of religious beliefs and practices, and privatization of religion (i.e. its marginalization form the public sphere)'.

The secularisation thesis is also closely related to the development of markets and consumer culture in modern society. As Gauthier and Martikainen (2013) demonstrate, the secularisation thesis denotes that market-generated consumerism gradually breaks down traditional religious norms as people immerse themselves in hedonism, materialism, and temporary and superficial relationships with market contents.

Modern advocates of the secularisation thesis often base their studies largely on the statistical analysis of church attendance in the west (implying a decrease) and also on the rise of secular movements (e.g. nationalist or liberal activism in religious countries and the secularisation of the forms of governance and nation-state relationships in Muslim countries such as Turkey) in the world. There are also those (e.g. Norris and Inglehart 2004) who believe that secu-larisation is indeed happening but not ubiquitously. For them, secularisation is a 'trend' that has been occurring 'most clearly among the most prosperous social sectors living in affluent and secure post-industrial nations' (Norris and Inglehart 2004, p. 5). Another key point that Norris and Inglehart's empirical study indi-cates is that religiosity is more evident in those strata of society that face existential risks; that is, those who feel vulnerable due to exposure to physical, societal and personal risks.

The de-secularisation thesis

As the term suggests, this thesis is the opposite of the secularisation process. As one of the key theorists of this stream, Berger (1999) rejects the thesis of secular-isation and argues that there has been a 'counter-secularisation' movement. As Karpov (2010, p. 234) indicates, de-secularisation theorists see 'the rise of Christianity in the "global South," the worldwide Islamic resurgence, the revitalization of religion in Russia and China, and other cases' as evidence for their argument. The de-secularisation thesis also differentiates between proper de-secularisation (i.e. counter-secularisation and religious resurgence) and the manifestations of religious resilience and vitality (i.e. survival and adaptation). Karpov's analysis of de-secularisation is particularly vital as he argues that the secularisation thesis fails to take into consideration some fundamental issues such as 'believing without belonging', 'material substratum' and 'cultural dynamics'.

By 'believing without belonging' he critiques the dominant statistical measurements of individuals' attendance in religious activities, such as churchgoing, and argues that not attending church does not mean that there is lack of belief in religion. Such individualistic self-reported surveys also ignore the importance of 'supra-individual' cultural and collective manifestations of religious presence. To explain this, he refers to Durkheim's (1915 [1912]) notion of 'material substratum' (the material and symbolic dimensions of religion in the cultural life; things such as artefacts) and asserts that the secularisation thesis needs to empirically study such manifestations. Last but not least, he uses Sorokin's (2006 [1957]) idea of 'cultural dynamics' to explain that in their everyday life situations people oscillate between 'ideational' (transcendental truth; e.g. religion) and 'sensate' (material, rational, and profane) realities of life.

Karpov then presents his definition of de-secularisation as follows:

> Desecularization is a process of counter-secularization, through which religion reasserts its societal influence in reaction to previous and/or co-occurring secularizing processes. The process manifests itself as a combination of some or all of the following tendencies: (a) a rapprochement between formerly secularized institutions and religious norms, both formal and informal; (b) a resurgence of religious beliefs and practices; (c) a return of religion to the public sphere ('de-privatization'); (d) a revival of religious content in a variety of culture's subsystems, including the arts, philosophy, and literature, and in a decline of the standing of science relative to a resurgent role of religion in world-construction and world-maintenance; (e) religion-related changes in society's substratum (including religiously inspired demographic changes, redefinition of territories and their populations along religious lines, reappearance of faith-related material structures, growing shares of religion-related goods in the overall economic market, and so on).
>
> (p. 250)

In sum, de-secularisation asserts that religion is actually making a return to social life. The resurgence of religion and religious movements (e.g. Russia and Eastern Europe, post-Revolutionary Iran, and some African countries) is used to support the thesis. Commodification of religious signs and symbols in society is also taken as a strong indicator of a counter-secularisation movement.

The religious reconfiguration thesis

This thesis doubts the usefulness of secularisation and de-secularisation theses, claiming that involvement in these debates will only deter researchers from understanding the real landscape of religion in everyday life situations. The gist of this stream can be seen in the work of Gauthier and Martikainen (2013), who propose that religion is neither disappearing nor returning; rather it is being reconfigured. The authors argue that 'the twin forces of neoliberalism and consumerism are penetrating and transforming the 'religious' worldwide, though in locally-embedded forms' (p. xv). Emphasising the importance of consumerism as a 'culturally dominant ethos' of modern society, Gauthier and Martikainen invite social theorists to 'understand and analyse a growing number of religio-cultural phenomena' through the lenses of the 'cultural phenomena that are born and have grown out of consumer cultures' (p. xv). In their view, seeing 'the world of religions through those lenses clarifies many discussions on contemporary religious change' (p. xv).

With reference to the concepts of 'liquid' and 'transient' (Bauman 1997, 2000; De Groot 2008; Beck 2010) realities of life, this thesis establishes that religion is not fading away; rather, it is the form of religiosity that is changing as people's needs are answered in different ways. Elsewhere (Jafari 2014) I have summarised Gauthier and Martikainen's notion of the changing form of reli-giosity as follows: 'in many societies (particularly western), there has been a shift towards 'more experiential rather than creed-based forms of religion', 'a move from a regime of orthodoxy towards a regime of orthopraxy' (p. 4).

> Other factors – such as the rapid growth of communication media, erosion of nation-state boundaries that historically described religion and prescribed religiosity, emergence of new forms of religiosities, and the transformation of traditional religious institutions – have collectively given rise to a homogenous form of religiosity that seeks salvation (not necessarily in the life hereafter but in this very worldly life and now) in different ways. The emergence of the notion of 'spiritual' (as an alternative for the 'religious') therefore signifies the rise of privatized experiences of religious authenticity.

This thesis recognises alternative religiosities and spiritualities as a form of religious reconfiguration which can theoretically explain the changing nature of religious practices and beliefs in secular and religious settings worldwide. On this basis, the notion of religiosity becomes a problematic term for labelling and measuring people's belief in religion, as is the case with the secularisation thesis.

Prevailing 'trends' and 'forces' in the landscape of religion

In light of the above theses and review of the extant literature, it could be argued that people's religious orientations happen somewhere between militant religionism (fighting the manifestations of the irreligious and anti-religious) (Ashouri 2011) and militant atheism (fighting the manifestations of the religious) (Kitcher 2011). These two extreme ideologies form two ends of an extensive spectrum that encompasses different types of religious, spiritual, secular and atheist tendencies (see Asad 2003, 2007; Roy 2004; Cimino and Smith 2007; Karpov 2010; Amarasingam 2010; Calhoun et al. 2011; Jafari and Süerdem 2012; Gauthier and Martikainen 2013). These trends are not always fixed; to borrow from Bauman (1997) and De Groot (2008), they are 'liquid' and 'transient'. That is, based on attitudinal and behavioural positions (e.g. conformism, innovation, ritualism, retreat and rebellion) (see Karpov 2010), people can switch between different religious trenches. The relationship between them is also an 'unintegrated' one (Karpov 2010) in the sense that the boundaries between them are loose and unstable.

These trends, however, are neither autonomous nor ubiquitous – that is, they are influenced by multiple forces and function differently in diverse socio-economic, cultural, and politico-ideological contexts. Karpov (2010) tactfully analyses such tendencies in the light of two mega forces of secularisation and de-secularisation that shape the two ends of the above-mentioned spectrum. These forces are either from 'above' (institutional) or from 'below' (the masses). From 'above', political and ideological regimes and actors (such as states, religious authorities and elite leaderships) that are equipped with sufficient institutional resources (e.g. finances, media, power, networks and education) can pursue their goal to either secularise or de-secularise society, either partially (i.e. at institutional level, such as central state) or entirely (i.e. public and private domains of life), depending on their goals and interests. From 'below', secularisation and de-secularisation movements occur on the part of the masses. For a variety of reasons (e.g. historical, political, economic and sociocultural), people may seek either a return to religion or the removal of religion from society. In this case, the masses are mobilised by activists such as religious (e.g. militant religionism) or anti-religious (e.g. militant atheism) individuals and groups. However, the success of these mass movements is highly dependent on access to resources: resourceless majority masses can be readily marginalised by better-resourced minority groups.

Vulnerability in consumer society

In contemporary society, opinions regarding religion are articulated by groups from both 'above' and 'below'. These opinions vary in terms of their logic, public acceptance and enforcement. Mass media (online and offline) and social networks in particular (Beck 2000) play a significant role in the way these forces receive, transmit, transform, interpret and react to such opinions in the global context. One's (un)deliberate (ir)religious opinion may be perceived as (un)pleasant to others. In societies where forces from 'above' purposefully and resourcefully pursue and accomplish secularisation or de-secularisation policies, there is little or no freedom for explicit ideological pluralism. In the presence of this form of governance, market contents (e.g. commodified symbolism, goods and services) and structures (e.g. governing bodies of the market and systems of production, promotion, distribution and disposition) can become potential sources of vulnerability for those who may (claim to) experience feelings of marginalisation, exclusion, stigma, disrespect, and so forth. In the absence of explicit freedom of expression, some people may embark on expressing their opinion through unorthodox engagement with the 'material substratum' (Durkheim 1915 [1912]) (e.g. underground anti-religious lifestyles in religious societies). That is, using religiously sensitive symbolic consumption and material manifestations to rebel against the dominant cultural order of society. An example of this can be underground lifestyles associated with witchcraft in Saudi Arabia (see Ali 2009).

Likewise, in societies where, in favour of freedom of expression, ideological pluralism is tolerated and/or encouraged, 'overwhelming emphasis on unlimited self-expression' (Karpov 2010, p. 243), verbally and/or through 'material substratum', can create the same issues of vulnerability (e.g. the case of Boycott Halal). Research on the sacred and the profane (see Jafari and Süerdem 2012 for a summary) has already established that markets and consumption practices can sacralise the profane and desacaralise the sacred. Nowadays, the increasingly endemic forces of neoliberalism are further loosening the boundaries between the sacred and profane. In such a landscape, where expressions of multiple opinions and life practices are allowed, new *rights* can be claimed by different groups (i.e. religious, irreligious, and anti-religious); for example, the right to practise one's belief through one's own work and life style. As such, even the most sophisticated monitoring bodies (e.g. the ASA, as described above) cannot convince all members of society. There will always be some people – somewhere in society, at some point in time – who claim to be experiencing vulnerability or discontent.

The anecdotal evidence I outlined earlier should be analysed within this framework. Why does a magazine image create so much anxiety in public? Why does an individual's tattoo receive so much media coverage? Why does a simple request for *halal* food at work become the subject of political debate? Why does the inclusion of some groups in a market result in others' exclusion from that market? It is wrong to assume that all of these are the creation of the media. The media is only a means. Stereotypes exist and so do issues of inclusion and exclusion, but these are not causes – they are consequences. Thus, research on vulnerability should endeavour to understand causes, the forces that pave the way for expressions and experiences of vulnerability.

Conclusion

In this essay I demonstrated that religion-related vulnerability is more complex than it might seem to be. Therefore, the phenomenon needs conceptualisation and empirical investigation. In particular, social researchers should study such vulnerability in the context of markets and consumption and in different socioeconomic, cultural and politico-ideological settings. As Karpov (2010) also contends, understanding 'material substratum' is essential to our analysis of the status of religion and the variety of forces that shape it. And 'material substratum' is most visible in the context of markets and consumption. It is also vital to understand: (1) whether such vulnerability is vicarious or actually lived out; (2) how, in everyday life situations, this kind of vulnerability comes into existence; (3) whether perceptions of religion and religiosity influence it; and (4) the forces and mechanisms that create or accelerate it.

References

Ali, A.J. (2009) 'Conducting Business in Saudi Arabia: A Brief for International Managers', *Global Business and Organizational Excellence*, 28, 6, pp. 64–84.

Amarasingam, A. (2010) *Religion and the New Atheism: A Critical Appraisal*. Leiden: Brill Academic Publishers.

Asad, T. (2003) *Formations of the Secular: Christianity, Islam, Modernity (Cultural Memory in the Present)*. Stanford, CA: Stanford University Press.

Asad, T. (2007) *On Suicide Bombing*. New York: Columbia University Press.

Ashouri, D. (2011) 'Creeping Secularism', *Comparative Studies of South Asia, Africa and the Middle East*, 31,1, pp. 46–52.

Baumann, G. (1999) *The Multicultural Riddle: Rethinking National, Ethnic and Religious Identities*. New York: Routledge.

Bauman, Z. (ed.) (1997) *Postmodernity and Its Discontents*. Oxford: Blackwell.

Bauman, Z. (2000) *Liquid Modernity*. Cambridge: Polity.

BBC.co.uk (2011) 'Phones 4U mobile phone Jesus advert banned', *BBC News*, 7 September. Available at: http://www.bbc.co.uk/news/business-14815616 (accessed 10 May 2014).

Beck, U. (2000) *What is Globalization?* Cambridge: Polity Press.

Beck, U. (2010) *A God of One's Own: Religion's Capacity for Peace and Potential for Violence*. Cambridge: Polity.

Berger, P.L. (ed.) (1999) *The Desecularization of the World: Resurgent Religion and World Politics*. Grand Rapids: William B. Eerdmans Publishing Company.

Bhargava, R. (2004) *Inclusion and Exclusion in South Asia: The Role of Religion*. United Nations Human Development Programme Report. Available at: http://hdr.undp. org/sites/default/files/hdr2004_rajeev_bhargava.pdf (accessed 11 May 2014).

Boycott Halal (2014) http://www.boycotthalal.com/ (accessed 11 May 2014).

Broderick, A.J., Demangeot, C., Adkins, N.R., Ferguson, N.S., Henderson, G.R., Johnson, G., Kipnis, E., Mandiberg, J.M., Mueller, R.D., Pullig, C., Roy, A. and Zúñiga, M.A. (2011) 'Consumer Empowerment in Multicultural Marketplaces: Navigating Multicultural Identities to Reduce Consumer Vulnerability', *Journal of Research for Consumers*, 19 (January), pp. 1–13.

Calhoun, C., Juergensmeyer, M. and VanAntwerpen, J. (2011) *Rethinking Secularism*. New York: Oxford University Press.

Casanova, J. (1994) *Public Religions in the Modern World*. Chicago: University of Chicago Press.

Cimino, R. and Smith, C. (2007) 'Secular Humanism and Atheism beyond Progressive Secularism', *Sociology of Religion*, 68, 4, pp. 407–424.

Cimino, R. and Smith, C. (2011) 'The New Atheism and the Formation of the Imagined Secularist Community', *Journal of Media and Religion*, 10, 1, pp. 24–38.

De Groot, C.N. (2008) 'Three Types of Liquid Religion', *Implicit Religion*, 11, 3, pp. 277–296.

Durkheim, E. (1915 [1912]) *The Elementary Forms of Religious Life*, trans. J.W. Swain. New York: Free Press.

Fam, K.S., Waller, D.S. and Erdogan, B.Z. (2004) 'The Influence of Religion on Attitudes Towards the Advertising of Controversial Products', *European Journal of Marketing*, 38, 5/6, pp. 537–555.

Gauthier, F. and Martikainen, T. (eds), (2013) *Religion in Consumer Society: Brands, Consumer and Markets*. Farnham, UK: Ashgate Publishing Limited.

Hastings, C. (2012) 'We won't eat halal meat, say MPs and peers who reject demands to serve it at Westminster', *Daily Mail*, 1 January. Available at: http://www.dailymail.co.uk/news/article-2080805/We-wont-eat-halal-meat-say-MPs-peers-reject-demands-serve-Westminster.html (accessed 11 May 2014).

Jafari, A. (2014) 'Review of *Religion in Consumer Society: Brands, Consumers and Markets* by François Gauthier and Tuomas Martikainen', *Consumption, Markets & Culture*, 17, 6, pp. 612–618.

Jafari, A. and Süerdem, A. (2012) 'An Analysis of Material Consumption Culture in the Moslem World', *Marketing Theory*, 12, 1, pp. 59–77.

Jafari, A., Özhan Dedeoğlu, A., Regany, F., Üstündağli, E. and Batat, W. (2014) 'Rethinking Religion in the Context of Ethnicity and Wellbeing', *Marketing Theory*. DOI: 10.1177/1470593114553329.

Jury, L. (1997) 'Nike to trash trainers that offended Islam', *The Independent*, 25 June. Available at: http://www.independent.co.uk/news/nike-to-trash-trainers-that-offended-islam-1257776.html (accessed 10 May 2014).

Karpov, V. (2010) 'Desecularization: A Conceptual Framework', *Journal of Church and State*, 52, 2, pp. 232–270.

Kitcher, P. (2011) 'Militant Modern Atheism', *Journal of Applied Philosophy*, 28, 1, pp. 1–13.

Linh, H.H. and Bouchon, F. (2013) 'The Relationship between Food Constraints and Destination Choice of Malaysian Muslim Travellers', *Asia-Pacific Journal of Innovation in Hospitality and Tourism*, 2, 1, pp. 69–86.

Luckmann, T. (1967) *The Invisible Religion: The Problem of Religion in Modern Societies*. New York: Macmillan.

Macchiette, B. and Roy, A. (1994) 'Sensitive Groups and Social Issues: Are You Marketing Correct?', *Journal of Consumer Marketing*, 11, 4, pp. 55–64.

Modood, T. (2005) *Multicultural Politics: Racism, Ethnicity and Muslims in Britain*. Edinburgh: Edinburgh University Press.

Mohamed, R.N. and Daud, N.M. (2012) 'The Impact of Religious Sensitivity on Brand Trust, Equity and Values of Fast Food Industry in Malaysia', *Business Strategy Series*, 13, 1, pp. 21–30.

Norris, P. and Inglehart, R. (2004) *Sacred and Secular: Religion and Politics Worldwide*. New York: Cambridge University Press.

Pechmann, C., Moore, E.S., Andreasen, A.R., Connell, P.M., Freeman, D., Gardner, M.P., Heisley, D., Lefebvre, R.C., Pirouz, D.M. and Soster, R.L. (2011) 'Navigating the Central Tensions in Research on At-Risk Consumers: Challenges and Opportunities', *Journal of Public Policy & Marketing*, 30, 1, pp. 23–30.

Polanyi, K. (2001 [1944]) *The Great Transformation: The Political and Economic Origins of Our Time*. Boston, MA: Beacon Press.

Rosenbaum, M.S., Moraru, I., and Labrecque, L.I. (2013) 'A Multicultural Service Sensitivity Exercise for Marketing Students', *Journal of Marketing Education*, 35, 1, pp. 5–17.

Roy, O. (2004) *Globalized Islam*. New York: Columbia University Press.

Sauer, E. (2003) *The Archaeology of Religious Hatred in the Roman and Early Medieval World*. Stroud, UK: The History Press Ltd.

Smith, J.M. (2011) 'Becoming an Atheist in America: Constructing Identity and Meaning from the Rejection of Theism', *Sociology of Religion*, 72, 2, pp. 215–237.

Sorokin, P. (2006 [1957]) *Social and Cultural Dynamics: A Study of Change in Major Systems of Art, Truth, Ethics, Law, and Social Relationships*. New Brunswick: Transaction Publishers.

Squires, N. (2009) 'Vatican condemns "immoral" church conversions', *The Telegraph*, 27 November. Available at: http://www.telegraph.co.uk/news/worldnews/europe/vaticancityandholysee/6670813/Vatican-condemns-immoral-church-conversions.html (accessed 11 May 2014).

The Advertising Standards Authority (ASA) (2013) *Public Perceptions of Harm and Offence in UK Advertising*. Available at: http://www.asa.org.uk/~/media/Files/ASA/Misc/ASAHarmOffenceReport.ashx (accessed 10 May 2014).

The Committees of Advertising Practice (CAP) (2014) *Religious Offence*. Available at: http://www.cap.org.uk/~/media/Files/CAP/Help%20notes%20new/religious_offence.ashx (accessed 12 May 2014).

The Telegraph (2010) 'Domino's Pizza scraps halal menu', 16 August. Available at: http://www.telegraph.co.uk/foodanddrink/foodanddrinknews/7946771/Dominos-Pizza-scraps-halal-menu.html (accessed 11 May 2014).

The Times of India (2013) 'Case against Dhoni for "hurting" religious sentiments'. 6 May. Available at: http://timesofindia.indiatimes.com/sports/off-the-field/Case-against-Dhoni-for-hurting-religious-sentiments/articleshow/19912916.cms (accessed 10 May 2014).

Wheeler, B. (2013) 'What happens at an atheist church?', *BBC News Magazine*, 4 February. Available at: http://www.bbc.co.uk/news/magazine-21319945 (accessed 14 May 2014).

Wilkes, D. (2009) 'The Domino's branch where you can't get a pepperoni pizza – because they only do halal', *Daily Mail*, 12 February. Available at: http://www.dailymail.co.uk/news/article-1142022/The-Dominos-branch-pepperoni-pizza–halal.html (accessed 11 May 2014).

15 Descent into financial difficulty and the role of consumer credit

Andrea Finney

Introduction

In the post-financial crisis environment of the late 2000s and early 2010s, UK household finances came under increasing pressure. This emerged from a deep and prolonged recession in 2008/9, rising unemployment and declining earnings (Office for Budget Responsibility, 2012). Inflation climbed to at least twice the Bank of England's target rate of 2 per cent in most months from mid-2008 onwards (Office for National Statistics, 2013). Meanwhile, the stock market crashed and the availability of credit to consumers was constricted (Office for National Statistics, 2012). The cut in the Bank of England base rate to an unprecedented low of 0.50 per cent in March 2009 (Bank of England, 2013) was the only source of reprieve for consumers with commercial borrowing, albeit creating problems for when the rates eventually rise (Whittaker, 2013).

The squeeze on living standards is now known to be longer and deeper than previously expected, and it is likely that 'an already difficult situation will get worse before it gets better' (Whittaker, 2013, p3). It is in the context of these straitened times that increased attention has turned to the ability of consumers – especially those from lower-income households, which have felt the squeeze the most (Bunn et al., 2012) – to make ends meet (Hirsch, 2013). In turn, this brings a sharper focus to bear on households' vulnerability to financial difficulties.

This paper considers households' vulnerability to financial difficulties in two substantive ways. First, it briefly examines evidence of the main factors that contribute to households' descent into financial difficulty in the context of the recent economic climate. Second, it explores the role played by non-mortgage borrowing in this process, considering how credit use and access to credit may contribute to or compound financial difficulty. It does so exclusively from the perspective of the consumer drawing on insights from recent qualitative research, the main focus of which was on low- or lower-income households. The focus on households – defined here broadly as a person living alone or a couple or a family with children occupying the same address – reflects a tendency for resources within households to be pooled to a greater or lesser extent.

Defining financial difficulty

Financial difficulty is referred to in the empirical and policy literature as being interchangeable with over-indebtedness. Over-indebtedness has been defined in research for the European Commission as the situation in which *a household cannot meet all of its contracted financial commitments on a prolonged or persistent basis without reducing it below the minimum standard of living accepted within society* (Davydoff et al., 2008). At the sharp end, it is characterised by households falling into arrears on their credit and other financial commitments. But it also encompasses a broader range of households which, while keeping up with their commitments, nonetheless struggle greatly to do so, perhaps only by cutting back their spending to below minimum acceptable standards or relying on help from friends and family (Finney and Davies, 2011).

Importantly, financial difficulty can extend beyond difficulties with credit commitments to include difficulty meeting rent or mortgage payments, utility and telecommunication bills and other financial commitments (e.g. court fines and tax payments). It can occur in the absence of borrowing (e.g. Kempson, 2002; Pyykkö, 2013). Nonetheless, highly leveraged households remain a particular concern for government.[1]

Levels of consumer borrowing and financial difficulty in the UK

From 2011 into 2012, consumer (non-mortgage) borrowing in the UK stood at around £160,500 million. This represented a steady fall from a peak of £208,300 million at the start of the financial crisis, bringing household borrowing in line with levels last seen in June 2003.[2] Research has consistently shown that just under a half of households in the UK have outstanding consumer credit commitments at any time (e.g. Office for National Statistics, 2012), although the households concerned change over time (Kempson et al., 2004).

National data show that 49.2 per cent of households in Britain in 2008/10 had outstanding consumer borrowing, a slight increase from 48.2 per cent in 2006/08 (ibid.). The median amount owed by those with any was £3,200, up from £2,800. Taking into account any arrears households owed on household bills (and on credit commitments held), some 51.0 per cent of households had some form of financial liability. Again, this was up slightly from 49.9 per cent of households in 2006/08.

A survey for the Bank of England has separately shown that rates of self-reported financial difficulty increased into 2011 (Kamath et al., 2011): 7.5 per cent of respondents had fallen behind with some or many bills or credit commitments, compared with just 4.1 per cent the previous year. The study's authors suggest that the increase reflected rises in the price of essentials, including utility bills, rather than the cost of servicing borrowing; there was a decrease in the proportion of households reporting finding unsecured debt a burden.

To the extent that there is movement in and out of borrowing by households over time, there is movement in relation to financial difficulty. Following a sample of people from the most over-indebted households in 2006/08, Bryan and colleagues (2010) found tentative evidence of substantial drops a year later in the proportions with arrears on unsecured debts and household bills. However, those that remained in arrears had more extensive arrears.

Method

Three complementary studies undertaken in 2011 and 2012 are the primary source of evidence consulted in this chapter. All involved qualitative research methods and focussed on people of working age living in households with low or lower (e.g. below median) incomes.

Facing the Squeeze

In *Facing the Squeeze*, Finney and Davies (2011) explored the impact of the recent economic climate on adults of working age living in households with a low (below 70 per cent median; n=13) or low-to-middle (90 per cent median to median; 17) income. Thirty depth interviews were undertaken in Bristol in summer 2011. By design, all participants were aged 18 to 55, were using one or more consumer credit commitments, and self-reported keeping up with all household bills and other commitments. The sample design also ensured a mix of participants by gender, age and employment status, household composition and housing tenure. Further provision was made to ensure that a broad range of financial situations were represented by recruiting participants from households with (13) and without (17) major drops in income in the last year. Participants received £30 in shopping vouchers.

Although participants self-reported keeping up with their bills and commitments, it emerged during the research that a few were in some degree of financial difficulty. Others were stretched financially, and even those who were managing reasonably comfortably were mostly 'feeling the pinch'.

Debt Advice Clients

Debt Advice Clients (Collard et al., 2012) focussed on the experiences of people who had sought debt advice from StepChange Debt Charity, a national provider of free-to-client independent debt advice. The scope of the study was on people living in working households (those with at least one earner). The average monthly income of all working households helped by StepChange in 2012 was £18,000 per year (compared with a national median income of £22,204 for a two adult household without children in 2011/12; Alzubaidi et al., 2013). An initial sample of 2000 eligible clients was contacted by StepChange inviting them to participate in the study. Of those who then consented to their details being passed to the research team, 20 were purposively selected to represent a range of people in their twenties to their sixties living in single adult and couple households with and without children. They also comprised equal numbers of men and women and those living in rented and mortgaged homes. Participants each received £20.

Undertaken in three locations across England (Reading/Slough, Birmingham and Manchester) in autumn 2012, each interview explored how vulnerability to debt problems built up over time, tipping points into unmanageable debt and coping strategies used. When participants first contacted StepChange, most of them had significant levels of unsecured debt, in many cases totalling over £40,000.

Early Intervention

Early Intervention (Collard, 2011) involved 36 depth interviews and four focus groups with customers of Barclays' Customer Review Team (CRT). The CRT offers pre-arrears support to customers of personal unsecured loans or overdrafts who are showing signs of financial difficulty. Based on Barclays' administrative data, four in ten of all CRT customers had a personal annual income of less than £12,000 per year and a further five in ten had incomes of up to £24,000. Participants interviewed in depth comprised a mix of customers who were contacted by the CRT (n=13) and those who, conversely, had contacted the CRT themselves for help or advice (26). In age they ranged between their twenties and their sixties and they comprised men (17) and women (19) living in a mixture of housing tenures and household compositions. Two-thirds of them (24) were working at the time of their interview for 16 or more hours per week. The depth interviews were conducted face-to-face in March and April 2011, in Bristol, Cardiff, Oxford, Reading and Twickenham. The focus groups – comprising CRT clients recruited along similar criteria – were conducted in May 2011 in London and Manchester. Participants each received £50.

The research explored the causes of financial difficulties among CRT customers and the impact of such difficulties on them and their families.

Methodological considerations

The particular strength of qualitative research is that it enables the experiences, attitudes and perceptions of consumers to be explored from the consumer's own perspective. It allows emergent issues to be explored interactively with participants and sees social life in context and in relation to processes (Snape and Spencer, 2003). In drawing on three qualitative studies, undertaken at a similar time and in a particular economic context, a greater breadth and depth of insight can be found than from one study alone. Together, the three studies represent consumers at different stages of financial difficulties and with different types and levels of intervention (if any) received.

How do low-income households fall into financial difficulty?

A long-standing body of research has found that no simple, single cause of over-indebtedness exists (Davydoff et al. 2008). Instead, underlying risk factors such as a low-income work in combination with trigger events, such as a change in circumstances, to bring about consumer financial difficulty. Other contributors, such as poor money management and over-borrowing, can compound the problems households face, the relative contribution of each factor tending to change depending on the economic context.

When change leads to difficulty

Facing the Squeeze explored the ways in which households on lower incomes had been affected by the post-recession macroeconomic situation. Although the study had a particular focus on changes in the last 12 months, longer-term changes of up to two or three years previously continued to impact on households. Where households had experienced a drop in income, these included work-related income drops imposed upon them, principally through job loss, reduced hours and pay cuts and increasingly infrequent employment. In other instances it arose through the departure of an income-earner from the household, the loss of child maintenance payments or changes in eligibility for social security benefits or tax credits.

Increased expenditure was also a factor for *Facing the Squeeze* households, whether from the costs of an expanding family, increased rent, or the sustained rise in the cost of living. Some participants even identified the cost of living as the foremost change they had experienced:

> Even if you are cutting down you're probably spending the same amount as you were a year ago.
>
> (*Facing the Squeeze*; Man, early thirties)

One woman estimated that the effect of inflation on her family's grocery shop alone was £100 each month.

However, even those households that were markedly worse off as a result of major events could continue to manage relatively comfortably so long as they were limited to a reduction in hours and a change in household structure or the increase in the cost of living. Where households had been affected by multiple drops in income, one compounding the other, they were generally in some degree of financial strain. And what seemed to distinguish the households in actual difficulty was lack of any permanent or full-time work in the household. One man with children, whose wife was unable to work due to long-term illness, had been made redundant without pay 12 months earlier when his employer went into liquidation; in the previous six months his pay cheques had routinely bounced. Notably, the impact of the increased cost of living was hidden from view for these householders because of the other major challenges they faced.

While *Facing the Squeeze* highlighted the lasting impact of longer-term changes on households, *Early Intervention* identified how a gradual decline in income made it difficult for people to determine when their households' problems had really started. Instead, their money worries had accumulated over a protracted period of time, as borne out by participants in the other studies:

> I think it's a combination of not earning any more money, things going up and probably over spending when we didn't realise we were … . You expect to be able to live a basic lifestyle when you're working full-time without going over the top, without having to struggle.
>
> (*Facing the Squeeze*; Man, early thirties)

In turn, this was a new experience for them, bringing acute anxiety, which partly explains the difficulty some had in taking constructive action to address their money worries.

The role of credit in financial difficulty

While consumer credit is a legitimate tool for helping smooth out the ebbs and flows of income and expenditure, the use of consumer credit is an important factor in consumer vulnerability to financial difficulty. Research has shown, for example, that the more consumer credit commitments households have the more likely they are to become over-indebted (Berthoud and Kempson, 1992; Kempson et al., 2004). This is true even when taking into account other major contributors to financial difficulties, such as a drop in income. The use of consumer credit is therefore rather more complex than the economic utility of borrowing suggests.

The legacy of borrowing

UK households entered the financial crisis in 2007 with average total (non-mortgage) borrowing of £8,856 (Credit Action, 2007). Major income shocks, like those described above, can impact on households' ability to meet their consumer credit commitments accumulated in better times (Dearden et al., 2010; Green, 2012). *Facing the Squeeze* and *Early Intervention* found that when faced with a drop in earnings, some households borrowed more to bridge the gap between their income and expenditure.

Debt Advice Clients found that households continued to use credit to plug gaps left by income shocks for two main reasons. First, they believed their downturn in fortune was only temporary, so short-term use of credit to maintain existing lifestyles was easily justified. People were, however, over-optimistic about their ability to get back into employment or their salaries on returning to work:

> That's when the credit cards started going back up again, because I was then thinking, well long-term I can get, I can climb back up the ladder as I'd done previously and get to a point where I can clear them… it's next month's problem.
>
> (*Debt Advice Clients*; Woman, late thirties)

Second, some were compulsive spenders and were accustomed to using credit to fund this. Partly this materialised through comfort spending following a traumatic event, such as relationship breakdown, crime victimisation, or serious illness. In some instances these events had also resulted in a loss of income in their own right, which the use of credit again compensated for. Or it was driven by an underlying need to maintain a positive self-image or portray to others the impression of success:

> He [husband] felt it was so important that he had a Jag … then people would think he was successful.
>
> *(Debt Advice Clients*; Woman, late fifties)

Facing the Squeeze also identified a group characterised by impulsive spending. Although it was common for impulsive spenders to have reined in their spending in response to changes in their circumstances, their disposition towards spending nonetheless remained strong in many cases:

> My attitude hasn't really changed really, again if I had the money then I'd go back to spending it how I used to.
>
> *(Facing the Squeeze*; Man, early thirties)

In other words, over-spending was a pattern that would, in all likelihood, be repeated.

Debt Advice Clients and *Early Intervention* highlighted how some people's financial difficulties were *entirely* attributable to over-spending fuelled by credit use. Some of the initial borrowing *Debt Advice Clients* had accrued had built up during periods of work stability because either they expected their earning potential to increase more than it did, or they had over-estimated the spending power their existing incomes gave them; or they had over-spent on consumer goods and services out of a sense of self-worth and deserving.

Escalating credit use

Some participants in *Facing the Squeeze* had reduced the amounts they owed in commercial borrowing over the preceding 12 months. For some, this reflected a conscious decision to reduce their credit burden in response to or in anticipation of financial strain. The more typical picture, however, was one of increasing levels of indebtedness. Sometimes this reflected 'big ticket' purchases, but more often a gradual increase in the sums owed as a result of everyday expense. One participant, who owed around £25,000 in unsecured credit for example, perceived that about a half of this had accrued within the previous year, on petrol, parking and day-to-day living, after her husband had been forced to cut his hourly rate.

Facing the Squeeze participants expressed concern about this 'creeping debt', some feeling that they had in effect borrowed more than they could afford.

This related especially to the balances on revolving credit commitments: credit cards, overdrafts and store cards. While participants felt they had been using these commitments with the same frequency and for the same reasons as before, they had not been able to repay the balances to the same extent. Where this was predominantly credit card based, participant households were at least stretched financially if not over-indebted. Some whose balances had increased were resigned to the possibility that their level of borrowing would continue to escalate:

> We've probably run up, since Christmas, probably about nearly £4,000 on, just on petrol, different things like that, petrol, shopping … . I think we're just going to have to keep going the way we're going at the moment, just making sure things are paid on time.
>
> (*Facing the Squeeze*; Woman, early forties)

In some cases the gradual build up of borrowing had caused households to draw on lines of credit they preferred not to use, including those kept only for 'emergencies', and there was evidence of people over-stepping their 'personal limits', set below their actual credit limits. In one extreme case, it had meant turning to multiple credit and store cards and an overdraft that had previously been thought of as only for emergency use just to make ends meet.

Access to credit now and in the future

The use – and sometimes heavy use – of credit among *Facing the Squeeze* participants obscured the concern many participants had about their ability to access credit in the future. In keeping with the macroeconomic picture, there was a widespread perception that credit was now generally harder to access than it had been in previous years. Interviews were peppered with evidence of a heightened awareness of the importance of credit ratings and how household circumstances influenced access to and the cost of credit. This made people feel vulnerable about their situations.

The concern participants felt led some to self-constrain their access to credit. One had cancelled several unused credit cards; another had asked the bank to remove an overdraft facility. This extended to avoiding making new applications for credit for fear that a refusal would damage their credit history. However, the fear also led others to use high-cost credit because they perceived that they did not have a good credit rating or that this was easier to access than mainstream credit. Crucially, it also deterred people from seeking debt advice:

> I think we would [consider getting advice] but I don't want to rock the boat and go on payment plans … because if you write to them apparently they can freeze your interest and everything like that, but I'm worried in case it goes against the credit rating … because we need to keep the credit rating.
>
> (*Facing the Squeeze*; Woman, early forties)

Furthermore, it led some people to stockpile unused balances on revolving lines of credit. Many participants in *Facing the Squeeze* had unused credit available, ranging from as little as £100 on an overdraft to £5,000 or more on a credit card. Retaining unused balances, and in some cases whole facilities, reduced the need for people to apply for credit or to expect to have to do so in the near future, or run the risk of having their applications rejected when they needed to access credit the most. In reality, however, unused balances were not something everyone could rely on when they felt they needed to call on them: one participant found that her credit card provider substantially reduced the credit limit on her card just when she needed to call on it. Additionally, the dependence some participants had on credit to make ends meet or fund the lifestyle they desired had already led them to draw on one or more of these facilities in the previous year – as we saw above – against their better judgement.

Despite this, there was little objective evidence in *Facing the Squeeze* that lower-income credit users were 'credit-constrained'. Where participants had applied for credit in the previous year, most had been successful, even if they had found there to be more 'rigmarole' than previously, and it was not unusual for them to have been given a higher credit limit than they had requested.

From credit to debt

While people's concern and frustration at 'creeping balances' was evident, many *Facing the Squeeze* households were nonetheless meeting their minimum contracted credit payments. However, compounding the situation for some was the accrual of charges for late or missed payments. Where this was the case it related to the use of unauthorised overdrafts or direct debits that had 'bounced' due to lack of funds. This was echoed by participants in the other studies:

> It was the bank charges that were killing me. Sometimes I'd have 100 and odd pounds a month bank charges. Yeah and that every month added on top of it.
>
> (*Early Intervention*; Woman, early twenties)

Some had turned to sources of high-cost credit to avoid such charges. However, a separate study of high-cost credit users found that the use of payday loans in particular when struggling to make ends meet had ultimately only added to most consumers' difficulties (although it had enabled a few to stabilise and ease their situations, at least temporarily; Collard et al., 2013). The study also found that pawnbroking and payday loans were sometimes used as a substitute for revolving credit, including where people had exhausted all their existing lines of credit, but, with interest charges adding to people's overall debt, this only perpetuated the need to borrow. Some had been encouraged to take out repeat loans at the instigation of lenders.

In *Debt Advice Clients,* several 'signals' that households' borrowing had become unmanageable were identified. There was a clear tendency for *Debt Advice Clients* to have lost touch with the true extent of their indebtedness. They had little or no idea about the amounts they were accumulating and did not look across their commitments to consider the total amount they owed.

> I recognised that it was bad, but I thought it could get better … . Until you suddenly tot it all up and think, well we can sort that one out maybe but then gosh there's that one and the other one, so when you realise that, you know.
>
> (*Debt Advice Clients*: Woman, early fifties)

Instead, they preferred to focus on what they had to pay every month to each lender and felt they were managing their credit as long as they could pay at least the minimum contractual amount. They also focussed on the fact that they were keeping up with priority payments such as rent or mortgage. Some participants confessed to being in denial about their situation. People's continued over-optimism about their ability to repay their accruing debts was also pervasive.

One of the clearest signs that people had over-borrowed was the practice of using credit to repay credit. Credit cards were used to pay off other credit cards, balances were juggled between credit cards and overdrafts, or credit card balances were transferred to 0% deals. This reflected efforts to manage the debt and avoid charges for default or unauthorised overdraft use, or at least deflect attention from lenders:

> So you were taking cash out or doing whatever you could to kind of move the money, keep moving it around … and we were coming up with all sorts of ingenious ways to try and keep them [creditors] appeased.
>
> (*Debt Advice Clients*; Man, mid-thirties)

These strategies were mirrored in *Facing the Squeeze*, as was the consolidation of credit commitments. This can be a convenient way of organising debts into one payment. But those in vulnerable situations risk escalating their situation further if they do not take decisive action to curb further use of existing credit facilities. All *Debt Advice Clients* who had consolidated their debts had, without exception, started using credit again within a relatively short period when they were either sent a replacement credit card or were short of money:

> I didn't cut up the credit cards after I took the [debt consolidation] loans so and you know, after a couple of months, oh I'm a little bit short I haven't got enough for petrol this month so I'll start using one of the cards and then within six months that's it … all the cards are full again.
>
> (*Debt Advice Clients*; Woman, mid-thirties)

In effect, some lenders had been complicit in households' descent into difficulty by enabling an additional loan to be taken out at a time when customers were already struggling with debt or allowing unauthorised overdrafts to escalate:

> For some reason it [the authorised overdraft] allowed me to go over it and very irresponsibly I kind of took advantage of it and I went right overboard.
>
> (*Early Intervention*; Woman, late twenties)

Some participants had approached their creditors for help with their debts, but instead of being helped to reduce what they owed had been offered more credit. Equally, however, other participants had hidden the scale of their borrowing when consolidating their debts or asking for help from friends or family or kept one or more credit cards secret from a partner. In these cases, there was a tacit acknowledgement that their borrowing was out of control, even if they were unable or unwilling to admit that they could not resolve their situations themselves.

Discussion and conclusions

Although the primary function of borrowing is to ease disparities between income and expenditure, the evidence points to a clear, if nuanced, role of consumer credit in compounding households' vulnerability to financial difficulties. In large part this is not directly attributable to consumer over-borrowing but reflects the intersection of: a difficult economic context impacting on households; the legacy of a booming credit market and consumer culture; a mismatch between the supply of credit by lending institutions and consumer needs; and consumers' responses to changing situations.

Consumer vulnerability in the context of financial difficulty derives from all four of these sources. It partly reflects a determination or expectation that households remain self-sufficient and resolve their problems by themselves and remain 'below the parapet' in order to protect their future interests, both of which result in their isolation from the sources of potential help that exist. This also makes consumers vulnerable to systemic practices of lending – including in the over- and under-supply of credit – and debt management. Vulnerability is also partly realised through a poor awareness by consumers (and the frontline staff they come into contact with day to day) of the risk factors, triggers and signals of financial difficulty and the independent help and advice that is available. More broadly, it reflects the gradual contraction of state-based welfare and the financialisation of everyday life through the increased diversity, complexity, accessibility and immediacy of financial services provision.

A number of implications emerge from this evidence. There is a strong case for lenders to holistically oversee product design and operational practices and procedures to avoid the escalation of debt wherever possible. There is also a need for greater involvement from government and lenders (including via the new Financial Conduct Authority) in helping consumers recognise and respond to early signs of financial difficulty and prevent their situations spiralling. Consumers could benefit from the development of new tools that enable them to look across multiple forms of borrowing to see the totality of their borrowing and link directly to support to deal with unmanageable debt. Consumers also need a better understanding of the help and support they should expect from particular lenders as well as the short-, medium- and longer-term consequences of the action (and inaction) they take in relation to their credit use. More consistent communication to consumers of lending codes of practice – by both government and individual lenders – has a key role to play here. Moreover, lenders' contact with borrowers places them uniquely to intervene when consumers get into difficulty and signpost them to help manage their debts, whether provided internally or by independent debt-advice organisations. Pre-collections action by creditors is an area of growing activity, and one which might be facilitated further within the industry through the sharing of good practice and increased links with external advice organisations.

Notes

1 There is, for example, an All-Party Parliamentary Group on Debt and Personal Finance.
2 From the Bank of England 'Money and lending' interactive database, accessed July 2013: www.bankofengland.co.uk.

References

Alzubaidi, H, Carr, J, Councell, R and Johnson, G (2013) *Household below average income: an analysis of the income distribution 1994/95–2011/12.* Newport: Office for National Statistics.
Berthoud, R and Kempson, E (1992) *Credit and debt: the PSI report.* London: Policy Studies Institute.
Bryan, M, Taylor, M and Veliziotis, M (2010) *Over-indebtedness in Great Britain: an analysis using the Wealth and Assets Survey and Household Annual Debtors Survey.* London: Department for Business, Innovation and Skills.
Bunn, P, Le Roux, J, Johnson, R and McLeay, M (2012) 'Influences on household spending: evidence from the 2012 NMG Consulting Survey', *Bank of England Quarterly Bulletin* 4; pp. 332–342.
Collard, S (2011) *Understanding financial difficulty: exploring the opportunities for early intervention.* London: Barclays.
Collard, S, Finney, A and Davies, S (2012) *Working households' experiences of debt problems.* London: StepChange Debt Charity.
Collard, S, Finney, A and Kempson, E (2013) *The impact on business and consumers of a cap on the total cost of credit.* London: Department for Business, Innovation and Skills.
Credit Action (2007) *Debt facts and figures*, September. Accessed March 2014: http://themoneycharity.org.uk/media/september-2007.pdf.
Davydoff, D., Dessart, E, Naacke, G, Jentzsch, N, Figueira, F, Rothemund, M, Mueller, W, Kempson, E, Atkinson, A, Finney, A and Anderloni, L (2008) *Towards a common operational European definition of over-indebtedness.* Brussels: European Commission.

Dearden, C, Goode, J, Whitfield, G, and Cox, L (2010) *Credit and debt in low-income families*. York, UK: Joseph Rowntree Foundation.

Finney, A and Davies, S (2011) *Facing the Squeeze 2011: A qualitative study of household finances and access to credit*. London: Money Advice Trust.

Green, K (2012) *Life on a low income*. London: The Resolution Foundation.

Hirsh, D (2013) 'Will future tax cuts reach future working households?'. Briefing, April. London: The Resolution Foundation

Kamath, K, Reinold, K, Nielsen, M and Radia, A (2011) 'The financial position of British households: Evidence from the 2011 NMG Consulting survey', *Bank of England Quarterly Bulletin*, 4, pp. 305–318.

Kempson, E (2002) *Overindebtedness in Britain*. London: Department of Trade and Industry.

Kempson, E., McKay, S and Willits, M (2004) 'The characteristics of families in debt and the nature of indebtedness', *DWP Research Report 211*. Leeds: Corporate Document Service.

Office for Budget Responsibility (2012) *Economic and fiscal outlook, March 2012*. London: Office for Budget Responsibility.

Office for National Statistics (2012) 'Financial Wealth 2008/10', in *Wealth in Great Britain 2008/10*, Part II, Chapter 3. Newport: Office for National Statistics.

Office for National Statistics (2013) 'Consumer Price Inflation, June 2013', *ONS Statistical Bulletin*. Newport: Office for National Statistics.

Pyykkö, E (2013) in Chmelar, A (2013) 'Household debt and the European crisis', *ECRI Research Report 13*. Brussels: European Credit Research Institute.

Snape, D and Spencer, L (2003) 'The foundations of qualitative research', in J Ritchie and J Lewis (eds) *Qualitative Research Practice: a guide for social science students and researchers*. London: Sage.

Whittaker, M (2013) *Squeezed Britain 2013*. London: Foundation for Credit Counselling.

16 Poverty, shame and the vulnerable consumer

Elaine Chase and Robert Walker

This chapter illustrates how findings from research on the connection between poverty and shame (Walker 2014; Chase and Bantebya-Kyomuhendo 2014) connect with Baker et al.'s (2005) perception that people's lack of control and power within the 'market' place (understood broadly here) may be heightened by how others, those either in positions of authority and power or within more immediate social interactions, respond to them. Such 'consumer vulnerability' therefore stems from the fact that a) certain 'consumption goals' cannot be fulfilled, and b) the experience of failing to meet them affects personal and social perceptions of the self (Baker et al. 2005). Situated within the disciplines of social policy, sociology and anthropology, the study was executed without any real cognisance of the concept of the 'vulnerable consumer'. Yet post hoc interactions with scholars in marketing and related fields revealed that much of what had evolved from this work resonated with the idea of consumer vulnerability. After presenting evidence of how the 'vulnerable consumer', though not previously named as such, clearly emerges from this research, the chapter ends with some reflections on the links between these distinct bodies of work and the possibilities for disciplinary cross-over in terms of the implications of its findings.

The relevance of shame

Shame is a self-conscious emotion entailing a sense of low self-worth made with reference to one's own aspirations and the perceived expectations of others (Tangney et al. 2007). It is therefore, an inherently social emotion (Scheff 2000, 2003; Chase and Walker 2013). In the context of poverty, shame is important not only because it causes psychological pain (Ho et al. 2004) but because it is frequently experienced in situations over which individuals have no control and from which there is therefore no escape. Shame causes people to withdraw socially, erodes self-confidence and reduces human agency. Besides being internally felt, shame is also externally imposed by others, by society and inevitably by the structures, systems and policies with which people in poverty interact (Chase and Walker 2013). The complex relationship between poverty and shame

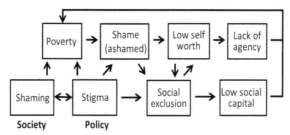

Figure 16.1 The poverty–shame nexus
Source: Walker 2014, 66.

and the role that shame might play in exacerbating poverty and undermining human agency, the 'poverty–shame nexus', is depicted in Figure 16.1.

Much of the evidence on poverty and shame comes from a study that explored Sen's idea (1983) that shame is universally associated with poverty. It was deliberately undertaken in settings that contrasted sharply in terms of socio-economic, cultural, political and policy profiles. They included urban Britain and urban and small-town Norway; rural India and Uganda; urban China; South Korea; and rural and urban Pakistan. The research was driven by two questions: first, was shame an essential part of the lived experience of poverty in each of these contexts; and second, if it was, what were the implications for anti-poverty policies? The work shifted the focus away from the measurement of poverty per se towards a greater emphasis on the psychosocial dimensions of poverty and their impact.

Cultural representations of the 'vulnerable consumer'

One can glimpse the cultural meaning of any complex phenomena by seeing them as *sensitising concepts* (Blumer 1969) and tracing their representation in literature, film and oral traditions (Coser 1963; Lewis et al. 2008; Sutherland and Felty 2010). Examining the depictions of 'poverty' and 'shame' in samples of these media from each of the seven countries (Chase and Bantebya-Kyomuhendo 2014) evoked a particular essence of the 'vulnerable consumer'.

The vulnerable consumer emerges prominently as someone who needs to maintain social standing and keep up appearances at all costs. Not having the necessary resources to meet such aspirations was a dilemma repeatedly faced by hard-up protagonists in film and literature across the different cultural contexts. In the Urdu short story, *Chothi ka jora*, an entire family conspires to spend beyond their means to impress a future son-in law (Choudhry 2014a). In the British film *The Full Monty* (Cattaneo 1997, cited in Chase et al. 2014), the character Gerald cannot face admitting to his wife that he's lost his job and keeps up the pretence of going to work every day for a full six months before she finds out. Similarly, the South Korean film, *The Day a Pig Fell into the Well* (1996, cited in Jo 2014), shows the characters becoming embroiled in a web of lies and deceit as they fabricate increasingly convoluted ways to hide their poverty. Likewise, across the samples of Norwegian literature, the pressure that women in particular feel to maintain appearances and avoid the label of poverty is a theme revisited over a hundred years. In the Chinese novel *A Pile of Wheat* (Tie 1986, cited in Yan 2014a) the protagonist goes so far as to offer a fellow villager the opportunity to sleep with his wife in exchange for a pair of Japanese boots.

Creative writers are well aware not only of the proneness of characters to feel inadequate about their impoverished circumstances but also of these characters' vulnerability to being ridiculed for their poverty in just about every social situation. In the Ugandan play *Wrinkled Faces* (Ssebanga 2010, cited in Bantebya-Kyomuhendo 2014a), the Isabiyre family is taunted daily because they have to ask others for salt. In the Indian film *Kanchivaram* (2008, cited in Pellissery and Mathew 2014a), Vengadam, despite his aspirations since childhood, fails to be the first person from his caste to marry a bride in a silk sari. As a result, on his wedding day he is taunted by his local community:

> **OLD LADY:** (taunting) Why is she in a cotton sari? Where is the silk sari? Since the age of five you've been singing to the whole village that when you marry, your bride will be in a silk sari, what happened? I thought you'd be marrying the lord's daughter.
> *VENGADAM doesn't respond, but puts his head down in shame.*
> **OLD LADY:** A silk weaver can only weave silk, not wear it.

At times, fictional characters are portrayed as 'shameless', either in the sense that degradation anaesthetises them to feeling any sense of shame or because they transgress social norms but refuse to acknowledge shame as society expects them to do. An example of the former scenario is the assertion of the Urdu poet Nazeer Akbarabadi (1740–1830) that 'The poor know no politeness or formality / They fall upon food with uninhibited alacrity / Risking their lives for a piece of loaf / And fighting like dogs over every bone' (cited in Choudhry 2014a). The British film *Riff Raff* (Loach 1991, cited in Chase et al. 2014) illustrates the second kind of shamelessness. In it the character Stevie, having fallen on hard times, steals a power drill from the building site where he is working and sells it on to someone in the pub during his lunch break.

The temporality of the 'vulnerable consumer'

Cultural media from some countries suggest that the 'vulnerable consumer' has become increasingly prominent over time. This was probably most clearly seen in the case of China and South Korea, countries which had historically rejected consumerism and wealth accumulation. Traditional Chinese society, for example, was embedded in the cultural values of Confucianism, Daoism and Buddhism, which nominally at least accommodate the existence of poverty without attaching shame to those who are unable to consume. Literature from the era of the Communist Revolution went further to vilify the wealthy and their propensity to over-consume while honouring the majority who had little or nothing. Fictional works from the post-reform period, however, appear to signal a shift in cultural norms towards appraising poverty and the associated inability to consume as something shameful in the context of the legitimisation of growing socio-economic disparity and the glorification of wealth (Yan 2014a). In South Korea, popular films trace the decline in values, strong during the 1970s, which tended to reject consumerism and portray the rich as greedy and corrupt. By the 2000s, films were portraying poverty as a legitimate consequence of personal weaknesses and the inability to succeed and consume within the context of new economic opportunities and social expectations of prosperity (Jo 2014). Proverbs from Uganda trace a narrative suggesting that in traditional times the 'vulnerable consumer' was less prominent than in contemporary society, probably because the cash economy was less developed and poverty was so widespread. Increasingly, in a society of growing wealth disparity, modern proverbs appear to celebrate the accrual of money and frown upon people's failure to become successful consumers (Bantebya-Kyomuhendo 2014b). In Norway too, pre-modern literature conjures the vulnerable consumer as a product of structural causes rather than individual inadequacies, thus minimising any associated shame or stigma. However, more modern literature (post the introduction of the welfare state) suggests that the inability to conform to society's consumption norms is in fact the result of personal failure to make the most of the opportunities created by an egalitarian state (Gubrium 2014). By contrast, literature in Britain, spanning a period of more than 170 years, suggests that the vulnerable consumer (in the sense of feeling unable to conform to society's norms of consumption and being exposed to criticism as a result) is a fairly constant construct throughout that time period.

The lived experiences of the 'vulnerable consumer'

Interviews with adults and children living in poverty revealed a strong synergy between fictional sketches of the vulnerable consumer and their daily struggle to fit within society's norms of consumption and the reality of people's lives (Chase and Bantebya-Kyomuhendo 2014). Comparing the analyses across these different worlds revealed that people had very similar consumption aspirations in their lives. They all needed enough food and the right type of food; they were all concerned with the type and quality of accommodation they had, whether it met the needs of their families and whether it was affordable; they all wanted to be in control of their lives financially and to be able to live without being indebted to others; and they all aspired to maintain the health and wellbeing of their families. Poverty and the lack of resources it trailed persistently undermined these aspirations and people repeatedly spoke of how they hated living in poverty and felt bad about themselves because of their circumstances.

Yet beyond what might be termed as basic consumption needs, the vulnerable consumer emerges as someone who is constantly pressurised into patterns and standards of consumption which are collectively generated rather than, as classic economic theory would have us believe (Keynes 1936), determined by purchasing power or income. People with limited resources are proactively compelled by society's norms into purchases likely to be beyond their means and, because of the potential and power of the shaming process, are constantly forced to weigh up the social costs of failing to adhere to these norms for financial reasons. Adults and children interviewed repeatedly signalled how they were surrounded by pressures to live up to these collective demands and patterns of consumption, whether within the family, the school or the wider community. Integral to all of their aspirations to step up to these pressures was the desire to feel good about themselves and to be appreciated by others.

The 'vulnerable consumer' emerged in two major senses. In the first sense people described lacking the necessary resources to procure the goods and services (consumables) to lead the lives they aspired to and to play the roles that they expected of themselves or that society expected of them. This invariably resulted in feelings of inadequacy, embarrassment or shame (actual or anticipated) and a belief that they were not valued by others.

A woman living in rural Kerala (India) commented,

> There are certain practices we have to do somehow. But most of the time we may not have money to perform them ... . In the community, if our respect is at risk, everyone helps us. If we don't do it, we lose our respect and people will talk about us ... even if there is no money we borrow it and do.

In South Korea the cultural emphasis on children's educational attainment meant that parents felt a constant obligation to provide extra-curricular learning opportunities such as music, dance, sport and educational trips for their children on a par with their peers, even when they could not afford to do so. Parents spoke of how they went to inordinate lengths to meet the costs of these activities, skimping, saving, borrowing and taking on multiple jobs as necessary. Many spoke of how they inevitably went into debt as a result of these additional demands on the household budget (see Jo 2014).

Secondly, people's consumer vulnerability came from the exposure to judgement and treatment by others for not meeting the societal norms of consumption. Within nuclear and extended families there were numerous accounts of people feeling judged, discriminated against or ostracised because they were unable to meet material demands and expectations. Being unable to contribute the required resources or wear the right clothes to family or community rituals such as weddings, birth ceremonies, funerals and feasts were repeatedly described as a cause of shame, embarrassment and social exclusion. People spoke of either not attending these events in order to avoid the shame or of going out of a sense of duty, only to find themselves – often – ostracised or ignored by others who were better dressed or who could afford more elaborate gifts or larger amounts of money.

The school, for parents and children alike, became an arena where differences in material acquisition became magnified; parents felt inadequate either for not being able to provide what their children needed or because they didn't measure up to the wealthier parents; children described how they constantly felt compared to their peers in terms of what they wore, the toys they could afford or whether or not they were recipients of free school meals. Within the community, people frequently recounted experiences of being labelled, stigmatised or ignored by others who were wealthier or more powerful. And when people needed to access whatever social assistance was available, they spoke of how their dealings with officials frequently left them feeling that they had been reduced to a category or number and that they were somehow guilty for their inability to meet the consumption requirements of themselves and their families without falling back on state support. These experiences of feeling shame and being shamed within different arenas often intersected with other social cleavages such as gender, class, caste and age, with the result that some people, particularly women and those assigned to a stigmatised rung on the social hierarchy, were prone to feel its affects more acutely (see Chase and Bantebya-Kyomuhendo 2014).

Responses to shame

Faced with the social risks of failing to measure up to how and where they should consume, people living in poverty described how they adopted a range of different responses in order to save public face. In the first place, they did what they could to manage limited resources in a way that made them appear normal and enabled them to deflect the glare of shame. While this might be manageable in the short term, it was difficult to sustain. People were often prevented by limited skills and experience from furthering their employment career or they faced a structural lack of opportunities or frequent retrenchments. This meant that their reduced capacity to consume was not just a transitory phase but likely to last for a long period of time.

Yet, due to the dire social consequences of being singled out as not coping financially, the desire to keep up appearances and maintain the façade of credible consumer was extremely strong. This led some people to pretend that they were better off than they were in order to conceal their poverty and demonstrate that they were as capable as anyone else of maintaining the consumption norms that prevailed around them. In Uganda, women and men recounted how they endeavoured to camouflage their poverty by sacrificing everything else to dress smartly, style their hair, don jewellery and apply makeup. That way they could appear presentable in public and avoid the shame of looking shabby or unkempt, even if it meant they had nothing to eat when they got home. They also spoke of the importance of being seen to be successful consumers. For example, several reflected on how, whenever things were slightly easier financially and they could afford to buy 'luxuries' such as meat or cooking oil, they made sure that such purchases were made in full public view. One young man spoke of how, at a public fundraising function, he felt compelled to pledge money that he could not afford because he wanted the social recognition that such a pledge brought (Bantebya-Kyomuhendo 2014b). In Britain, people described pretending to others that they were working, to the extent of fabricating the type of job they were in, rather than admit that they were in receipt of social benefits. While such pretence might alleviate the immediate need for social acceptance, it also brought with it the potential hazard of being caught out (Chase and Walker 2014).

Avoiding social situations where a lack of resources might be discovered became a coping strategy which often led to increasing social withdrawal. One woman from Lahore (Pakistan) commented, 'When I get things from the store on credit, then I have to avoid passing through that road (where the shop is) … until I am able to return the loan' (Choudhry 2014b). In China another woman spoke of how, although as a recipient of *dibao* (the minimum standard of living allowance) she was entitled to a reduction in her daughter's tuition fees, she did not apply for the reduction because she believed it would make the girl 'feel ashamed'. Another spoke of how she would never invite the mother of her daughter's friend to her home because she felt ashamed of her poor furniture. And while classmates' reunions were repeatedly mentioned as an important social function in China, several participants spoke of how they no longer attended these because they did not want old school friends to learn the penury of their circumstances (Yan 2014b). And there were variations on this theme described by people from Norway, with a father emphasising the strain he felt when his teenage daughter wanted to have her more affluent friends over to their simple apartment because it contrasted so sharply with the nice, large houses that her friends lived in. A woman recounted how she had recently been snubbed for driving a rusty old car by another parent at her daughter's nursery school (Gubrium and Lødemel 2014).

Efforts to sustain appearances frequently meant that people became overstretched and fell into debt. The moneylender and debt collector were ubiquitous figures across the different cultural contexts. Loan companies were portrayed as routinely appearing on the doorstep in the first place and cranking up the pressure to borrow money, making people believe that financial loans were the norm and were affordable. When this proved to be not the case and people struggled to meet loan repayments, the moneylender was replaced by the debt collector, who put them under further pressure to pay back the borrowed money. People in poverty frequently spoke of how they wanted to hide away and how they lived in constant fear of possible coercion when they were unable to pay debts or of having their economic struggles publicly exposed. A woman in India spoke of how she felt no option but to pledge her house to a moneylender in order to raise cash for her daughter's marriage. Another commented, 'The other day also the bank manager called me and asked me to repay some of the money I owe … . This is the only thing I have. I can't afford to lose my house' (Pellissery and Mathew 2014b). In Britain, one man spoke of how he could not even get together the £90 required for a debt relief order which would enable him to wipe out £10,000 worth of debt and relieve him of the constant stress of 'bailiffs knocking on the door ..., people I owe money for bills and things phoning me up five times a day, even on a Sunday' (Chase and Walker 2014).

Importantly, focus group discussions with more affluent people in each of the countries revealed the common opinion that people living in poverty were often profligate and wasteful of the resources they had. Expenditures on clothes, gifts or gadgets were seen as unnecessary extravagances rather than rational actions carried out in order for people to save face and attain or protect their social credibility. These views are indicative of the perception that being a 'viable' rather than 'vulnerable' consumer is a rank that must be earned. Being 'worthy' of consumption is a status legitimately achieved through 'hard work' and perseverance, characteristics which were repeatedly referred to as lacking among people living in poverty by the better-off participants. Denying others the status of viable consumer enables those with wealth to differentiate themselves from people on low incomes, evidence of clearly defined consumption classes. The possibility that those with wealth actively strive to sustain this distinction arguably renders the low-income consumer even more 'vulnerable'.

People in poverty, particularly if they were facing debt and its consequences, frequently described feeling depressed and the need or desire to withdraw completely from society. Several people across different cultures spoke of how they had contemplated or even attempted suicide as a result of the constant stresses and strains of being unable to meet their own and others' expectations of them. Personal disintegration and sense of lack of control or agency were commonly described by research participants and observed by those conducting the research.

Children described similar fears and anxieties to those of adults when alluding to their consumer vulnerability. In Britain they recounted how they were subjected to calls of 'benefit bum' because they were consumers of free school meals. In India and in Uganda, children and young people refused to go for free meals at lunchtime because they were acutely aware of the stigma attached to being recipients of this service. In Uganda, the UK and India, children described how they would not bring friends home for a meal or to play because they were too 'ashamed' or 'embarrassed' about where they lived. School was essentially a space for consumer competition, where who could afford the latest and most expenses gadgets, phones, toys or clothes became evident. Some children, and especially boys, spoke of how they often felt angry and, although they were not always able to locate the cause of their anger, they knew that not being able to have or do what they wanted due to a lack of resources contributed to this feeling. On the whole, however, children and young people tended to express a greater sense of optimism than the adults interviewed and were hopeful that their futures would be brighter and that they would live successful lives as adult consumers.

Conclusions

The work cited here had the intention of shifting the focus away from a purely economic analysis of poverty towards a deeper understanding of its psychosocial elements and their impact. As such, poverty was examined through the lens of the potential for feeling or being subjected to shame. The importance of shame is that it forces people to withdraw socially, erodes self-confidence and reduces human agency, thus arguably perpetuating poverty. As evidenced here, there was a strong correlation between how the associations between poverty and shame were represented in different cultural media and how they were experienced in real life.

The spectre of the 'vulnerable consumer' comes readily to light in this analysis and it has two important dimensions. First, it signifies that people living in poverty lack the necessary resources to procure the goods and services (consumables) to lead the lives they aspire to and play the roles that they expect of themselves or that society expects of them. Second, it suggests that people living in poverty are constantly faced with or risk exposure to judgement and treatment by others for not meeting societal norms and patterns of consumption. Failure to consume in ways that are comparable to the norms of society has definite social, psychological and ultimately physical consequences.

The boundaries of the 'market place' within this analysis are no longer confined to spaces of financial transaction but permeate society as a whole and form an integral part of people's daily relations. Therefore, the person in poverty, redefined here as the 'vulnerable consumer', strives hard to adopt strategies to navigate the 'market place' and service market interactions in ways which enable them to retain a sense of control over their social standing. The market place thus becomes a potent arena for the experience of shame, dividing people between those who are deemed to be valued actors – the 'viable' consumers – and those, by implication, who are not viable. Moreover, those who believe they have legitimately acquired the status of 'viable consumers' employ shame, at least in how they refer to people living in poverty, as a means of maintaining the distinction between themselves and others who are not worthy of such a status because they have not worked hard enough for it. Acutely aware of these processes of shaming, the vulnerable consumer who repeatedly fails in the market place of society tends to retreat and, in doing so, reduces their potential to become valued as a 'viable consumer'.

Couched within the domains of international development and poverty alleviation, the research cited here drew its conclusions about the implications of these findings for re-evaluating anti-poverty policies through the lens of 'shame' and for conceptualising a rubric for shame-proofing future policies (see Gubrium et al., 2013). Applying these findings to the world of marketing will inevitably lead to the drawing of other conclusions and highlight other implications. Nonetheless, adding shame to the mix of how we understand the circumstances of the 'vulnerable consumer' may prove useful in any analysis which seeks to reconceptualise the market place as a space for the enhancement of social cohesion rather than one which serves to further marginalise its more 'vulnerable' participants.

References

Baker, S.M., Gentry, J.W. and Rittenburg, T.L. (2005), 'Building understanding of the domain of consumer vulnerability', *Journal of Macromarketing*, 25, 2, 128–139.

Bantebya-Kyomuhendo, G. (2014a), 'Oral tradition and literary portrayals of poverty: the evolution of poverty shame in Uganda'. In E. Chase and G. Bantebya-Kyomuhendo, *Poverty and Shame: Global Experiences*. Oxford: OUP.

Bantebya-Kyomuhendo, G. (2014b), '"Needy and vulnerable, but poverty is not my identity": Experiences of people in poverty in Uganda'. In E. Chase and G. Bantebya-Kyomuhendo, *Poverty and Shame: Global Experiences*. Oxford: OUP.

Blumer, H. (1969), *Symbolic Interactionism: Perspective and Method*. London: University of California Press.

Chase, E. and Walker, R. (2013), 'The co-construction of shame in the context of poverty: beyond a threat to the social bond,' *Sociology*, 47, 4, 739–754.

Chase, E., and Walker, R. (2014), 'The "shame" of shame: experiences of people living in poverty in the UK'. In E. Chase and G. Bantebya-Kyomuhendo, *Poverty and Shame: Global Experiences*. Oxford: OUP.

Chase, E. and Bantebya-Kyomuhendo, G. (2014), *Poverty and Shame: Global Experiences*. Oxford: OUP.

Chase, E., Walker, R. and Choudhry, S. (2014), 'Poverty and shame: seeking cultural cues within British literature and film'. In E. Chase and G. Bantebya-Kyomuhendo, *Poverty and Shame: Global Experiences*. Oxford: OUP.

Choudhry, S.A. (2014a), 'The wealth of poverty-induced shame in Urdu literature'. In E. Chase and G. Bantebya-Kyomuhendo, *Poverty and Shame: Global Experiences*. Oxford: OUP.

Choudhry, S.A. (2014b), 'Tales of inadequacy from Pakistan'. In E. Chase and G. Bantebya-Kyomuhendo, *Poverty and Shame: Global Experiences*. Oxford: OUP.

Coser, L. (1963), *Sociology through Literature*. Englewood Cliffs: Prentice-Hall International.

Gubrium, E. (2014), '"Then" and "now": literary representations of shame, poverty and social exclusion in Norway'. In E. Chase and G. Bantebya-Kyomuhendo, *Poverty and Shame: Global Experiences*. Oxford: OUP.

Gubrium, E. and Lødemel, I. (2014), 'Relative poverty in a rich, egalitarian state: experiences from Norway.' In E. Chase and G. Bantebya-Kyomuhendo, *Poverty and Shame: Global Experiences*. Oxford: OUP.

Gubrium, E., Pellissery, S. and Lødemel, I. (eds) (2013), *The Shame of It: Global Perspectives on Anti-poverty Policies*. Bristol: Policy Press.

Ho, D., Fu, W. and Ng, S. (2004), 'Guilt, shame and embarrassment: revelations of face and self', *Culture and Psychology*, 10, 1, 64–84.

Jo, Y.N. (2014), 'Disclosing the poverty–shame nexus within popular films in South Korea (1975–2010)'. In E. Chase and G. Bantebya-Kyomuhendo, *Poverty and Shame: Global Experiences*. Oxford: OUP.

Keynes, J.M. (1936), *The General Theory of Employment, Interest and Money*. New York/London: Harcourt, Brace and Co.

Lewis, D., Rodgers, D. and Woolcock, M. (2008), 'The fiction of development: literary representation as a source of authoritative knowledge', *Journal of Development Studies*, 44, 2, 198–216.

Lister, R. (2004), *Poverty*, Cambridge/Malden, MA: Polity.

Pellissery, S. and Mathew, L. (2014a), 'Film and literature as social commentary in India'. In E. Chase and G. Bantebya-Kyomuhendo, *Poverty and Shame: Global Experiences*. Oxford: OUP.

Pellissery, S. and Mathew, L. (2014b), "I am not alone": experience soft poverty-induced shame in a moral economy'. In E. Chase and G. Bantebya-Kyomuhendo, *Poverty and Shame: Global Experiences*. Oxford: OUP.

Scheff, T. (2000), *Shame and the Social Bond: A Sociological Theory*. Santa Barbara: University of California at Santa Barbara.

Scheff, T. (2003), 'Shame in self and society', *Symbolic Interaction*, 26, 2, 239–262.

Sen, A. (1983), 'Poor, relatively speaking', *Oxford Economic Papers*, 35, 153–169.

Sutherland, J.A. and Felty, K. (2010), *Cinematic Sociology: Social Life in Film*. Thousand Oaks, CA: Sage Publications.

Tangney, J., Stuewig, J. and Mashek, D. (2007), 'What's moral about the self-conscious emotions?'. In J. Tracy, R. Robins and J. Tangney (eds), *The Self-Conscious Emotions*, New York: Guilford Press.

Tracy, J. and Robins, R. (2007) 'The self-conscious emotions: a cognitive appraisal approach'. In J. Tracy, R. Robins and J. Tangney (eds), *The Self-Conscious Emotions*, New York: Guilford Press.

Walker, R. (2014) *The Shame of Poverty*. Oxford: OUP.

Yan, M. (2014a) 'Poverty and shame in Chinese literature'. In E. Chase and G. Bantebya-Kyomuhendo, *Poverty and Shame: Global Experiences*. Oxford: OUP.

Yan, M. (2014b) 'Experiences of poverty and shame in urban China'. In E. Chase and G. Bantebya-Kyomuhendo, *Poverty and Shame: Global Experiences*. Oxford: OUP.

17 Poverty-proofing the school day

Sara Bryson and Stephen Crossley

'Everything was fine until the dreaded lunch bell sounded'
Look there's Hope,
She's got holes in her shoes,
Pays nothing for dinners,
And holds up the queues,
Going home with a face full of sorrow,
But don't worry Hope,
We'll get you tomorrow.

> (Written by young people attending Children
> North East workshops exploring their shared
> experiences of growing up in poverty
> in the North East)

Introduction: child poverty and schooling

Despite a legally binding commitment to 'eradicate' child poverty by 2020, the number of children living in poverty in the UK is predicted to hit 3.4 million by 2020[1] if current policies are enacted and current trends continue. Talk of a 'cost of living crisis' has ensured that issues such as rising utility bills, housing costs and food prices at a time of low wage increases have received media and political attention. The UK government's most recent child poverty strategy, launched in June 2014, includes a number of proposals aimed at 'tackling' some of these issues in a chapter called 'Supporting families' living standards'. None of the proposals are aimed directly at improving the material conditions of children themselves, despite a large body of evidence highlighting the particularly detrimental impact of poverty on children (for a brief summary, see Ridge 2002: 22–7). The experience of children living in poverty is rarely considered. For example, it is unclear how children living in poverty in the UK today have contributed to or influenced the development of a policy allegedly aimed at improving their lives. Given that the official consultation took place entirely online via a government website, it could be inferred that few children knew about the opportunity to respond to initial proposals.

The role of school does feature prominently in the government's child poverty strategy and this is a theme which has continued since Tony Blair articulated his 'historic aim' to end child poverty 'within a generation' in 1999. In particular, the focus has been on the 'attainment gap' between poorer children (generally presented as those who are eligible for free school meals) and their better-off peers. The UK child poverty strategy for 2014–17 states that the government 'will continue to raise the educational attainment of poor children' through a range of measures including a 'Pupil Premium', holding schools to account for how well poor children do, providing 'targeted support' for children who 'fall behind' and supporting children to stay on in education after the school leaving age. This narrow focus on attainment appears to highlight a concern with the potential earnings of children when they become adults, which is afforded primacy over and above their experience of school as a child who may not have access to some of the resources of their peers.

Tess Ridge (2002) has highlighted a number of disparities between the school experience for poorer children and that of their better off peers, using both quantitative and qualitative methodologies. Analysing the British Household Panel Youth Survey (BHPYS) she shows that poorer children are more likely to face suspension or expulsion from school, are more likely to truant, and are also more likely to be worried about bullying or feel that their teachers are 'getting at' them.

Using semi-structured interviews with parents and children, Ridge also explores the social aspects of school and how a lack of resources can affect the participation in and enjoyment of school. The interviews highlighted children missing school trips because parents couldn't afford them (in one case a young person decided to pay for her own school trips if she thought they were of benefit), worries about non-uniform days and concerns about not being able to afford all the equipment and materials necessary to participate fully in some subjects, especially when group work is involved. Children and parents both highlighted free school meals (FSM) as 'a very specific and visible issue of difference' (2002: 83) which led to concerns about stigmatisation and bullying of children identified as being in receipt of FSM. Parents who had themselves received FSM as children remembered their own experiences of being labelled as 'poor' and this led to them being worried about their own children.

The potential for school to highlight disparities in income between pupils has also been noted more recently with work by researchers from Oxford University and other institutions suggesting that:

> school broadened horizons but the stark differences it exposed were a source of shaming: smartly dressed or not, more than one set of uniform or not, hungry or not, pocket money or not, the list was endless,
>
> (Walker et al. 2013: 225–6)

The research used interviews with adults and children from different countries to examine the cross-cultural and international links between poverty and shame. Children in the UK talked of their anger at peers gloating about their possessions and the authors noted that in every country involved with the research, with the possible exception of Pakistan, 'school was an engine of social grading, a place of humiliation for those without the possessions that guaranteed acceptance' (Walker et al. 2013: 224). Other research has shown that the lack of possessions can lead to children choosing not to study certain subjects, especially 'creative subjects' such as art, design and technology, and photography, which require extra materials and therefore carry additional costs (Farthing 2014: 4).

The relatively small amount of poverty-related research undertaken with children has highlighted that the school day is, despite an ostensibly 'free' education system in the UK, an area where consumption and material resources matter. Some research suggests that the 'cost' of a child going to school in the UK in 2013 was around £1,614 each year (Aviva 2013), with this cost including transport, out-of-school clubs/care, uniform, sports equipment and textbooks. Hamilton has also shown how parents often seek to protect their children from the stigma of poverty by purchasing branded items for them and making sacrifices in other areas of household expenditure. She suggests that this is particularly true for parents of school-age children and provides the following quote from 'Eva' by way of example:

> Now that everybody is going back to school after the summer holidays I couldn't get her ordinary shoes, it had to be Nike Air Max but that's because she's going to big school. If it had been at primary you could have got away with it but at 12 you couldn't.
>
> (Hamilton 2012: 83)

Parents and children living on low incomes are, therefore, acutely aware of the potential for children to experience stigmatisation and/or marginalisation at school as a result of the family's financial circumstances. In discussing this social exclusion of children at school, Ridge highlights the need to understand the structural and institutional processes which lead to children being marginalised or excluded, highlighting the importance of the school environment. She notes that economic considerations such as the cost of school trips, course books, etc. are:

> exacerbated by institutional processes: an insistence on uniforms and equipment, demanding examination criteria, deposit deadlines, meetings after school with no transport home and overly stigmatising bureaucratic processes of qualification and delivery in welfare support. ... Exclusion *from* school has long been recognised as a factor in children's likelihood of experiencing social exclusion; what is apparent ... is that exclusion *within* school may pose an equally grave danger for children from low-income families.
>
> (Ridge 2002: 142)

'Poverty-proofing the school day'

Children North East works within a children's rights framework and actively seeks the views and lived experiences of children and young people to inform its work. In seeking to understand how children experience poverty we found further evidence of children and young people experiencing stigma and discrimination during the school day. Young people told us if we could do anything to tackle the impact of child poverty, then we should poverty-proof the school day.

In partnership with the North East Child Poverty Commission we spent a year in four schools developing the programme. We worked with children and young people in two primary and two secondary schools. We began by exploring poverty in a UK context and by asking the simple question: 'Do you know who is poor in your school?' Across all four schools children and young people told us yes, they did know. We spent almost 12 months of intensive work in those schools trying to understand how it was possible for pupils to know the private financial circumstances of their peers. We walked and talked the school day from the moment they left home to when they returned home at the end of the day. What we discovered was a raft of shared experiences and policies and practices across the school day that often unintentionally stigmatised children from poorer backgrounds and created barriers to their learning. Examples are below.

Resources

Young people in a secondary school studying home economics were asked to bring in the ingredients required each lesson. Young people described to us the pressure to bring in the correct brand of goods and the bullying and teasing which took place if you used 'value' or supermarket-own brands. As a result young people would often 'forget' to bring in any ingredients. The school's response was to supply the ingredients to those pupils. However, at the end of the lesson, when students were able to eat what they had cooked, those pupils who hadn't provided their own ingredients saw their meals being thrown away. Teaching staff explained that this was to ensure pupils wouldn't 'forget' ingredients in the future. It had simply never occurred to staff that for some students the cost of the ingredients would be too great. In contrast, pupils were aware of this fact and throwing the prepared food away became another way in which the differences between pupils were highlighted and the poorest pupils humiliated and shamed.

Uniform and PE kits

In one secondary school it became compulsory to buy expensive branded tracksuit bottoms costing £40. Parents could no longer buy cheaper versions from supermarkets. The branding of the PE kit of course made no difference to pupil's performance. However, it once again drew stark differences between those who could and those who couldn't afford them. Some pupils would 'forget' their kit, avoid their lesson, or attend and suffer the punishment for turning up to lessons without the proper equipment.

Debt

We found that children and young people were acutely aware of the impact of poverty throughout their school day. In one primary school a pupil told us that her parents hated receiving the debt letters for school dinner money. All pupils knew when a debt letter was being issued as it was folded in a certain way and stapled closed. Pupils across all year groups told us about them. One child explained to us that she once folded the letter again and drew a picture on it, to soften the blow for her parents when she took it home. Similarly, pupils in secondary schools told us they would often hide letters about school trips as they knew their parents couldn't afford them and they didn't want to put further pressure on the family finances.

Black market economy

We also found examples of pupils being creative in their approach to the cost of the school day. With strict guidelines in schools around healthy eating, pupils aren't able to purchase chocolate, crisps or fizzy drinks on the school site. Across almost all secondary schools we found a profitable black market economy run by pupils. These young people bought food and drinks wholesale and made a profit selling them to their peers. In most cases this involved poorer pupils buying the goods wholesale and selling them on to their wealthier peers. The buying and selling of goods once again made apparent the differences between pupils. The punishments for students caught selling and buying goods were also different, with greater consequences for those caught selling. Thus, greater risk was involved for pupils from poorer backgrounds.

Unintentional stigmatisation through school policy and practice

Almost all of the cases we came across unintentionally discriminated against poorer children. Sometimes this was the policy of the school, such as issuing a gold card to pupils in receipt of FSM to access their dinners or giving out packed lunches in brown paper bags to those pupils in receipt of free school meals when going on a trip. Sometimes teachers acted in the best interest of pupils. In one secondary school staff used a budget underspend to buy a pencil case filled with resources for all pupils on free school meals in their school. They distributed them to pupils by going into classrooms, pulling pupils out of the class and sending them back in with their pencil case. They couldn't understand why pupils didn't want to bring them into school. The pencil case became another form of differentiation, a signifier that the pupils were different: entitled to free school meals or poor.

In response to our findings we developed a toolkit to poverty-proof the school day, to reduce the stigma and remove the barriers to learning. The toolkit consists of an audit for each individual school, questioning pupils, staff, parents and governors. The result is an action plan tailored to each individual school to address any stigmatising policies or practices. We also offer training to staff and governors on poverty and its impact on education. As schools now have more control over their own policies, practice and budget we have found that changes have been quickly made. Each school is different but so far the array of changes that have taken place have included: introducing cashless systems to ensure free school meals are distributed anonymously; replacing the brown paper bags for packed lunches with a variety of packed lunch boxes or issuing brown paper bags to all pupils; replacing the requirement for expensive uniforms such as branded tracksuit bottoms, dry-clean-only blazers or branded t-shirts with plain and affordable ones; calculating the requirement for additional resources from pupils from across the whole school; ensuring systems work for parents, appointing a member of staff to deal with any concerns relating to financial circumstances; appointing governors with responsibility for the appropriate use and monitoring of pupil premium spending. To find out more, visit www.povertyproofing.co.uk.

Summary

In the 1970s Basil Bernstein argued that education could not compensate for society, noting that education systems primarily represent the values, beliefs and priorities of the societies in which they are situated. More recently, Diane Reay has argued that 'Capitalist neo-liberal societies beget capitalist neo-liberal education systems' (2011: 2), and in recent years we have observed an increased role for the market in education, through parental choice and developments such as academies and free schools in parts of the UK. The research highlighted above suggests that this role is not limited to structural changes to the education system. The daily life of schools and their participants is increasingly being shaped by market forces, with pupils and parents acutely aware of the consumption 'choices' they are offered if they want to participate fully and equally in school life. A long-standing concern about 'having the "right" trainers' is now accompanied by concerns about having the officially endorsed branded school tracksuits, the 'right' ingredients for home economics lessons and the appropriate resources for the study of creative subjects.

However, such a view suggests that little can be done about the increasingly pervasive effects of the market into the education of our children. Education might not be able to compensate for society, but it need not reflect all aspects of society, good and bad, and the relative autonomy that some schools enjoy should enable them to resist and negotiate some of the consumption and material issues that have been highlighted. Steven Gorard has noted that 'Schools, in their structure and organisation, can do more than simply reflect the society we have; they can try to be the precursor of the kind of society that we wish to have' (Gorard 2010).

The action research undertaken in the North East of England has shown that involving children in discussions about their lived experience of poverty can uncover situations which may not be priorities to adults or have occurred to them. Focusing on the day-to-day experiences of children also creates an opportunity to ameliorate some of the (sometimes hidden) effects of poverty. The consumption that takes place within school or is required for participation in school life has been neglected by many researchers, policy makers and politicians. This situation requires addressing, without forgetting that the priority should be to eradicate child poverty, not enable children to live with it more successfully.

Note

1   http://www.guardian.co.uk/society/2013/may/07/uk-children-poverty-2020-thinktank

References

Aviva (2013) *Family Finances Report* [Online]. Available at http://www.aviva.co.uk/healthcarezone/document-library/files/ge/gen5175.pdf [accessed 3 August 2014]

Bernstein, B. (1970) Education cannot compensate for society, *New Society*, 15, 387: 344–347

Blair, T. (1999) *Beveridge Lecture* [Online]. Available at http://www.bristol.ac.uk/poverty/downloads/background/Tony%20Blair%20Child%20Poverty%20Speech.doc [accessed 3 August 2014]

Farthing, R. (2014) *The Costs of Going to School, From Young People's Perspectives* [Online]. Available at http://www.cpag.org.uk/sites/default/files/The%20Costs%20of%20Going%20to%20School%20FINAL.pdf [accessed 3 August 2014]

Gorard, S. (2010) Education can compensate for society – a bit, *British Journal of Educational Studies*, 58, 1: 47–65

Hamilton, K. (2012) Low-income families and coping through brands: inclusion or stigma?, *Sociology*, 46, 1: 74–90

Reay, D. (2011) Schooling for democracy: a common school and a common university? A response to 'Schooling for Democracy', *Democracy and Education*, 9, 1: 1–4

Ridge, T. (2002) *Childhood Poverty and Social Exclusion: From a Child's Perspective*, Bristol: Policy Press

Walker, A., Kyumohendo, G. B., Chase, E. Choudhry, S., Gubrium, E. K., Nicola, J. Y., Lodemel, I., Mathew, L., Mwiine, A., Pellissery, S. and Ming, Y. (2013) Poverty in global perspective: is shame a common denominator?, *Journal of Social Policy*, 42, 2: 215–233

Index

Italics are used to indicate tables or figures.

For Product Safety Concerns and Information please contact our EU
representative GPSR@taylorandfrancis.com
Taylor & Francis Verlag GmbH, Kaufingerstraße 24, 80331 München, Germany

www.ingramcontent.com/pod-product-compliance
Ingram Content Group UK Ltd.
Pitfield, Milton Keynes, MK11 3LW, UK
UKHW020959180425
457613UK00019B/745